CHILDREN OF TRAUMA

International Universities Press
Stress and Health Series

Edited by
Leo Goldberger, Ph.D.

Monograph 8

Children of Trauma
Stressful Life Events and Their Effects on Children and Adolescents

edited by

Thomas W. Miller, Ph.D.

International Universities Press, Inc.
Madison   Connecticut

Library of Congress Cataloging-in-Publication Data

Children of trauma : stressful life events and their effects on
   children and adolescents / edited by Thomas W. Miller.
      p.   cm.—(International Universities Press stress and health
series ; monograph 8)
   Includes bibliographical references and indexes.
   ISBN 0-8236-0810-7
   1. Psychic trauma in children. 2. Stress in children. 3. Posttraumatic stress disorder in children. I. Miller, Thomas W.,
1943-   . II. Series: Stress and health series ; monograph 8.
   [DNLM: 1. Stress, Psychological—in infancy & childhood.
2. Stress, Psychological—in adolescence. 3. Stress Disorders, Posttraumatic—in infancy & childhood. 4. Stress Disorders, Posttraumatic—in adolescence. 5. Life Change Events.   W1 ST799K
monograph 8 1998 / WS 350 C5364 1998]
RJ506.P66C47   1998
618.92'8521—dc21
DNLM/DLC
for Library of Congress   97-15597
                                                                                      CIP

Manufactured in the United States of America

This book is dedicated to
David and Jeanine
and to children around the world
who seek liberation from trauma
in all its forms

Contents

Contributors

Aniat Azarian, Ph.D., Director, Child Psychotherapy Center, Research Institute of Pedagogics, Yeravan, Armenia; Visiting Professor, Child Development Center, Brown University, Providence, Rhode Island.

Allan Beane, Ph.D., Department of Special Education, Murray State University, Murray, Kentucky.

Sandra A. Brown, Ph.D., Professor, Department of Psychiatry, University of California and VA Medical Center, San Diego, California.

Duncan B. Clark, Ph.D., M.D., Department of Psychiatry, University of Pittsburgh Medical Center, Pittsburgh, Pennsylvania.

Erik J. de Wilde, Ph.D., Professor, University Hospital for Children and Adolescents, University of Utrecht, The Netherlands.

John A. Fairbank, Ph.D., Research Triangle Institute, Durham, North Carolina.

Kelly Hill, M.D., Assistant Professor, Department of Psychiatry, University of Kentucky, Lexington, Kentucky.

Ineke C. W. M. Kienhorst, Ph.D., Department of Pediatrics, University Hospital for Children and Adolescents, University of Utrecht, The Netherlands.

Catherine A. Martin, M.D., Associate Professor, Child and Adolescent Division, Department of Psychiatry, University of Kentucky, Lexington, Kentucky.

Richard J. McNally, Ph.D., Associate Professor, Department of Psychology, Harvard University, Cambridge, Massachusetts.

Thomas W. Miller, Ph.D., A.B.P.P. Professor, Department of Psychiatry, University of Kentucky, Lexington, Kentucky, and Department of Psychology, Murray State University, Murray, Kentucky.

Paula Raines, J.D., Ph.D., Department of Psychiatry, University of Kentucky, Lexington, Kentucky.

ix

Phillip A. Saigh, Ph.D., Professor and Chair, Doctoral Program in School Psychology, Graduate School of City University of New York, New York City.

Vitali Skriptchenko-Gregorian, Ph.D., Child Psychotherapy Center, Research Institute of Pedagogics, Yeravan, Armenia; Visiting Professor, Child Development Center, Brown University, Providence, Rhode Island.

Roland Summit, M.D., Professor, Department of Psychiatry, Harbour-UCLA Medical Center, University of California, Los Angeles, California.

Lane J. Veltkamp, M.S.W., B.C.D., Professor and Director, Family Violence Clinic, Department of Psychiatry, University of Kentucky, Lexington, Kentucky.

Peter Vik, Ph.D., Department of Psychiatry, University of California and VA Medical Center, San Diego, California.

Richard Welsh, M.S.W., Professor, Child and Adolescent Division, Department of Psychiatry, University of Kentucky, Lexington, Kentucky.

Anastasia Yasik, B.A., City University of New York Graduate School and University Center, New York City.

William Yule, Ph.D., Professor, Department of Psychology, Institute of Psychiatry, University of London, London, U.K.

Foreword

This series on *Stressful Life Events* is designed to provide the theoretician, clinician, and researcher with the latest information related to our understanding of stressful life events and their impact on our lives. Theoretical formulations and hypotheses, issues, and implications related to the validity and reliability of life stress measurement, and its applications to both medical and mental health–related concerns, are addressed here. Furthermore, special attention is given to individuals and how they function within various life settings. This book views the person as both the producer of stress and a reactor to stress and attempts to identify a variety of sources of stressful life experiences from within and beyond the individual's life space.

The chapters herein are directed toward the myriad of health care theoreticians, practitioners, and researchers, and brings together a representative sample of the authorities in each of the areas presented. Many of the individuals have pioneered extremely fruitful clinical research activities and their understanding of certain ethnogenic mainstream concepts have become important ingredients in defining, analyzing, and treating stress-related disorders. There are several rich perspectives that effectively integrate the variety of generalizations about functional and dysfunctional aspects of stress.

MATTHEW J. FRIEDMAN, M.D., PH. D.

Acknowledgments

Appreciation is extended to several individuals for their significant contributions to our understanding and to the knowledge base of this most important problem. The published contributions of several scholars and clinicians, such as Lenore Walker, Roland Summit, David Finkelhor, Anne Burgess, Nicholas Groth, Susan Sgroi, and B. Gomez-Schwartz, are hereby recognized. Appreciation is also extended to Aline Ludwig, Betty Downing, Tag Heister, Arnold Ludwig, Cathy Smith, Celena Cooper, Janeen Klaproth, Shannon Nelson, Linda Brown, Heather Hosford, Virginia Lynn Morehouse, Janet Saier, and Betty Lawson for their assistance in the preparation of this manuscript.

Acknowledgments

Introduction

Thomas W. Miller, Ph.D., A.B.P.P.

Stressors that produce traumatization in children have been widely recognized most often in cases of domestic violence, sexual abuse, natural disasters, and warfare, but also related to crimes of violence, victims of accidents, severe burn patients, and ferry boat disasters. In most cases, the symptoms but not the syndrome of posttraumatic stress disorder (PTSD) emerge, as for example, in ferry boat disasters (Yule and Williams, 1990), natural disasters (Green, Grace, Vary, Kramer, Gleser, and Leonard, 1994), war-related trauma (Saigh, Green, and Korol, 1991; Boehnlein, Kinzie, and Fleck, 1992), violent crime (Pynoos and Nader, 1988; Schwartz and Kowalski, 1991), and domestic violence and child abuse (Miller and Veltkamp, 1996). While these stressful life experiences often produce symptoms of traumatic stress in children, but without the full-blown syndrome, the research literature (Spitzer, Williams, and Gibbon 1993) suggests that exposure to violence triggers symptoms of PTSD in children more consistently than other types of traumatic events. The realization that symptoms but not the syndrome emerge is within the diagnostic nomenclature of the American Psychiatric Association in its fourth edition (DSM-IV; APA, 1996).

Revised diagnostic criteria have emerged for what has come to be called Acute Stress Disorder by the American Psychiatric Association. The criteria for an acute stress reaction include children who have been exposed to traumatic events in which the child has experienced, witnessed, or been confronted with an event or events that involve actual or threatened death, various types of injury, or threats to their physical well-being or that of others, and as a result of this experience intense fear, helplessness or horror. Recognition of various forms of dissociative symptoms, persistent experiencing and reexperiencing of the stressor, recognized avoidant behaviors related to recollections of the trauma, and symptoms of anxiety, including sleep disturbance, irritability, poor concentration, hypervigilance, or exaggerated startle response, help to formulate the increased recognition that traumatization may have a significant impact on the person who either experiences, witnesses, or has been confronted with a stressful life event. For those who have been victims of prolonged, repeated victimization and violence, Judith Herman (1992) has argued for a syndrome entitled "Disorders of Extreme Stress Not Otherwise Specified." Survivors of repeated and prolonged victimization, particularly survivors of childhood abuse, suffer the dissociative states and ego fragmentation often associated with perpetual revictimization and prolonged trauma. This whole area clearly warrants further exploration.

The diagnostic nomenclature of the American Psychiatric Association (DSM-IV; 1994) yields newly defined criteria for PTSD (309.81). It recognizes that as with acute stress disorder, the person exposed to a stressful life experience not only must have experienced, witnessed, or been confronted with an event which involved actual or threatened death or serious injury, but also to have had as a response to this experience, intense fear, helplessness, and horror. Or as in children, disorganized or agitated behavior. As with acute stress disorder, the traumatization or PTSD must be persistently reexperienced in at least one of five ways that can include recurrent and intrusive distressing recollections, dreams, acting or feeling as if the traumatic event were recurring, intense physiological distress and exposure, or physiological reactivity. Furthermore, criteria that address avoidance of stimuli associated with the trauma, numbing of general responsiveness, as well as sleep disturbance, irritability, difficulty concentrating, hypervigilance, and exaggerated startle response are recognized as symptoms associated with this syndrome.

Special attention to the way in which children respond to trauma is noted in DSM-IV. Special attention is given to the ways in which the symptomatology may show itself in child victims. In young children, for example, repetitive play may occur in which themes or aspects of the trauma are expressed, showing that the child is reexperiencing the traumatic event. Likewise, in children there may be frightening dreams without recognizable content, and in young children there may be the recognition of a trauma-specific reenactment of the traumatization or the reaction to the traumatization. In the examination of children and trauma, a continuum emerges which recognizes that modifying effects of predisposing vulnerability, learned behavior, and various personality characteristics, as well as the presence of support systems and locus of control play a critically important ingredient in adjustment, adaptation, and accommodation to stressful life events. Questions which emerge about children and stress are not unlike those we have explored in previous volumes about adults. These include: How are the trauma and its symptoms diagnosed? How do we assess the impact of life stress events? How do children process trauma from life stress? Are there ethnocultural variances related to stressful life experiences? What treatment models are most helpful in dealing with traumatized children? What research is needed in the next decade to aid clinicians in the treatment of this disorder? The chapters which follow explore each of these questions over the spectrum of traumatizing situations that uniquely impact children and adolescents.

In the opening chapter, Clark and Miller examine various theoretical models of stress adaptation as they relate to children. Specific emphasis is placed on psychological and physiological responses of children and adolescents to severe stressors. The authors recognize the importance of developmental issues for child adaptation to trauma and focus on the relevance of developmental stages to stress response and adaptation theories.

In chapter 2, Richard McNally examines measures used to assess children's reactions to stressful life events. In this chapter, he addresses some of the new structured clinical interviews and questionnaires designed to remedy deficiencies in earlier generations of measures used in the assessment of traumatized children. The current measures have been designed to accommodate the new criteria sets from the *Diagnostic and Statistical Manual* of the American Psychiatric Association thereby meeting assurances that criteria of psychiatric disorders are measured across populations. Efforts to assure standardization for comparison purposes is addressed.

Roland Summit joins with Miller and Veltkamp to discuss the issues and implications of the child sexual abuse accommodation syndrome in understanding the impact of child sexual abuse on adaptation. The five-stage model developed by Dr. Summit becomes the focus of examining issues related to delayed disclosure, feelings of helplessness and entrapment experienced by children seen in the clinical setting. Syndrome validity issues are discussed.

Paula Raines provides a legal perspective as she joins with Thomas W. Miller and Lane J.Veltkamp to address the trauma of family violence. Examined are recent clinical and research data addressing family violence. Criteria useful in the identification of victims of family violence are explored with specific attention given to clinical indicators and the abusing family profile. Guidelines for mental health and medical practitioners are explored.

Azarian and Skriptchenko-Gregorian, psychologists who developed a psychotherapy center for the treatment of children who were survivors of the Armenian earthquake, discuss the broader aspects of traumatization that are the result of natural disasters. The two clinician researchers, who are now Visiting Fellows at Brown University, present the clinical and research issues essential to consider in addressing the needs of child survivors of a natural disaster. Case vignettes to assist in understanding the impact of trauma in children and subsequent adaptation are offered.

Saigh, Fairbank, and Yasik examine war-related posttraumatic stress disorder among children and adolescents. Addressed in this chapter is the reactivity of children and adolescents who have experienced various war-related stressors. A historical review of war-related stress reactions among children and adolescents is presented as is information involving the validity of posttraumatic stress disorder as a psychiatric classification. Suggestions are made for future research directions on traumatic stress among youth.

Adolescent pregnancy as a stressful life event is examined by Martin, Hill, and Welsh. Psychological issues faced by a pregnant adolescent are discussed as are clinical data and a case presentation. Clinical issues with the stressed pregnant teen are explored as are issues and import for the treating practitioner.

Erik de Wilde and Ineke Kienhorst examine stressful life events and adolescent suicidal behavior. Scientific inquiry into the evaluation of a group of adolescent suicide attempters, a group of depressed adolescents who have never attempted suicide, and a control group are explored. Discriminative values for stressful life events among the members of these adolescent groups is discussed as are the results of a multiple regression analysis for events and suicidal behavior among the clinical sample studied. Comparison with other research findings is examined.

Peter Vik and Sandra Brown of the University of California at San Diego examine stressful life events and substance abuse usage during adolescence. Emphasized are various characteristics of adolescent stress including severity, chronicity, and developmental aspects of life stressors. Patterns of usage along with family stressors and adolescent substance abuse are examined. Mechanisms of stress and the stress-vulnerability model as it applies to adolescents is discussed.

Allan Beane examines the impact of bullying behavior as a stressful life event. This author examines the complexity of understanding peer rejection and other "bullying" behavior on the child's ability to adapt to the school environment. Practical prevention and intervention suggestions for the clinician, teacher and researcher are explored.

William Yule addresses in the final chapter posttraumatic stress disorder in children and its treatment. This internationally recognized scholar and clinician provides a cross-cultural perspective. Examined are the similarities and differences between the *International Classification of Disorders* and the *Diagnostic and Statistical Manual* of the American Psychiatric Association with respect to criteria for posttraumatic stress disorder. A summary of published studies are provided as are treatment and prevention models for clinical care. Case examples provide important reference points for examining the impact of stressful life events and subsequent pathology in children and adolescents.

REFERENCES

American Psychiatric Association (1994), *Diagnostic and Statistical Manual of mental Disorders* (DSM-IV), 4th ed. Washington, DC: American Psychiatric Press.

Boehnlein, J. K., Kinzie, J. D., & Fleck, J. (1992), DSM diagnosis of posttraumatic stress disorder and cultural sensitivity: A response. *J. Nerv. Ment. Dis.*, 180:597–599.

Green, B., Grace, M., Vary, M., Kramer, T., Gleser, G., & Leonard, A. (1994), Children of disaster in the second decade: A 17-year follow-up of Buffalo Creek survivors. *J. Amer. Acad. Child & Adol. Psychiatry*, 33:71–79.

Herman, J. L. (1992), *Trauma and Recovery*. New York: Basic Books.

Miller, T. W., & Veltkamp, L. J. (1996), Theories, assessment and treatment of domestic violence. In: *Directions in Clinical and Counseling Psychology*. New York: Hatherleigh.

Pynoos, R. S., & Nader, K. (1988), Children who witness the sexual assaults of their mothers. *J. Amer. Acad. Child & Adol. Psychiatry*, 27:567–572.

Saigh, P. A., Green, B., & Korol, M. (1996), The history and prevalence of posttraumatic stress disorder with special reference to children and adolescents. *J. School Psychol.*, 34(2):107–131.

Schwartz, E. D., & Kowalski, J. M. (1991), Posttraumatic stress disorder after a school shooting: Effects of symptom threshold selection and diagnosis by DSM-III, DSM-III-R, or proposed DSM-IV. *Amer. J. Psychiatry*, 148:592–597.

Spitzer, R. L., Williams, J. B., & Gibbon, M. (1993), *Structured Clinical Interview for DSM Diagnosis*. Washington, DC: American Psychiatric Press.

Yule, W., & Williams, R. (1990), Post traumatic stress reactions in children. *J. Traum. Stress*, 3:279–295.

Children of Trauma

Chapter 1
Stress Response and Adaptation in Children: Theoretical Models

Duncan B. Clark, Ph.D., M.D., and
Thomas W. Miller, Ph.D.

Increased awareness in our society that children and adolescents are commonly subjected to severe stressors has underscored the importance of understanding responses to stress in formative stages of development. There is evidence that children and adolescents are traumatized more often than adults. For example, according to a Justice Department, Bureau of Justice Statistics study of 11 states and the District of Columbia for 1992, adolescents, ages 12 to 17, were the most common victims of violent crime in America, being raped, robbed, or assaulted at five times the rate of adults 35 or older. In a longitudinal study of 386 Caucasian working-class adolescents (mean age 17.9 years), the lifetime prevalence of posttraumatic stress disorder (PTSD) was 6.3 percent while it was 5.8 percent for working class adults (Reinherz, Giaconia, Lefkowitz, Pakiz, and Frost, 1993). These statistics from U.S. samples document that in our society trauma and its consequences are unfortunately common early in life.

Acknowledgments. Dr. Clark was supported by grants from NIAAA (P50-AA08746) and NIDA (DA05605) during manuscript preparation.

Responses to stressors in children, as in adults, involve psychological and physiological mechanisms which may be viewed from several theoretical perspectives. Acute and chronic psychological and physiological responses to stressors may result in distressing symptoms and physical illness, or may result in positive adaptations. The term *adaptation* has a positive connotation and refers in the present context to the child's responses to stressors. The child attempts through its responses to tolerate effectively and manage the stressor's psychological and physiological consequences. When successful, the responses enable the child to continue without a major deviation in developmental trajectory (Pynoos, 1993).

Stressors and responses to stressors exist along a continuum. Psychological responses to stressors involve graded symptomatic reactions such as anxiety and depression, and syndromal disorders such as PTSD. Psychological responses also involve adaptive, cognitive, affective, and behavioral changes. Physiological responses to stressors involve a variety of central nervous system, peripheral nervous system, and neuroendocrine activities. These responses can be modified by many diverse psychological, social, and biological factors. While responses to mild stressors have been studied through controlled experimentation in children, the relevance of such experiments to clinical circumstances is questionable and this literature will not be reviewed here. Ethical considerations, of course, obviate the presentation of severe stressors to humans for controlled experimentation. Clinical research has primarily focused on responses to naturally occurring severe stressors or trauma.

PSYCHOLOGICAL RESPONSES TO STRESSORS

Responses to stressors within this developmental period range from mild distress to severe psychopathology, with a spectrum of symptoms being more common than syndromally defined reactions such as PTSD (Kinzie, Sack, Angell, Manson, and Rath,

1986; Green, Korol, Grace, Vary, Leonard, Gleser, and Smithson-Cohen, 1991; Miller and Başoğlu, 1992). Psychopathological reactions to stressors include depression, anxiety, conduct problems, dissociative reactions, and psychotic symptoms (Friedman, 1981; Nadelson, Notman, Zackson, and Gornick, 1982; Lindberg and Distad, 1985; Gomes-Schwartz, Horowitz, and Sauzier, 1985; Sansonnet-Hayden, Haley, Marriage, and Fine, 1987; Sanders and Giolas, 1991). Suicide attempts in adolescents have been found to be associated with the stressors of social instability in the context of a childhood abuse history (De Wilde, Kienhorst, Diekstra, and Wolters, 1992). Syndromes not primarily identified with traumatic experiences, including affective disorders, somatoform disorders, dissociative disorders, and anxiety disorders other than PTSD also commonly occur in response to stressors (Herman, 1993), but the classically recognized syndromal response to severe stressors is PTSD.

PTSD AND ACUTE STRESS DISORDER

Definitions

Posttraumatic stress disorder (PTSD) is defined by the American Psychiatric Association in DSM-III-R (1987) and DSM-IV (1994) as the emergence of persistent symptomatology following a traumatic event outside the range of usual human experience. The event must be such that it would be considered markedly distressing to almost anyone. Symptomatic criteria include reexperiencing of the event, which can be manifested by intrusive recollections, distressing dreams, sudden feeling as if the event were recurring, or intense distress at exposure to events that recall the traumatic incident. Stimuli associated with the event are avoided. Signs of increased arousal must also be present. For the diagnostic criteria of PTSD to be met, the symptoms must be present for at least one month. In DSM-IV, the revised criteria acknowledge that children may have frightening dreams without recognizable content, and may exhibit trauma-specific reenactment as a form of reexperiencing the traumatic event. The reliability and validity of PTSD measures with child and adolescent samples has been reviewed elsewhere (Clark, Smith, Neighbors, Skerlec, and Randall, 1994).

DSM-IV adds the diagnosis category of Acute Stress Disorder to the psychiatric nomenclature. In acute stress disorder, a traumatic event and symptoms of reexperiencing the event, avoidance, increased arousal, and functional impairment are required, as in PTSD. For acute stress disorder, however, the symptoms must occur within 4 weeks of the traumatic event and have a maximum duration of 4 weeks. The reasoning behind the inclusion of this diagnostic category has been described (Brett, 1993), although data have not been presented concerning the characteristics of acute stress disorder defined in this way for children and adolescents. Delayed stress symptoms may not show themselves for months or years after the traumatic event.

Stressors and Psychoactive Substance Abuse

Stressful life events have long been hypothesized to lead to alcohol abuse in some individuals (see Clark and Sayette, 1993, for review), but the complexities of studying this relationship have resulted in conflicting results. Animals models involving lower species of mammals, such as rats, have not been particularly helpful in clarifying issues relevant for humans in this area. However, a more relevant primate model concerning the relationships among early parenting, proximal stress, and alcohol consumption has been developed. Higley and colleagues (Higley, Hasert, Suomi, and Linnoila, 1991) reared rhesus monkeys in the first 6 months of life either without access to adults (i.e., peer-reared) or with their mothers (mother-reared). At 50 months old, monkeys were given access to ethanol solution before, during, and after social separation. Peer-reared subjects showed more alcohol consumption before and after social separation. During social separation, while the difference between the peer- and mother-reared groups was diminished, there were positive correlations between biological and behavioral indices of distress and alcohol consumption. Biological indices of stress were higher in peer-reared monkeys during separation. This animal model suggests that stressors involving both early experience and proximal social stress may be associated with increased alcohol consumption.

Stressors have been found to be positively correlated with adolescent alcohol and other psychoactive substance abuse (e.g., Labouvie, 1986). An association between PTSD and alcohol use disorders in adolescents has also been described. Clark and colleagues (Clark, Bukstein, Smith, Kaczynski, Mezzich, and Donovan, in press) studied 43 adolescents hospitalized for alcohol abuse or dependence; PTSD was seen in 7 of 22 females and 2 of 21 males.

Clark and Neighbors (in press) have suggested that the association between alcohol abuse and internalizing disorders observed in adolescents may be related to trauma history. Traumatic experiences in childhood and adolescence may increase the likelihood of alcoholism through attempts to use alcohol to reduce symptoms of PTSD and other comorbid conditions, including anxiety and depression. Alcohol consumption may acutely reduce sleep disturbances, particularly traumatic nightmares and sleep latency (Keane, Caddell, and Taylor, 1988). The interaction between early childhood social experience and proximal stressors needs to be further considered in developing models for the relationship between stress and psychoactive substance abuse.

FACTORS INFLUENCING TRAUMA RESPONSE

Trauma Characteristics

The occurrence of PTSD and other responses among traumatized children and adolescents may be influenced by trauma characteristics. High prevalences of PTSD have been reported following natural disasters (39%; Green et al., 1991). Accidents may also lead to PTSD (severe burns, 30%, ages 7–19 years; Stoddard, Norman, Murphy, and Beardslee, 1989; injury due to speedboat crash, 60%; Martini, Ryan, Nakayama, and Ramenofsky, 1990).

Interpersonal violence may be more likely to produce PTSD in children than other types of traumatic events (McNally, 1993). Examples include kidnapping or attempted kidnapping (33%, ages 2–7 years; Terr, 1983), witnessing the murder of a parent (100%, ages 5–10; Malmquist, 1986), witnessing the sexual assault of a parent (100%, ages 5–17; Pynoos and Nader, 1988), exposure to shootings (77%, ages 5–13 years; Pynoos, Frederick, Nader, Arroyo, Steinberg, Eth, Nunez, and Fairbanks, 1987; 27%, ages 5–14 years; Schwartz and Kowalski, 1991). The relationship between the child victim and the perpetrator may be important. In a study of sexually abused children, PTSD was present in 75 percent of the children abused by natural fathers, 67 percent abused by strangers, 25 percent abused by trusted adults, and none abused by older children (McLeer, Deblinger, Atkins, Foa, and Ralphe, 1988).

Several more general characteristics of traumatic events have also been found to have a role in determining psychological responses. Characteristics correlating with increased symptom severity include threat to life and loss of significant others (Wilson, Smith, and Johnson, 1985; Clark et al., 1994). For example, Green and colleagues (1991) found that, among children and adolescent survivors evaluated 2 years after a dam collapse, there were significant correlations between PTSD symptoms and life threat.

The effects of trauma may vary also with developmental stage. Van der Kolk (1985) reported that a sample of Vietnam veterans diagnosed with PTSD were significantly younger (mean age = 18.3) during their exposure to combat than a control group without PTSD (mean age = 22.8). The psychological responses of children to traumatic stress have been observed to differ from those of adults. Terr's (1983) report of the Chowchilla school-bus kidnapping highlights this point. The children, ages 5 to 14 years, were driven at gunpoint, then buried alive for 16 hours. Four years after this incident, these children did not report experiencing amnesia, psychic numbing, or flashbacks. Trauma reenactment, time skew, and the belief that their futures would be limited, however, were common. Terr (1983) stressed that the responses of these children, regardless of age, were remarkably similar. Lyons (1987) also indicates that children rarely experience flashbacks, but instead reexperience the traumatic event through nightmares or behavioral reenactment.

Gender Differences

The exposure of boys and girls to various types of traumas differs. Girls are more often the victims in sex-related crimes, including rape and sexual child abuse. Half of the females who reported being raped in 1992 were under 18, and 1 out of 6 was under 12 years old, according to the U.S. Justice Department, Bureau of Justice Statistics (1992). The offender was typically a relative. In response to trauma, girls tend to report more symptoms of psychological distress than boys. For example, in a study of 179 children ages 2 to 15 who were exposed to a dam collapse, PTSD symptoms were more common in girls than boys (Green et al., 1991). It remains unclear whether this observed effect is due to cultural discouragement of male expression of symptoms or more fundamental gender differences in responding to stressors.

Protective Factors

Stress resistant children, according to Garmezy (1985) and colleagues (Masten, Best, and Garmezy, 1990), are characterized by three protective factors: (1) personality characteristics such as autonomy, self-esteem, and a positive social orientation; (2) family cohesion, warmth, and an absence of discord; and (3) external support systems that encourage and reinforce a child's coping efforts (see also Garmezy, 1985).

Individual characteristics influence response to stressful situations (see Rutter, 1990, for review). Resilience to stressors has been found to be associated with a positive relationship with a competent adult, skill at problem solving, and previous successful experiences (Pynoos, 1993; Masten et al., 1990). The ability of the individual to resist or effectively cope with stressors has been conceptualized as "psychological hardiness" (Kobasa, 1979).

Both human (Rutter, 1971) and animal studies (Hinde and Spencer-Booth, 1971; Hinde and McGinnis, 1977) show that family interactions influence responses to stressful stimuli, although the adverse influence of family discord can be modified by particular intrafamilial characteristics. For example, the presence of one good parent–child relationship reduces psychiatric risk associated with family discord (Rutter, 1978).

PHYSIOLOGICAL RESPONSES TO TRAUMA

Stress is known to increase activity of the hypothalamic–pituitary–adrenal axis (HPA), the sympathetic nervous system (SNS), and the adrenal medulla (see Friedman, Clark, and Gershon, 1992; Dorn and Chrousos, 1993, for reviews). Biochemical models have been discussed in detail in the first volume of this three-volume series and the reader is encouraged to review the chapter entitled "Theoretical Models of Stress Adaptation" (Miller and Kraus, 1995). While the theoretical models concerning physiological responses to stress have been primarily developed with reference to adults, these principles also generally apply to children.

THE HYPOTHALAMIC–PITUITARY–ADRENAL AXIS

The HPA axis is critical to the physiological response to stressors. The response begins with corticotropin-releasing hormone (CRH) secretion from the hypothalamus, which selectively stimulates pituitary adrenocorticotropin hormone (ACTH) secretion. This leads to increased cortisol secretion from the adrenal cortex as well as increased SNS activity. In addition, CRH and the locus coeruleus (LC) participate in a positive feedback loop (Chrousos and Gold, 1992). Attenuated ACTH response to exogenously administered CRH reflects dysregulation of the HPA axis (Gold, Goodwin, and Chrousos, 1988), and has been reported in adult samples with PTSD (Smith, Davidson, Ritchie, Kudler, Lipper,

Chapell, and Nemeroff, 1989). DeBellis, Lefter, and Trickett (1994) have reported attenuated plasma ACTH responses to CRH in sexually abused girls. These results suggest that sexually abused girls manifest an HPA axis regulatory disorder.

CATECHOLAMINERGIC SYSTEMS

Through both animal and human studies with adults, the physiological changes in catecholamine systems occurring in response to stress have been extensively investigated. Stressful stimuli increase locus coeruleus (LC) and peripheral sympathetic nervous system activities (SNS; Simson and Weiss, 1988). The nucleus paragigantocellularis (PGi), in the rostral ventral medulla, may be a key brain region in this dual response; PGi simultaneously activates LC and SNS in response to unexpected or urgent stimuli (Aston-Jones, Valentino, Van Bockstaele, and Meyerson, 1994). Through the coordinating influence of the PGi, LC and SNS may serve, respectively, as the catecholaminergic stress effector system's central and peripheral limbs (Murburg, Ashleigh, Hommer, and Veith, 1994).

Locus coeruleus is the major noradrenergic (NE) nucleus in the brain (Chronister and DeFrance, 1981). Increased responsiveness of LC neurons increases NE turnover in specific brain regions, including LC, hypothalamus, hippocampus, amygdala, and cerebral cortex, brain regions associated with cardiovascular regulation, memory, and emotion (Glavin, 1985; Tsuda and Tanaka, 1985; Murburg et al., 1994). Peripheral sympathetic system activation results in increased heart rate, elevated blood pressure, and other physiological changes (Chrousos and Gold, 1992). Stress also enhances the release and metabolism of DA in the prefrontal cortex (Charney, Deutch, Krystal, Southwick, and Murburg, 1993), a response which has been hypothesized to enhance adaptive coping (Deutch and Roth, 1989). Dysregulation of the catecholamines has been implicated in the pathophysiology of anxiety disorders, including PTSD (Friedman, Clark, and Gershon, 1992; Charney et al., 1993). Changes in central catecholaminergic systems have been implicated in the pathophysiology of several PTSD symptoms, including exaggerated startle (Rausch, Geyer, Jenkins, Breslin, and Braff, 1994), anhedonia (Zacharko, 1994), sleep difficulty (Aston-Jones et al., 1994), hypervigilance (Aston-Jones et al., 1994), and flashbacks (Charney, Southwick, Krystal, Deutch, Murburg, and Davis, 1994).

While understanding the CNS specific processes involved in the stress response is clearly important, peripheral measures are more than CNS activity approximations. The function of CNS activity is, in this context, to direct musculoskeletal, endocrine, and autonomic effector systems to respond to threat (Giller, 1994). Urinary excretion of NE, E, DA, and its metabolites reflects end organ functional activity of the CNS, the peripheral sympathetic system, and the adrenal medulla (Maas, Koslow, Davis, Katz, Frazer, Bowdewn, Berman, Gibbons, Stokes, and Landis, 1987; Goodwin and Jamison, 1990). Peripheral measures of physiological changes, such as heart rate, may be conceptualized as assessing the results accomplished by CNS activity (Mason, Giller, and Kosten, 1990).

There is evidence that traumatized individuals have increased systemic CA activity. Increased basal urinary catecholamines (Kosten, Mason, and Giller, 1987) have been found in adults with PTSD compared with control subjects. Debellis, Lefter, and Trickett (1994) measured 24-hour urinary catecholamines and metabolites in 12 sexually abused and nine control girls, ages 8 to 15. The abused subjects excreted significantly greater amounts of MN, VMA, and HVA and had greater total catecholamine synthesis compared with controls. After controlling for difference in height, the HVA difference remained significant, and the other findings exhibited positive trends. Only one of these traumatized girls met criteria for PTSD, and she showed more extreme results on several measures.

CARDIOVASCULAR REGULATION

As cardiovascular regulation is, in part, mediated by catecholaminergic systems, one would expect that increased CA activity would be reflected in heart rate. Increased tonic heart rate (Pitman, van der Kolk, Orr, and Graenberg, 1990), and greater heart rate increases in response to loud tones (Shalev, Orr, and Pitman, 1992) have been found in adults with PTSD compared with control subjects. Similarly, children with PTSD have been reported to have resting tachycardia and increased cardiovascular lability to orthostatic challenge (Perry, 1994).

Immune functioning

Stressors have been found to increase the risk for infectious diseases and other illnesses in children and adolescents (Boyce, Jensen, Cassel, Collier, Smith, and Ramey, 1977; Jacobs and Charles, 1980). It has been suggested that this effect may be through stress induced alterations in immune functioning, as stressors have been found to be associated with changes in cellular immunity in adults (Herbert and Cohen, 1993). In a sample of 54 adolescents, Birmaher, Rabin, Garcia, Jain, Whiteside, Williamson, Al-Shabbout, Nelson, Dahl, and Ryan (1994) recently found that the sum of lifetime adverse events was negatively correlated with natural killer cell activity.

CNS FUNCTIONING

There is limited evidence that maltreatment alters CNS functioning in children and adolescents. Several studies have found EEG abnormalities in abused children (Green, Voeller, and Gaines, 1981; Davies, 1979). Ito and colleagues (Ito, Teicher, Glod, Harper, Magnus, and Gelbard, 1993) found increased electrophysiological and conventional electroencephalographic (EEG) abnormalities in children with histories of psychological, physical, or sexual abuse compared with nonabused patients (Ito et al., 1993). Abnormal electrophysiological findings were noted in 27 percent of controls, 43 percent of cases with psychological abuse, 60 percent of cases with likely physical or sexual abuse, and 72 percent of cases with definite serious physical or sexual abuse.

THEORETICAL MODELS

Theories developed in the first half of this century primarily concerned acute physiological stress responses. An early modern theory of the acute stress reaction was developed by Walter B. Cannon (1929), who characterized the response to stress as an "emergency reaction" that results in the physiological and behavioral changes described as the "fight or flight" response. While initially adaptive, Cannon proposed that physical illness would result from prolonged activation of the fight or flight system. This prediction has been the subject of renewed interest, with more recent theories suggesting that elevated cortisol leads to immunosuppression with resulting diminished resistance to illness (DeBellis and Putnam, 1994). Figure 1.1 presents a schematic view of some of the initial biological changes that occur in response to stressors. Although this model is necessarily simplified, the figure represents a basic starting point to which additional complexities can be appended.

Hans Selye (1936, 1952) studied the long-term responses to chronic stressors, and developed a model termed the *general adaptation syndrome* (Figure 1.2). Selye observed that an organism, when exposed to a noxious agent, responds with physiological and behavioral changes which occur in stages. In other words, the responses of the organism change over time. The initial alarm reaction leads to a stage of resistance, during which the organism adaptively copes with the stressor. With concentrated exposure to the stressor, the state of resistance can be maintained for only a finite period. The duration of the resistance stage depends on the stressor characteristics and individual variables. Following the stage of resistance, the acquired adaptation is lost and a third stage emerges. This third stage is a state of exhaustion in which the organism fails to maintain an ability to cope with the stressful situation.

The stages of adaptation to stressful life events specific to humans, and likely common to both children and adults, have been further elaborated upon by other theorists. Among these models

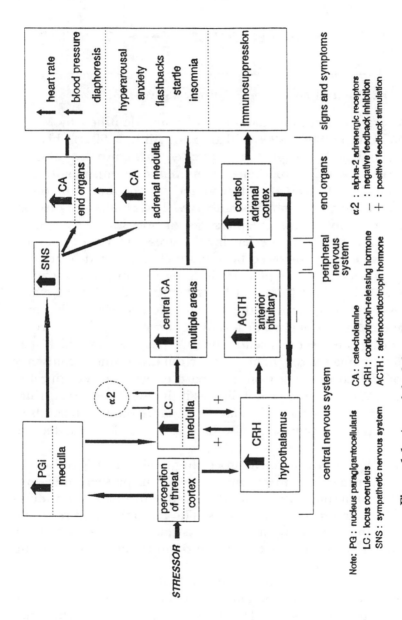

Figure 1.1. A model of the effect of stressors on biological systems.

Figure 1.2. General Adaptation Syndrome (Selye, 1936)

is the Trauma Accommodation Syndrome, identified by Miller and Veltkamp (1988, 1993; Veltkamp and Miller, 1994). This syndrome and its five stages are presented in Figure 1.3. Stage I concerns the child's experience of an event or events that involve threatened death, actual or threatened serious injury, or other threats to the child's physical integrity. The child's response in stage II may involve fear, helplessness, or horror.

The initial stages of experiencing the stressful life event and the acute response are followed by a phase characterized by trauma reenactment, repetitive play, frightening dreams, or avoidance. The key component in stage III is a recurrence of intrusive and distressing recollections of the stressful life experience that may include images, thoughts, or less direct forms. In children, reexperiencing often shows itself through repetitive play which may include trauma-related themes. Recurrent distressing dreams may be considered to result from trauma even without recognizable content. When a young child feels as if the event were recurring, trauma-specific reenactment may occur. More often with children than with adults, there may also be disorganized or agitated behavior.

Stage IV involves cognitive processing, wherein a triggering life experience may lead to trauma reevaluation or reexamination. There is often some effort toward reasoning through reconsideration of the traumatization process. The reasoning and reevaluation of the psychological and physical traumatization allow revisitation, better understanding, and mourning to occur in the traumatized child.

The final stage of trauma accommodation in the child involves stage V wherein either the child accommodates or is able to resolve the traumatic issues. The development of coping strategies

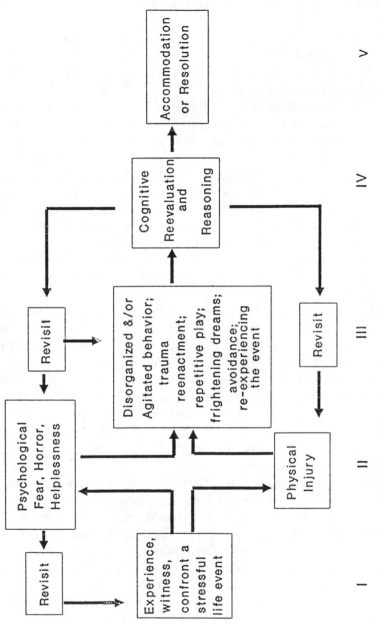

Figure 1.3. Trauma Accommodation in Children

may allow the child to accept and resolve, without doubt or guilt, the meaning of the traumatization to his or her identity.

Specifically concerning accommodation of victimization and child sexual abuse, Summit (1983) proposed a model called the Child Sexual Abuse Accommodation Syndrome. This model acknowledges that children who are sexually abused are often fearful and confused about the implications of abuse disclosure. The perpetrator has often convinced the child victim that they will be rejected or suffer dreadful and, perhaps, life-threatening consequences if they reveal the crime. Furthermore, the child may have been socialized to believe that discussing sexual topics is wrong. Parents and significant others may communicate to the child that he or she will not be readily believed. In response to these influences, the child often delays disclosure for extended periods of time, despite the on-going threat and harm imposed by the sexual abuse. If disclosure is met with resistance or disbelief, children may retract their allegation rather than suffer rejection by significant others.

Within the sexual abuse accommodation syndrome, Summit identified five phases. These include stages of secrecy, helplessness, accommodation, delayed disclosure, and retraction. It is in the accommodation phase that children may suffer dissociative experiences and repress recent and remote memories about the abuse. These accommodations are often reinforced if the child's eventual disclosure is met with disbelief, rejection, increased abuse, or threats of violence by the perpetrator. The trauma is thus accommodated through distorted cognition and maladaptive emotional functioning.

While theories concerning adaptation to stressors have been developed which may explain long-term psychological changes, biological models have primarily focused on acute physiological changes. Retrospective studies suggest that early traumatic experiences may lead to lifelong psychological and physiological changes, although data from prospective studies are not yet available to demonstrate their specific nature. Nevertheless, biological theories which attempt to explain long-term physiological changes in response to stressors are emerging.

Post (1992) has suggested that sensitization to stressors becomes encoded at the level of gene expression. In a theory developed to explain the relationship between psychosocial stress and recurrent affective disorder, he postulates that stressors resulting in affective and physiological responses can induce specific genes and related transcription factors, which in turn influence the expression of neurotransmitters, neurotransmitter receptors, and neuropeptides. In this way, a biological mechanism is hypothesized whereby psychosocial stressors may result in long-term changes in CNS responsivity.

DEVELOPMENTAL ISSUES

While these psychological and biological theories model the changes in adaptive responding with time, they do not account for possible differences in responses with maturation. Furthermore, the possible influences of stressors and stress responses on developmental processes need to be addressed when constructing theoretical models applicable to children and adolescents.

The data available to date strongly suggest that preadolescent children differ from adults in their psychological responses to severe stressors. For example, Goodwin (1988) has observed that, in response to incest, preschool children will exhibit "frozen watchfulness," with children ages 4 to 6 years being more afraid of being punished than toddlers. The preadolescent, ages 7 to 13 years, shows well-differentiated fears of retaliation by the sexually intrusive parental figure.

It remains unclear to what extent adolescents may primarily manifest adult or child PTSD expressions. Previous research on psychic trauma has pointed out that there may be unique adolescent responses, including impaired identity formation, premature entrance into adulthood, acting out behavior, interpersonal difficulties, and poor work values (Krener, 1985; Eth and Pynoos, 1985; Malmquist, 1986). Lyons (1987) points out that traumatized adolescents may become very compliant and withdrawn, or alternately may become aggressive, abuse psychoactive substances, and act out sexually. She also notes that guilt and secretiveness are more prominent among adolescents than younger trauma victims.

Physiological responses may also differ across age groups. While the HPA axis plays a primary role in the stress response, other endocrine systems are influenced by its output (Dorn and Chrousos, 1993). Hormones influenced by the HPA axis activity include gonadal hormones, growth hormone, and thyroid hormone. These endocrine systems are central to growth and pubertal development. Chronic changes in these systems during critical periods of development, which may occur in response to stressors, may be particularly problematic for individuals actively undergoing maturation.

There have been attempts to construct developmentally informed stress adaptation theories. Pynoos (1993) points out that, as children get older, their interaction with their social environment changes in a variety of ways which may modify their risk for encountering stressors. As adolescents become more independent, they rely more on their own assessment of threat, and increasingly come under peer influence. While younger children may express reenactment through play, adolescents may engage in risk-taking behavior as a form of trauma reenactment, thereby increasing the probability of encountering additional stressors. Approaches to adaptive coping are also likely influenced by developmental stages. Children who are in later stages of development when severe stressors occur may be better equipped psychologically and socially to respond to the effects.

Pynoos (1993) proposes that traumatic stress may affect both proximal and distal development. With regard to proximal developmental effects, recently acquired competencies may be vulnerable to disruption, and selective attention resulting from reexperiencing phenomena may interfere with new skill acquisition. Intense distress may result in fear of emotions, adversely influencing the capacity to experience and express affect. Trauma related avoidant behavior may interfere with the achievement of autonomy.

Sexual trauma may distort the child's psychosexual maturation. With regard to distal developmental effects, traumatic experiences in childhood may influence the emerging personality through changes in perception of internal and external dangers, inner representation of the self and other, and cognitive and emotional regulation. Negative self-attributions may be reactivated with exposure to stressors in adulthood. Pynoos also speculates that increases in stress hormones in early childhood may influence neural network formation.

Several theorists have hypothesized that early childhood traumatization may alter CNS development. Teicher, Glod, and Surrey (1993) have suggested that early child abuse causes abnormal limbic system maturation, leading to affective instability, inability to modulate anger, poor impulse control, and other psychological abnormalities. Van der Kolk and Greenberg (1987) have proposed that the adverse effects of repeated traumatization may be due to amygdaloid kindling. Ito and colleagues (1993) speculate that early abuse results in elevated levels of glucocorticoid levels, resulting in damage to specific brain areas during development.

CONCLUSION

Within the biopsychosocial framework, there exist several perspectives that have applicability to our growing understanding of the responses of children to stressful life events. Early theoretical models focused on the acute response to stressors, such as Cannon's description of the fight or flight reaction. More recently developed theories have focused on psychological and physiological adaptation to the effects of trauma over a more extended time period. As it is increasingly clear that children differ in their responses, variable accounting for individual variations are increasingly being incorporated into theoretical models. A developmental framework can provide an approach toward accommodating changes in children's responses with maturation, another important consideration in theory construction. As theories become more comprehensive, however, they necessarily become more complex.

The development of theoretical models concerning the responses and adaptation of children to the effects of stressors is not simply an intellectual exercise. Theoretical models serve as the stepping stones to the next generation of clinical and research activities on traumatization. Improved understanding of the psychological and physiological responses to stressors will lead to more effective psychological and pharmacological treatments to alleviate the distress resulting from traumatization. The hypothesis that early childhood traumatization alters later responses to stressors supports the importance of prevention efforts, including programs designed to improve child rearing and to prevent child abuse. Comprehensive theoretical models concerning the impact of stressors on children have the potential for directing the attention of society on the adverse influence stressors have on the next generation.

REFERENCES

American Psychiatric Association (1987), *Diagnostic and Statistical Manual of Mental Disorders* (DSM-III-R), 3rd ed., rev. Washington, DC: American Psychiatric Press.
———(1994), *Diagnostic and Statistical Manual of Mental Disorders* (DSM-IV), 4th ed. Washington, DC: American Psychiatric Press.
Aston-Jones, G., Valentino, R. J., Van Bockstaele, E. J., & Meyerson, A. T. (1994), Locus coeruleus, stress, and PTSD: Neurobiological and clinical parallels. In: *Catecholamine Function in Posttraumatic Stress Disorder: Emerging Concepts*, ed. M. M. Murburg. Washington, DC: American Psychiatric Press, pp. 17–62.
Birmaher, B., Rabin, B. S., Garcia, M. R., Jain, U., Whiteside, T. L., Williamson, D. E., Al-Shabbout, M., Nelson, B.C., Dahl, R. E., & Ryan, N. D. (1994), Cellular immunity in depressed, conduct disorder, and normal adolescents: Role of adverse life events. *J. Amer. Acad. Child & Adol. Psychiatry*, 33:671–978.
Boyce, T. W., Jensen, E. W., Cassel, J. C., Collier, A. M., Smith, A. H., & Ramey, C. T. (1977), Influences of life events and family routines on childhood respiratory tract illness. *Pediatrics*, 60:609–615.

Brett, E. A. (1993), Classifications of posttraumatic stress disorder in DSM-IV: Anxiety disorder, dissociative disorder, or stress disorder? In: *Posttraumatic Stress Disorder: DSM-IV and Beyond*, ed. J. R. Davidson & E. B. Foa. Washington, DC: American Psychiatric Press, pp. 191–204.

Cannon, W. B. (1929), *Bodily Changes in Pain, Hunger, Fear and Rage*. Boston: C. T. Branford.

Charney, D. S., Deutch, A. Y., Krystal, J. H., Southwick, S. M., & Murburg, M. M. (1993), Psychobiological mechanisms of posttraumatic stress disorder. *Arch. Gen. Psychiatry*, 50:294–305.

—— Southwick, S. M., Krystal, J. H., Deutch, A. Y., Murburg, M. M., & Davis, M. (1994), Neurobiological mechanisms of PTSD. In: *Catecholamine Function in Posttraumatic Stress Disorder: Emerging Concepts*, ed. M. M. Murburg. Washington, DC: American Psychiatric Press, pp. 284–296.

Chronister, R. B., & DeFrance, J. F. (1981). Functional organization of monoamines. In: *Neuropharmacology of Central Nervous System and Behavioral Disorders*, ed. G. C. Palmer. New York: Academic Press, pp. 437–446.

Chrousos, C. P., & Gold, P. W. (1992), The concepts of stress and stress systems disorders: Overview of physical and behavioral homeostasis. *J. Amer. Med. Assn.*, 267:1244–1252.

Clark, D. B., Bukstein, O. G., Smith, M. G., Kaczynski, N. A., Mezzich, A. C., & Donovan, J. E. (in press), Anxiety disorders in hospitalized adolescents with alcohol abuse or dependence. *Hosp. & Commun. Psychiatry*.

—— Neighbors, B. (in press), Adolescent substance abuse and internalizing disorders. *Child Psychiatric Clin. N. Amer.*

—— Sayette, M. A. (1993), Anxiety and the development of alcoholism: Clinical and scientific issues. *Amer. J. Addictions*, 2:59–76.

—— Smith, M. G., Neighbors, B. D., Skerlec, L. M., & Randall, J. (1994), Anxiety disorders in adolescence: Characteristics, prevalence, and comorbidities. *Clin. Psychol. Rev.*, 14:113–137.

Davidson, J. R. T., Hughes, D. L., & Blazer, D. G. (1991), Posttraumatic stress disorder in the community: An epidemiological study. *Psycholog. Med.*, 21:713–721.

Davies, R. K. (1979), Incest: Some neuropsychiatric findings. *Internat. J. Psychiatry & Med.*, 9:117–121.

DeBellis, M. D., Lefter, L., & Trickett, P. (1994), Urinary catecholamine excretion in sexually abused girls. *J. Amer. Acad. Child & Adol. Psychiatry*, 33:320–327.

—— Putnam, F. W. (1994), The psychobiology of childhood maltreatment. *Child & Adol. Psychiatric Clin. N. Amer.*, 3:1–16.

Deutch, A. Y., & Roth, R. H. (1989), The determinants of stress-induced activation of the prefrontal cortical dopamine system. In: *The Prefrontal Cortex: Its Structure, Function, and Pathology*, ed. H. B. M. Uylings, C. G. Van Eden, & M. A. DeBruin. Amsterdam: Elsevier Science.

De Wilde, E. J., Kienhorst, I. C. W. M., Diekstra, R. F. W., & Wolters, W. H. G. (1992), The relationship between adolescent suicidal behavior and life events in childhood and adolescence. *Amer. J. Psychiatry*, 149:45–51.

Dorn, L., & Chrousos, G. (1993), The endocrinology of stress and stress system disorders in adolescence. *Endocrinol. & Metabol. Clin. N. Amer.*, 22:685–700.

Eth, S., & Pynoos, R. S. (1985), Developmental perspective on psychic trauma in childhood. In: *Trauma and Its Wake*, ed. C. R. Figley. New York: Brunner/Mazel, pp. 36–52.

Friedman, E. S., Clark, D. B., & Gershon, S. (1992), Stress, anxiety, and depression: Review of biological, diagnostic, and nosologic issues. *J. Anxiety Disord.*, 6:337–363.

Friedman, M. (1991), Neurological alterations associated with posttraumatic stress disorder. Teleconference Report prepared for the National Center for PTSD, Clinical Laboratory and Education Division.

Friedman, M. J. (1981), Post-Vietnam syndrome: Recognition and management. *Psychosomatics*, 22:931–943.

Garmezy, N. (1985), Stress-resistant children: The search for protective factors. In: *Recent Research in Developmental Psychopathology*, ed. J. E. Stevenson. *Journal of Child Psychology and Psychiatry* book, Vol. 4. Oxford: Pergamon Press, pp. 213–233.

Giller, E. L. (1994), Foreword. In: *Catecholamine Function in Posttraumatic Stress Disorder: Emerging Concepts*, ed. M. M. Murburg. Washington, DC: American Psychiatric Press.

Glavin, G. B. (1985), Stress and brain noradrenaline: A review. *Behav. Neurosci. Rev.*, 9:233–243.

Gold, P. W., Goodwin, F. K., & Chrousos, G. P. (1988), Clinical and biochemical manifestations of depression: Relation to the neurobiology of stress, part II. *N. Eng. J. Med.*, 319:413–420.

Gomes-Schwartz, B., Horowitz, M. J., & Sauzier, M. (1985), Severity of emotional distress among sexually abused preschool, school age, and adolescent children. *Hosp. & Commun. Psychiatry*, 36:503–508.

Goodwin, F., & Jamison, K. (1990), *Manic-Depressive Illness*. New York: Oxford University Press.

Goodwin, J. (1988), Post-traumatic symptoms in abused children. *J. Traum. Stress*, 1:475–488.

Green, A. H., Voeller, K., & Gaines, R. W. (1981), Neurological impairment in maltreated children. *Child Abuse & Neglect*, 5:129–134.

Green, B. L., Korol, M., Grace, M. C., Vary, M. G., Leonard, A. C., Gleser, G. C., & Smithson-Cohen, S. (1991), Children and disaster: Age, gender, and parental effects on PTSD symptoms. *J. Amer. Acad. Child & Adol. Psychiatry*, 30:945–951.

Herbert, T. B., & Cohen, S. (1993), Stress and immunity in humans: A meta-analytic review. *Psychosom. Med.*, 55:364–379.

Herman, J. (1993), Sequelae of prolonged and repeated trauma: Evidence for a complex posttraumatic syndrome (DESNOS). In: *Posttraumatic Stress Disorder: DSM-IV and Beyond*, ed. J. R. T. Davidson & E. B. Foa. Washington, DC: American Psychiatric Press, pp. 213–228.

Higley, J. D., Hasert, M. F., Suomi, S. J., & Linnoila, M. (1991), Nonhuman primate model of alcohol abuse: Effects of early experience, personality, and stress on alcohol consumption. *Proc. Nat. Acad. Sci.*, 88:7261–7265.

Hinde, R. A., & McGinnis, L. (1977), Some factors influencing the effects of temporary mother–infant separation in rhesus monkeys. *Psycholog. Med.*, 7:197–212.

———— Spencer-Booth, Y. (1971), Effects of brief separation from mother on rhesus monkeys. In: *Primate Ethology*, ed. D. Morris. London: Weidenfeld & Nicolson, pp. 267–286.

Ito, Y., Teicher, M. H., Glod, C. A., Harper, D., Magnus, E., & Gelbard, H. A. (1993), Increased prevalence in children with psychological, physical and sexual abuse. *J. Neuropsychiatry & Clin. Neurosci.*, 5:401–408.

Jacobs, T. J., & Charles, E. (1980), Life events and the occurrence of cancer in children. *Psychosom. Med.*, 42:11–24.

Keane, T., Caddell, J., & Taylor, K. (1988), Mississippi Scale for combat-related post traumatic stress disorder: Studies in reliability and validity. *J. Consult. & Clin. Psychol.*, 56:85–90.

Kinzie, J. D., Sack, W. H., Angell, R. H., Manson, S., & Rath, B. (1986), The psychiatric effects of massive trauma on Cambodian children: I. The children. *J. Amer. Acad. Child & Adol. Psychiatry*, 25:370–376.

Kobasa, S. C. (1979), Stressful life events, personality, and health: An inquiry into hardiness. *J. Personal. & Soc. Psychol.*, 37:1–11.

Kosten, T., Mason, J., & Giller, E. (1987), Sustained urinary norepinephrine and epinephrine elevation in post-traumatic stress disorder. *Psychoneuroendocrinol.*, 12:13–20.

Krener, P. (1985), After incest: Secondary prevention. *Amer. Acad. Child Psychiatry*, 24:231–234.

Labouvie, E. W. (1986), Alcohol and marijuana use in relation to adolescent stress. *Internat. J. Addict.*, 23:333–345.

Lindberg, F. H., & Distad, L. J. (1985), Post-traumatic stress disorders in women who experience childhood incest. *Child Abuse & Neglect*, 9:329–334.

Lyons, J. A. (1987), Posttraumatic stress disorder in children and adolescents: A review of the literature. *Develop. & Behav. Pediatrics*, 8:349–356.

Maas, J., Koslow, S., Davis, J., Katz, M., Frazer, A., Bowdewn, C., Berman, N., Gibbons, R., Stokes, P., & Landis, D. (1987), Catecholamine metabolism and disposition in healthy and depressed subjects. *Arch. Gen. Psychiatry*, 44:337–344.

Malmquist, C. P. (1986), Children who witness parental murder: Posttraumatic aspects. *J. Amer. Acad. Child & Adol. Psychiatry*, 25:320–325.

Martini, D. R., Ryan, C., Nakayama, D., & Ramenofsky, M. (1990), Psychiatric sequelae after traumatic injury: The Pittsburgh Regatta accident. *J. Amer. Acad. Child & Adol. Psychiatry*, 29:70–75.

Mason, J., Giller, E. J., & Kosten, T. (1990), Psychoendocrine approaches to the diagnosis and pathogenesis of PTSD. In: *The Biological Assessment and Treatment of Posttraumatic Stress Disorder*, ed. E. L. J. Giller. Washington, DC: American Psychiatric Press, pp. 65–86.

Masten, A. S., Best, K. M., & Garmezy, N. (1990), Resilience and development: Contributions from the study of children who overcome adversity. *Develop. & Psychopathol.*, 2:425–444.

McLeer, S. V., Deblinger, E., Atkins, M. S., Foa, E. B., & Ralphe, D. L. (1988), Post-traumatic stress disorder in sexually abused children. *J. Amer. Acad. Child & Adol. Psychiatry*, 27:650–654.

McNally, R. J. (1993), Assessment of intrusive cognition in PTSD: Use of modified troop paradigm. *J. Traum. Stress*, 6:33–41.

Miller, T. W., & Başoğlu, M. (1992), Posttraumatic stress disorder: The impact of life stress events on adjustment. *Integrat. Psychiatry*, 7:207–215.
—— Kraus, R. F. (1995), Stress adaptation in children: Theoretical models. *J. Contemp. Psychother.*, 25:5–14.
—— Veltkamp, L. J. (1988), The abusing family in rural America. *Internat. J. Fam. Psychiatry*, 9:259–275.
—— —— (1993), Family violence: Clinical indicators in military and post military personnel. *Milit. Med.*, 86:384–395.
Murburg, M. M., Ashleigh, E. A., Hommer, D. W., & Veith, R. C. (1994), Biology of catecholaminergic systems and their relevance to PTSD. In: *Catecholamine Function in Posttraumatic Stress Disorder: Emerging Concepts*, ed. M. M. Murburg. Washington, DC: American Psychiatric Press, pp. 3–16.
Nadelson, C. C., Notman, M. T., Zackson, H., & Gornick, J. (1982), A follow-up study of rape victims. *Amer. J. Psychiatry*, 139:1266–1270.
Perry, B. D. (1994), Neurobiological sequelae of childhood trauma: PTSD in children. In: *Catecholamine Function in Posttraumatic Stress Disorder: Emerging Concepts*, ed. M. M. Murburg. Washington, DC: American Psychiatric Press, pp. 233–256.
Pitman, P. K., van der Kolk, B. A., Orr, S. P., & Graenberg, M. S. (1990), Naloxone-reversible analgesic response to combat-related stimuli in posttraumatic stress disorder. *Arch. Gen. Psychiatry*, 47:541–544.
Post, R. M. (1992), Transduction of psychosocial stress into the neurobiology of recurrent affective disorder. *Amer. J. Psychiatry*, 149:999–1007.
Pynoos, R. S. (1993), Traumatic stress and developmental psychopathology in children and adolescents. In: *Review of Psychiatry*, ed. J. M. Oldham, M. B. Riba, & A. Tasman. Washington, DC: American Psychiatric Press, pp. 205–238.
—— Frederick, C., Nader, K., Arroyo, W., Steinberg, A., Eth, S., Nunez, F., & Fairbanks, L. (1987), Life threat and posttraumatic stress disorder in school-age children. *Arch. Gen. Psychiatry*, 44:1057–1063.
—— Nader, K. (1988), Children who witness the sexual assaults of their mothers. *J. Amer. Acad. Child & Adol. Psychiatry*, 27:567–572.
Rausch, J. L., Geyer, M. A., Jenkins, M. A., Breslin, G., & Braff, D. L. (1994), Neurobiology of startle response abnormalities in PTSD. In: *Catecholamine Function in Posttraumatic Stress Disorder: Emerging Concepts*, ed. M. M. Murburg. Washington, DC: American Psychiatric Press, pp. 279–292.
Reinherz, H. Z., Giaconia, R. M., Lefkowitz, E. S., Pakiz, B., & Frost, A. K. (1993), Prevalence of psychiatric disorders in a community population of older adolescents. *J. Amer. Acad. Child & Adol. Psychiatry*, 32:369–377.
Rutter, M. (1971), Parent–child separation: Psychological effects on the children. *J. Child Psychol. & Psychiatry*, 12:233–260.
—— (1978), Language disorder and infantile autism. In: *Autism: A Reappraisal of Concepts and Treatment*, ed. M. Rutter & E. Schopler. New York: Plenum Press, pp. 85–104.
—— (1990), Commentary: Some focus and process considerations regarding effects of parental depression on children. *Develop. Psychol.*, 26:60–67.
Sanders, B., & Giolas, M. H. (1991), Dissociation and childhood trauma in psychologically disturbed adolescents. *Amer. J. Psychiatry*, 148:50–54.

Sansonnet-Hayden, H., Haley, G., Marriage, K., & Fine, S. (1987), Sexual abuse and psychopathology in hospitalized adolescents. *J. Amer. Acad. Child & Adol. Psychiatry*, 26:753–757.

Schwartz, E. D., & Kowalski, J. M. (1991), Malignant memories: PTSD in children and adults following a school shooting. *J. Amer. Acad. Child & Adol. Psychiatry*, 30:936–944.

Seligman, M. E. F. (1975), *Helplessness*. San Francisco: W. H. Freeman.

Selye, H. (1936), A syndrome produced by diverse nocuous agents. *Nature*, 138:32.

———— (1952), *The Story of the Adaptation Syndrome*. Montreal, Canada: Acta Inc.

Shalev, A., Orr, S., & Pitman, P. (1992), Psychophysiologic response during script-driven imagery as an outcome measure in posttraumatic stress disorder. *J. Clin. Psychiatry*, 53:324–326.

Simson, P. E., & Weiss, J. M. (1988), Altered activity of the locus coeruleus in an animal model of depression. *Neuropsychopharmacology*, 1:287–295.

Smith, M. A., Davidson, J., Ritchie, J. C., Kudler, H., Lipper, S., Chapell, P., & Nemeroff, C. B. (1989), The corticotropin-releasing hormone test in patients with posttraumatic stress disorder. *Biolog. Psychiatry*, 26:349–355.

Stoddard, F. J., Norman, D. K., Murphy, J. M., & Beardslee, W. R. (1989), Psychiatric outcome of burned children and adolescents. *J. Amer. Acad. Child & Adol. Psychiatry*, 28:589–595.

Summit, R. C. (1983), The child sexual abuse accommodation syndrome. *Child Abuse & Neglect*, 7:177 193.

Teicher, M. H., Glod, C. A., & Surrey, J. (1993), Early childhood abuse and limbic system ratings in adult psychiatric outpatients. *J. Neuropsychiatry & Clin. Neurosci.*, 5:301–306.

Terr, L. (1983), Chowchilla revisited: The effects of psychic trauma four years after a school bus kidnapping. *Amer. J. Psychiatry*, 140:1543–1550.

Tsuda, A., & Tanaka, M. (1985), Differential changes in noradrenaline turnover in specific regions of rat brain produced by controllable and uncontrollable shocks. *Behav. Neurosci.*, 99:802–807.

van der Kolk, B. A. (1985), Adolescent vulnerability to posttraumatic stress disorder. *Psychiatry*, 48:365–370.

———— Greenberg, M. S. (1987), The psychobiology of the trauma response: Hyperarousal, constriction, and addiction to traumatic reexposure. In: *Psychological Trauma*, ed. B. van der Kolk. Washington, DC: American Psychiatric Press, pp. 63–87.

Veltkamp, L. J., & Miller, T. W. (1994), *Clinical Handbook of Child Abuse and Neglect*. Madison, CT: International Universities Press.

Wilson, J. P., Smith, W. K., & Johnson, S. K. (1985), A comparative analysis of PTSD among various survivor groups. In: *Trauma and Its Wake*, ed. C. R. Figley. New York: Brunner/Mazel, pp. 142–172.

Zacharko, R. M. (1994), Stressors, the mesocorticolimbic systems, and anhedonia: Implications for PTSD. In: *Catecholamine Function in Posttraumatic Stress Disorder: Emerging Concepts*, ed. M. M. Murburg. Washington, DC: American Psychiatric Press, pp. 211–215.

Chapter 2
Measures of Children's Reactions to Stressful Life Events

RICHARD J. MCNALLY, PH.D.

Although most assessment research on posttraumatic stress disorder (PTSD) has concerned adults exposed to combat or rape, clinical investigators have increasingly attended to the evaluation of children exposed to traumatic events (McNally, 1991, 1993, in press). Facilitating this trend, the third, revised edition of the *Diagnostic and Statistical Manual of Mental Disorders* (DSM-III-R) (APA, 1987) incorporated age-specific features into the criteria for PTSD, and traumatologists have endeavored to devise systematic measures for determining whether children satisfy these criteria. The purpose of this chapter is to provide an overview of measures for assessing children exposed to traumatic events and to describe new instruments currently undergoing validation. These new structured interviews and questionnaires are designed to remedy deficiencies in the first generation of assessment measures, and are designed to accommodate DSM-IV diagnostic criteria (APA, 1994).

STRUCTURED INTERVIEWS

The "gold standard" for establishing PTSD caseness is the structured (or semistructured) clinical interview. Investigators have developed instruments for interviewing traumatized children directly, and instruments for interviewing adults about the signs and symptoms of PTSD exhibited by children under their care.

INTERVIEWS WITH CHILDREN

One method for evaluating PTSD in children is simply to add questions to existing interview schedules to broaden their scope. For example, researchers have inserted questions from the modified Diagnostic Interview Schedule (DIS; Robins and Smith, 1984) into the Diagnostic Interview for Children and Adolescents (DICA; Welner, Reich, Herjanic, Jung, and Amado, 1987) to enable diagnosis of PTSD (Earls, Smith, Reich, and Jung, 1988). Thus, Earls et al. used the DICA to evaluate 39 children one year after a flood ravaged their rural Missouri community. Some children exhibited PTSD symptoms, but none met full criteria for the disorder.

Applying the same instrument, Stoddard and colleagues assessed 30 children, aged 7 to 19 years, who had been severely burned in house fires, half of them before the age of 2 years (Stoddard, Norman, Murphy, and Beardslee, 1989). Thirty percent met lifetime criteria for DSM-III PTSD, but only 6.7 percent had current PTSD. Stoddard et al. reported an interrater reliability of 92 percent for the DICA-based PTSD diagnosis.

DIS-based assessment of childhood PTSD is likely to become increasingly uncommon for several reasons. First, the DIS has a sensitivity of only 25 percent for detecting cases of PTSD in Vietnam combat veterans (Kulka, Schlenger, Fairbank, Hough, Jordan, Marmar, and Weiss, 1988), and its sensitivity for detecting cases of childhood PTSD is unlikely to be much better. Second, the DIS is an epidemiologic instrument designed for use by lay interviewers, not trained clinicians. Third, it is based on DSM-III criteria.

Saigh (1989a,b) has developed the Children's Posttraumatic Stress Disorder Inventory (CPTSDI), a structured interview for diagnosing DSM-III PTSD. Using this instrument, Saigh and his colleagues evaluated 840 Lebanese children, ranging from 9 to 13 years old, who had been referred for psychological assessment following their exposure to war-related traumatic events. Of these children, 273 met criteria for PTSD. Two experienced clinicians reviewed the written and taped interview transcripts and concluded that 231 (27.5%) of the children did, indeed, qualify for a PTSD diagnosis. PTSD cases scored higher than nonclinical control subjects on the Revised Children's Manifest Anxiety Scale (RCMAS; Reynolds and Richmond, 1978), the Children's Depression Inventory (CDI; Kovacs, 1985), and the Conners Teacher Rating Scale (CTRS; Conners, 1969). Thus, PTSD was associated with a wide range of psychological disturbance.

Saigh (1988) used the CPTSDI to diagnose PTSD in 24 Lebanese adolescents exposed to war-related traumatic events. These children scored higher than nonclinical control subjects and higher than students with test anxiety on the RCMAS and the CDI, but scored lower than test anxious students on the Test Anxiety Inventory (TAI; Spielberger, 1980).

Using DSM-III-R criteria, McLeer and her colleagues developed an interview to diagnose psychiatric disorders in 31 sexually abused patients ranging in age from 3 to 16 years (McLeer, Deblinger, Atkins, Foa, and Ralphe, 1988). McLeer et al. diagnosed PTSD in 48 percent of the children, in 75 percent of those abused by their biological father, in 67 percent of those abused by strangers, in 25 percent of those abused by trusted adults, and in none of those abused by an older child. Many of the children who did not qualify for a PTSD diagnosis nevertheless exhibited some PTSD symptoms.

Perhaps the most widely used instrument for diagnosing childhood PTSD is the Post-Traumatic Stress Disorder Reaction Index (PTSD-RI; Frederick, 1985, 1986; Pynoos, Frederick, Nader, Arroyo, Steinberg, Eth, Nunez, and Fairbanks, 1987). Investigators have used the 20-item PTSD-RI to evaluate children who witnessed the sexual assaults of their mothers (Pynoos and Nader, 1988), who were exposed to gunfire (Pynoos, Frederick et al., 1987; Schwartz and Kowalski, 1991a,b), and who were injured in a severe boating accident (Martini, Ryan, Nakayama, and Ramenofsky, 1990). Researchers have endeavored to simplify the wording of this instrument to ensure its comprehension by school-age children, and the current version incorporates DSM-III-R criteria. Pynoos, Frederick et al. (1987) have reported a correlation between .91 between clinically ascertained cases of PTSD and PTSD-RI scores. Brent, Perper, Moritz, Friend, Schweers, Allman, McQuiston, Boylan, Roth, and Balach (1993) have further modified the PTSD-RI for use with adolescents.

Using an early version of the PTSD-RI, Pynoos, Frederick et al. (1987) interviewed 159 children, ranging in age from 5 to 13 years old, who were exposed to a fatal sniper attack on their elementary school playground in Los Angeles. Of those youngsters on the playground during the attack, 77 percent had moderate to severe levels of PTSD. These researchers reinterviewed 10 children about one week later, and reported an average interrater agreement of 94 percent for the PTSD-RI items.

Schwartz and Kowalski (1991b) used the PTSD-RI to interview 64 children, exposed to varying degrees to a fatal shooting at an elementary school near Chicago. They found that 27 percent of the children qualified for a DSM-III-R PTSD diagnosis.

To evaluate stress responses in sexually abused children, V. V. Wolfe, Gentile, Michienzi, Sas, and D. A. Wolfe (1991) developed the Children's Impact of Traumatic Events Scale-Revised (CITES-R), a structured interview for ascertaining the perceptions and attributions of children concerning their abuse as well as for evaluating PTSD symptoms per se. Although an early version of this instrument did not tap the full range of DSM-III-R symptoms, these researchers nevertheless detected syndromal PTSD in 49 percent of sexually abused children referred to a witness preparation program (D. A. Wolfe, Sas, and Wekerle, in press).

McLeer, Callaghan, Henry, and Wallen (1994) incorporated a DSM-III-R PTSD module into the Schedule for Affective Disorders and Schizophrenia for School-Age Children—Epidemiologic

Version (K-SADS-E; Orvaschel, Puig-Antich, Chambers, Tabrizi, and Johnson, 1982). They calculated an interrater reliability of 85.7 percent for the diagnosis of PTSD in an outpatient sample of 22 children, many of whom had been sexually abused.

STRUCTURED INTERVIEWS WITH PARENTS

Nader and Pynoos (1989) have developed the Child Post-Traumatic Stress Disorder Inventory (CPTSD-I), a structured interview for questioning parents about PTSD symptoms exhibited by their children. The CPTSD-I covers trauma history, PTSD symptoms, associated features, and personality traits. Nader and Pynoos interviewed the parents of children exposed to the Los Angeles sniper attack and compared parental report with the children's self-report of symptoms. Children reported more subjective symptoms than did parents (e.g., intrusive thoughts, avoidance of feelings), whereas parents reported more objective symptoms than did the children (e.g., irritability, aggression).

In the wake of the aforementioned Missouri flood, Earls et al. (1988) administered the DICA-P (i.e., parents' version) to the parents of children exposed to this disaster. Earls et al. found that parents identified fewer symptoms in their children than the children reported for themselves.

The K-SADS-E interview, including the PTSD module, has been administered to parents of traumatized children as well to the children themselves (McLeer et al., 1994). Discrepancies between the child's and the parent's report of the child's symptoms are resolved through subsequent additional questions. McLeer et al. have cogently argued that integration of child and parental reports may provide the most valid assessment of PTSD in the child.

QUESTIONNAIRES

To assess traumatized children, investigators have traditionally used questionnaires that measure symptoms of depression (e.g., CDI), anxiety (e.g., State-Trait Anxiety Inventory for Children,

STAIC; Spielberger, 1973), low self-esteem (e.g., Self-Esteem Inventory, SEI; Coopersmith, 1986), or general psychological disturbance (e.g., Child Behavior Checklist, CBCL; Achenbach and Edelbrock, 1983). These questionnaires provide useful information about associated features of PTSD (e.g., depressed mood, acting-out behavior), but do not provide any information about DSM PTSD symptoms per se. Their role in trauma assessment is, accordingly, auxiliary.

In an effort to rectify this limitation, investigators have occasionally added "PTSD-like" items to standardized questionnaires. For example, to evaluate Australian children whose community had been ravaged by a severe brushfire, McFarlane (1987) had parents and teachers complete Rutter's behavior scales to evaluate psychopathology in their children and students, respectively (Rutter and Graham, 1967). McFarlane added several items concerning nightmares, posttraumatic play, becoming upset by reminders of the fire, and spontaneous talk about the fire. Unfortunately, these augmented Rutter scales failed to capture the full range of PTSD symptoms, rendering it difficult to establish PTSD caseness.

Investigators have documented the utility of the Impact of Events Scale (IES; Horowitz, Wilner, and Alvarez, 1979) as a measure of childhood PTSD. This instrument includes subscales for Intrusion and Avoidance/Numbing and is often used as a measure of posttraumatic stress response in adults. Malmquist (1986) used the IES to evaluate 16 children, aged 5 to 10 years, who had witnessed the murder of a parent. He administered it as an interview rather than having the children complete it as a questionnaire. Their scores were comparable to those of traumatized adults.

Yule and Williams (1990) administered the IES as a questionnaire to 10 adolescent survivors of a capsized ship. Twelve to 15 months after the shipwreck, these subjects exhibited scores approximately equivalent to those of traumatized adults in Horowitz's stress disorder clinic.

Unfortunately, the IES may fail to discriminate between PTSD and grief in traumatized children who have lost a friend or family member (Pynoos, Nader, Frederick, Gonda, and Stuber, 1987).

In the Los Angeles sniper attack study, Pynoos, Nader et al. (1987) found that exposure to gunfire was related to PTSD, whereas acquaintance with the murdered girl was related to elevated scores on a grief reaction inventory. Close friends of the slain girl, who were directly exposed to the gunfire, exhibited both PTSD and grief. These findings imply that IES scores may reflect PTSD, grief, or both.

Schwarzwald, Weisenberg, Waysman, Solomon, and Klingman (1993) revised the PTSD-RI to ensure coverage of all DSM-III-R PTSD symptoms, and administered it as a questionnaire to 492 Israeli children and adolescents exposed to SCUD attacks during the Persion Gulf War. Rates of PTSD were higher among children who lived in areas hit by SCUDS (24.9%) than among children who resided in areas merely threatened by SCUD attacks (12.9%). Elementary schoolchildren qualified for PTSD significantly more often than did junior high or high school children.

DSM-IV and New Developments in Childhood PTSD Assessment

The aforementioned research on childhood PTSD assessment was based on DSM-III (APA, 1980), and sometimes DSM-III-R, criteria. Accordingly, all of the aforementioned instruments have suddenly become obsolete as of May 1994 when DSM-IV (APA, 1994) appeared, especially because some the diagnostic changes concern the assessment of children. Moreover, DSM-IV includes a new category, acute stress disorder. In this section, I will highlight nosological changes relevant to children, and will describe two important ongoing projects involving development of new instruments for diagnosing DSM-IV PTSD in children.

DSM-IV Diagnostic Changes Relevant to Childhood PTSD

DSM-IV still requires exposure to a traumatic event, but it no longer insists that it be "outside the range of everyday experience." Indeed, many of the events associated with childhood

PTSD are not uncommon (e.g., violence, sexual abuse). Although exposure to life-threat is strongly associated with PTSD in children (McNally, 1993), DSM-IV now explicitly allows as qualifying stressors "developmentally inappropriate sexual experiences without threatened or actual violence or injury" (APA, 1994, p. 424). DSM-IV, however, requires that the person's reaction to the stressor be characterized by intense fear, helplessness, or horror, but it acknowledges that children may instead exhibit disorganized or agitated behavior. Extant assessment instruments do not explicitly code for the person's immediate emotional reaction to the stressor.

Regarding criterion B ("reexperiencing") symptoms, DSM-IV notes that young children may reexperience the traumatic event through repetitive play rather than through recurrent intrusive thoughts. Moreover, unlike traumatized adults who often experience "instant-replay" nightmares of the event, children may suffer from terrifying dreams without any recognizable content or connection to the traumatic event.

Included for the first time in the DSM is Acute Stress Disorder, a syndrome characterized by dissociative symptoms (e.g., derealization, amnesia) and at least one symptom each from the PTSD clusters of reexperiencing, avoidance/numbing, and hyperarousal. Symptoms must be present for at least two days in the wake of a traumatic event, and must not last longer than one month. Little systematic research has been done on acute stress disorder, and none involving children or adolescents suffering from it. Accordingly, DSM-IV provides no guidelines for diagnosing children.

THE REVISED CHILDREN'S POSTTRAUMATIC STRESS DISORDER INVENTORY (CPTSDI)

Saigh (1994) has revised his CPTSDI to ensure coverage of the DSM-IV PTSD criteria, and has been piloting the new version to ensure its understandability to school-age children. For example, he read each item to a series of 8-year-old schoolchildren, none traumatized, in a Catholic school in Brooklyn, and had them paraphrase the meaning of each question in their own words. In this manner, he was able to reduce potential ambiguities in the wording of the questions. In a further effect to enhance validity, Saigh has developed multiple questions for some of the more abstract PTSD symptoms (e.g., foreshortened future). Each item is scored as either "yes" or "no."

The DSM-IV-based CPTSDI has been used to evaluate English-speaking children in South Africa who had been raped, and further field trials are being planned (P. A. Saigh, personal communication, August 5, 1994). With his colleagues at New York City's Bellevue Hospital, Saigh plans to incorporate the new CPTSDI in a study of children who have survived motor vehicle accidents. With his colleagues in the Middle East, he plans to test this instrument with English-speaking children who had been exposed to war-related stressors in Lebanon and Kuwait. Saigh, a trilingual scholar, plans to develop Arabic and French versions to replace the Arabic and French versions of the original CPTSDI.

THE CHILDHOOD PTSD INTERVIEW

K. E. Fletcher of the Department of Psychiatry at the University of Massachusetts Medical Center has been developing three new measures of childhood PTSD (Fletcher, 1994) that incorporates DSM-IV criteria. His validation sample includes children from central Massachusetts who have been exposed to a wide range of domestic and urban traumatic events. The Childhood PTSD Interview (Fletcher, 1991a) is designed for schoolchildren, and is worded accordingly. Response options include "yes," "no," and "don't know." Fletcher has included multiple questions for each symptom. In contrast to Saigh, who has confined the scope of the revised CPTSDI to the DSM-IV criteria, Fletcher has incorporated additional questions to capture associated features of PTSD. These include depression, omens (e.g., "Do you ever think that something that happened before [the stressor] was a warning to you that [the stressor] was going to happen?''), survivor guilt, general guilt/self-blame (e.g., ''Do you ever feel like what happened was your fault?''), fantasy denial (e.g., ''Do you ever imagine or pretend that things happened differently from what really happened?''), self-destructive behavior, dissociation, antisocial behavior, and risk-taking behavior. As Fletcher (1994) has emphasized, DSM criteria were developed in reference to adults and modified for children, raising the possibility that what constitutes PTSD in children may have been prematurely closed with regard to diagnostic criteria. To guard against missing significant, non-DSM aspects of childhood stress response, Fletcher assesses for a wide range of associated features.

To accompany the Childhood PTSD interview, Fletcher (1991b) has devised the Parent Report of the Child's Reaction to Stress. Noting that children are better informants about internalizing symptoms, whereas their parents are better informants about externalizing symptoms, Fletcher's ongoing validation study includes both instruments. Parents are asked about the full range of DSM-IV PTSD symptoms and associated disturbances exhibited by their children. Unlike the Childhood PTSD Interview, response options are on 5- and 6-point Likert scales (e.g., ''Never'' to ''Always''), plus ''don't know.''

Finally, Fletcher (1992) is also validating a childhood PTSD questionnaire entitled ''When Bad Things Happen.'' This 93-item instrument includes multiple questions for each DSM-IV symptom, plus questions to cover the full range of associated disturbances. Response options are ''never,'' ''some,'' and ''lots.'' The motivation for its development stems from limitations in the IES, the PTSD questionnaire most often used with children. The IES does not cover the full range of DSM symptoms, nor does it tap associated features.

CONCLUSIONS

Concurrent with the publication of DSM-IV, new, improved instruments for the assessment of childhood PTSD are being validated, and will doubtlessly supersede earlier questionnaires and interview schedules. Unlike many early instruments used in child-hood stress research (e.g., PTSD-RI, IES), the instruments being validated by Saigh and by Fletcher are not modified versions of interview schedules originally devised for adults. These investigators have tested whether the wording of the questions is clearly understandable by children. Multiple questions have been developed to evaluate each PTSD symptom rather than relying on a single question to provide information about the presence of a particular symptom. Saigh is making efforts to test the cross-cultural validity of his instrument, and Fletcher has developed a parent form of his interview, plus a questionnaire for children that will supersede the IES.

In conclusion, great strides have been made in the systematic assessment of childhood PTSD since the classic phenomenologic work of Terr (1979). The new generation of interview schedules and questionnaires ought to provide a valid basis for diagnosing children, and ought to provide a foundation for case identification for psychopathology and treatment research.

REFERENCES

Achenbach, T. M., & Edelbrock, C. S. (1983), *Manual for the Child Behavior Checklist and Revised Child Behavior Profile.* Typescript.

American Psychiatric Association (1980), *Diagnostic and Statistical Manual of Mental Disorders* (DSM-III), 3rd ed. Washington, DC: American Psychiatric Press.

——— (1987), *Diagnostic and Statistical Manual of Mental Disorders* (DSM-III-R), 3rd ed. rev. Washington, DC: American Psychiatric Press.

——— (1994), *Diagnostic and Statistical Manual of Mental Disorders* (DSM-IV), 4th ed. Washington, DC: American Psychiatric Press.

Brent, D. A., Perper, J., Mortiz, G., Friend, A., Schweers, J., Allman, C., McQuiston, L., Boylan, M. B., Roth, C., & Balach, L. (1993), Adolescent witnesses to a peer suicide. *J. Amer. Acad. Child & Adol. Psychiatry,* 32:1184–1188.

Conners, C. K. (1969), A teacher rating scale for use in drug studies with children. *Amer. J. Psychiatry,* 126:884–888.

Coopersmith, S. (1986), *Manual for the Self-Esteem Inventories.* Palo Alto, CA: Consulting Psychologists Press.

Earls, F., Smith, E., Reich, W., & Jung, K. G. (1988), Investigating psychopathological consequences of a disaster in children: A pilot study incorporating a structured diagnostic interview. *J. Amer. Acad. Child & Adol. Psychiatry*, 27:90–95.

Fletcher, K. E. (1991a), *Childhood PTSD Interview*. Worcester, MA: University of Massachusetts Medical Center.

—— (1991b), *Parent Report of the Child's Reaction to Stress*. Worcester, MA: University of Massachusetts Medical Center.

—— (1992), *When Bad Things Happen*. Worcester, MA: University of Massachusetts Medical Center.

—— (1994), *What We Know about Children's Posttraumatic Stress Responses: A Meta-analysis of the Empirical Literature*. Submitted.

Frederick, C. J. (1985), Selected foci in the spectrum of posttraumatic stress disorders. In: *Perspectives on Disaster Recovery*, ed. J. Laube & S. A. Murphy. East Norwalk, CT: Appleton-Century-Crofts, pp. 110–130.

—— (1986), Posttraumatic stress disorder and child molestation. In: *Sexual Exploitation of Patients by Mental Health Professionals*, ed. A. Burgess & C. Hartman. New York: Praeger, pp. 133–142.

Horowitz, M., Wilner, N., & Alvarez, W. (1979), Impact of Event Scale: A measure of subjective stress. *Psychosom. Med.*, 41:209–218.

Kovacs, M. (1985), The Children's Depression Inventory (CDI). *Psychopharmacol. Bull.*, 21:995–998.

Kulka, R., Schlenger, W. E., Fairbank, J. A., Hough, R. L., Jordan, B. K., Marmar, C. R., & Weiss, D. S. (1988), *National Vietnam Veterans Readjustment Study (NVVRS): Description, Current Status, and Initial PTSD Prevalence Estimates*. Research Triangle Park, NC: Research Triangle Institute.

Malmquist, C. P. (1986), Children who witness parental murder: Posttraumatic aspects. *J. Amer. Acad. Child & Adol. Psychiatry*, 25:320–325.

Martini, D. R., Ryan, C., Nakayama, D., & Ramenofsky, M. (1990), Psychiatric sequelae after traumatic injury: The Pittsburgh Regatta accident. *J. Amer. Acad. Child & Adol. Psychiatry*, 29:70–75.

McFarlane, A. C. (1987), Posttraumatic phenomena in a longitudinal study of children following a natural disaster. *J. Amer. Acad. Child & Adol. Psychiatry*, 26:764–769.

McLeer, S. V., Callaghan, M., Henry, D., & Wallen, J. (1994), Psychiatric disorders in sexually abused children. *J. Amer. Acad. Child & Adol. Psychiatry*, 33:313–319.

—— Deblinger, E., Atkins, M. S., Foa, E. B., & Ralphe, D. L. (1988), Posttraumatic stress disorder in sexually abused children. *J. Amer. Acad. Child & Adol. Psychiatry*, 27:650–654.

McNally, R. J. (1991), Assessment of posttraumatic stress disorder in children. *Psycholog. Assess.*, 3:531–537.

—— (1993), Stressors that produce posttraumatic stress disorder in children. In: *Posttraumatic Stress Disorder: DSM-IV and Beyond*, ed. J. R. T. Davidson & E. B. Foa. Washington, DC: American Psychiatric Press, pp. 57–74.

—— (in press), Assessment of post-traumatic stress disorder in children and adolescents. *J. School Psychol.*

Nader, K., & Pynoos, R. S. (1989), *Child Post-Traumatic Stress Disorder Inventory: Parent Interview*. Typescript.

Orvaschel, H., Puig-Antich, J., Chambers, W., Tabrizi, M. A., & Johnson, R. (1982), Retrospective assessment of child psychopathology with the Kiddie-SADS E. *J. Amer. Acad. Child Psychiatry*, 21:392–397.

Pynoos, R. S., Frederick, C., Nader, K., Arroyo, W., Steinberg, A., Eth, S., Nunez, F., & Fairbanks, L. (1987), Life threat and posttraumatic stress disorder in school-age children. *Arch. Gen. Psychiatry*, 44:1057–1063.

—— Nader, K. (1988), Children who witness the sexual assaults of their mothers. *J. Amer. Acad. Child & Adol. Psychiatry*, 27:567–572.

—— —— Frederick, C., Gonda, L., & Stuber, M. (1987), Grief reactions in school age children following a sniper attack at school. *Israeli J. Psychiatry & Rel. Sci.*, 24:53–63.

Reynolds, C. R., & Richmond, B. O. (1978), What I think and feel: A revised measure of children's manifest anxiety. *J. Abnorm. Child Psychol.*, 6:271–280.

Robins, L. N., & Smith, E. M. (1984), *Diagnostic Interview Schedule/disaster supplement.* St. Louis, MO: Washington University School of Medicine.

Rutter, M., & Graham, P. (1967), A children's behaviour questionnaire for completion by teachers: Preliminary findings. *J. Child Psychol. & Psychiatry*, 8:1–11.

Saigh, P. A. (1988), The validity of the *DSM-III* posttraumatic stress disorder classification as applied to adolescents. *Profess. School Psychol.*, 3:283–290.

—— (1989a), The validity of the *DSM-III* posttraumatic stress disorder classification as applied to children. *J. Abnorm. Psychol.*, 98:189–192.

—— (1989b), The development and validation of the Children's Posttraumatic Stress Disorder Inventory. *Internat. J. Spec. Ed.*, 4:75–84.

—— (1994), *The Children's PTSD Inventory*, rev. ed. New York: City University of New York.

Schwartz, E. D., & Kowalski, J. M. (1991a), Posttraumatic stress disorder after a school shooting: Effects of symptom threshold selection and diagnosis by *DSM-III, DSM-III-R,* or proposed *DSM-IV. Amer. J. Psychiatry*, 148:592–597.

—— —— (1991b), Malignant memories: Posttraumatic stress disorder in children and adults following a school shooting. *J. Amer. Acad. Child & Adol. Psychiatry*, 30:936–944.

Schwarzwald, J., Weisenberg, M., Waysman, M., Solomon, Z., & Klingman, A. (1993), Stress reaction of school-age children to the bombardment by SCUD missiles. *J. Abnorm. Psychol.*, 102:404–410.

Spielberger, C. D. (1973), *Manual for the State-Trait Anxiety Inventory for Children.* Palo Alto, CA: Consulting Psychologists Press.

—— (1980), *Test Anxiety Inventory.* Palo Alto, CA: Consulting Psychologists Press.

Stoddard, F. J., Norman, D. K., Murphy, J. M., & Beardslee, W. R. (1989), Psychiatric outcome of burned children and adolescents. *J. Amer. Acad. Child & Adol. Psychiatry*, 28:589–595.

Terr, L. C. (1979), The children of Chowchilla: A study of psychic trauma. *The Psychoanalytic Study of the Child*, 34:547–623. New Haven, CT: Yale University Press.

Welner, Z., Reich, W., Herjanic, B., Jung, K. G., & Amado, H. (1987), Reliability, validity, and parent-child agreement studies of the Diagnostic Interview for Children and Adolescents (DICA). *J. Amer. Acad. Child & Adol. Psychiatry*, 26:649–653.

Wolfe, D. A., Sas, L., & Wekerle, C. (in press), Factors associated with the development of posttraumatic stress disorder among child victims of sexual abuse. *Child Abuse & Neglect.*

Wolfe, V. V., Gentile, C., Michienzi, T., Sas, L., & Wolfe, D. A. (1991), The Children's Impact of Traumatic Events Scale: A measure of post-sexual-abuse PTSD symptoms. *Behav. Assess.*, 13:359–383.

Yule, W., & Williams, R. M. (1990), Post-traumatic stress reactions in children. *J. Traum. Stress*, 3:279–295.

Chapter 3
The Child Sexual Abuse Accommodation Syndrome: Clinical Issues and Forensic Implications

Roland C. Summit, M.D., Thomas W. Miller, Ph.D., A.B.P.P., and Lane J. Veltkamp, M.S.W., B.C.D.

The impact of stressful life events on physical and mental health has been the focus of clinicians and researchers alike. Considerable attention has been given to the growing understanding of how victimized individuals process their victimization. The responses and reactions common to violence in our society, and particularly to sexual abuse, are often in conflict with normal developmental reactions to other life stressors. The reactions which might be unique to children who experience trauma have tended until recently to be ignored or discounted by adult theoreticians and researchers, with no personal experience of trauma. This disparity between child experience and adult acceptance is compounded by the fact that child victims tend not to complain about victimization because they are fearful about the repercussions of disclosure.

In the search for understandable metaphors for emerging concepts of the dynamics of victimization, various authors have organized descriptive models or syndromes relating to child sexual abuse. Since any attempt to explain child sexual abuse impacts on such diverse fields as ethology, child development, psychology, psychopathology, traumatology, criminology, jurisprudence, victim advocacy, prosecution, criminal defense, and legislative politics, any such innovation is bound to provoke controversy. While clinicians, researchers, and legal experts may be equally interested in understanding the human realities of traumatization, each interest group will have intra- and extramural disagreement over the validity of a proposed interdisciplinary synthesis.

Descriptive syndromes such as the General Adaptation Syndrome (Selye, 1967), Rape Trauma Syndrome (Burgess, Holmstrom and McCausland, 1978), the Child Sexual Abuse Accommodation Syndrome (CSAAS; Summit, 1983), and others, do not constitute medical diagnoses but serve to provide a framework for understanding what otherwise appear to be illogical and irrational responses to various types of stressful life experiences. Of particular interest in the study of sexually abused children is the CSAAS, developed in 1979 and published in 1983 by Roland Summit. This model observes that the child who is sexually abused is often fearful and confused about the outcome of disclosure in sexual abuse situations. For various reasons children tend to believe that the topic is not to be discussed openly and that they will be rejected or suffer dreadful and perhaps even life-threatening consequences if they do disclose the events which have occurred. In addition, parents, health care professionals, and law enforcement agencies offer little support and tend to send children a message that they are not readily believed.

The Child Sexual Abuse Accommodation Syndrome describes a constellation of conditions (Akiskal, 1989) which offer a state-of-the-art working model allowing clinicians to better evaluate the disparity between child reality and adult presumption which occurs as a child attempts to accommodate to the traumatization of sexual abuse. Whitcomb (1992) notes that while there is no clear and exclusive pattern of behavior or psychological symptoms that automatically prove that a child sexual abuse situation has occurred, the CSAAS is a clinical delineation between low-confidence and high-confidence indicators. It is clearly recognized that children do not react uniformly to sexual abuse. Any observable responses of children to trauma such as this can vary according to the gender, age, ethnicity, culture, and education of the child and the variables of relationship, threat, force, and perversity introduced by the intruder.

THE CHILD SEXUAL ABUSE ACCOMMODATION SYNDROME

Summit (1983) developed the CSAAS to describe the dilemma faced by the child victims in attempting to communicate their experience to those who may potentially help them. Recognizing that its usefulness would be in helping observers understand why children may delay disclosure and provide inconsistent details, and having observed these phenomena from a social and community focus rather than from a strictly psychiatric point of view, Summit did not describe this as a medical syndrome. The CSAAS was presented not as a diagnostic checklist of signs and symptoms for identifying sexual abuse but rather as a guide to understanding a child's limited options for coping in the face of prevailing adult indifference and disbelief. In the course of processing the traumatization which occurs during sexual abuse there is compromise not only by the intrinsic victim–perpetrator interaction but also by the isolation and psychological distancing (orphaning) unwittingly imposed on the child by adults who fail to recognize the fact that sexual abuse is occurring (e.g., the mother who is too intimidated by a father who is abusing a teenage daughter).

Within this concept of dual stressors, five categories are identified. The first two, secrecy and helplessness, are closely linked as basic handicaps of any normal child in the face of an unprecedented sexual assault. The other three phases, entrapment and accommodation, delayed, conflicted, and unconvincing disclosure, and retraction, describe sequential responses to abuse that may be typical for children but which are regarded by skeptical adults as contradictory to normal, credible victim behavior. Summit has pointed out that the persistent rejection by adult society of a child's natural reactions constituted a prejudicial myth (1983, p. 177):

Evaluation of the responses of normal children to sexual assault provides clear evidence that societal definitions of "normal" victim behavior are inappropriate and procrustean, serving adults as mythic insulators against the child's pain. Within this climate of prejudice, the sequential survival options available to the victim further alienate the child from any hope of outside credibility or acceptance. Ironically, the child's inevitable choice of the "wrong" options reinforces and perpetuates the prejudicial myths [p. 177].

SECRECY

As enumerated in the CSAAS, the fundamental reality for children is that of silence or secrecy. The nearly universal failure of the child to voice a spontaneous and immediate complaint jeopardizes the credibility of any later protest and burdens the victim with a lifelong sense of being trapped in guilty complicity. The noncomplaining victim becomes the custodian of a secret that must never be disclosed. The failure to complain can be developmentally determined for the victim who is too young to use language to describe the trauma and socially determined for early adolescents who have never been allowed a nonobscene vocabulary or a cognitive framework for any form of sexual act. A child may feel guilty for having touched or been touched in the "no-no" places. Hardt and Stoller (1990) note that in most cultures, secrecy is the norm where sexuality, especially sexual perversion, is concerned.

Perhaps the most profound basis for silence is the paralyzing confusion produced by the context of the abusive experience, which is inevitably isolated and different from any human interaction the child has ever experienced. No one else is present to explain or to validate the situation. The only mentor for this occasion is someone who is generally well known to the child and reliable, but who in this private (secret) context is behaving out of character and with unrecognizable urgency and passion. After the intrusion, and outside of the private place, that same person returns to normal, giving no hint of what has perplexed the child in private. It is not surprising that some children conclude they only dreamed the experience, while others may believe they have been visited by some kind of a monstrous double for the person they know in the outer world. Thus a child may be trapped in confused silence without any spoken instructions or threats from the abuser.

The one who controls and creates the reality of the child's private experience may be full grown or only a few years older, but is infinitely wiser and more powerful in having the advantage of greater knowledge. If words are shared at all, the child is led to believe that this is a unique relationship, too precious to be shared, or that either or both of the conspirators (i.e., child and abuser) will suffer disastrous consequences if anyone else finds out. Threats of destruction may be directed toward the child and toward anything essential to a child's emotional survival: home, parents, siblings, and pets. The offender claims incredible, even supernatural power in these transactions while the victim is offered secrecy as the only antidote for annihilation. Secrecy, which may seem to outsiders an unreasonable and incomprehensible evasiveness, becomes so central to the child's survival that it may trigger elaborate behavioral and mental mechanisms of concealment.

HELPLESSNESS

The second category of the CSAAS is helplessness. It should go without saying that no child is a match for the test-proven blandishments of a child molester. But our post-Victorian society tends to hold any victim responsible for precocious and illicit sexual experience. Perhaps it is also more expedient to scapegoat the victim than to ferret out and confront the responsible adult.

In order to challenge traditional prejudice, it is therapeutically vital to recognize that children cannot be consenting partners in the sophisticated sexual agendas imposed by older people (Finkelhor, 1979). Beyond the intrinsic juvenile handicaps of naiveté, gullibility, and small stature, any child faced with sexual seduction or assault is overpowered by the isolation and paralysis imposed by the conspiracy of silence. The first and second categories of the CSAAS combine therefore to recognize the immense vulnerability of the child who is rendered still more speechless and powerless through sexual exploitation.

The CSAAS has been helpful in restructuring both the social tendency toward blaming the victim and the self-denigration of survivors who have condemned themselves for allowing the abuse. The simple message of the CSAAS, a truism which has been muddied and bitterly contested in intellectual and forensic discourse, is that it is normal for a child to submit to sexual assault without effective protest. The accommodation concept asserts that it is also normal for otherwise caring adults to reinforce the secrecy and helplessness of victimized children through traditional cues of avoidance, disbelief, and denial. As with the imaginary monsters in their closets, it is natural for children not to speak of things that adults cannot accept or believe in. Children learn somehow to cope for themselves with problems for which their parents are no help.

ENTRAPMENT AND ACCOMMODATION

The isolation and perverse education peculiar to the abuse experience leaves the molested child caught up in the maddening dilemmas described in categories 3, 4, and 5 of the CSAAS. The third category, entrapment and accommodation, explores several of the coping mechanisms or accommodations which are natural for molested children but which are likely to be regarded by adult observers as self-impeaching pathology if weighed against an eventual disclosure. These mental and behavioral options are not advanced in the CSAAS as diagnostic symptoms of abuse, though some of the same features have been listed in purportedly diagnostic "child sexual abuse syndromes." Most cannot be authenticated as exclusive to sexually abused children as opposed to other classes of stressed or troubled individuals.

While some of the options listed, such as substance abuse, self-harming, and sexually exploratory behaviors, are at least generally accepted as real and positively correlated with some kind of stress, one aspect of adjustment has provoked astonishment and sometimes mean-spirited protest, that is, a child's ability to completely hide the abuse. Despite the lawyer-inspired insistence that there are no symptoms which identify a sexually abused child, the same voices attack as a fraud any child or adult who was abused as a child and who managed to get by without apparent pathology.

Some children deliberately conceal their distress and determine to be well adjusted and successful at all costs. Others manage to *dissociate* the specifically stressful events in their lives, emerging from each incident as if it never happened, enduring repeated abuse with no conscious awareness of the dark side of their lives. Marilyn Van Derber Atler, Miss America of 1958, eminently successful college scholar, athlete, and motivational speaker, explains (1991): "In order to survive, I split into a day child, who giggled and smiled, and a night child, who lay awake in a fetal position, only to be pried apart by my father. Until I was 24, the day child had no conscious knowledge of the night child. During the day, no embarrassing or angry glances ever passed between my father and me . . . because I had no conscious knowledge of what he was doing to me" (p. 90).

The ability of children to accommodate to ongoing abuse without complaining, whether through self-harm, antisocial behavior, psychological distortions, or by sheer guts, excites remarkable scorn and rejection if they claim later to have been abused. The American idealization of pioneering individualism turns sour against such late complainers. Rather than gaining respect for their personal courage and inventive ability to survive in a dark, uncharted wilderness, survivors are rejected as liars or whiners. Adult society has a demonstrated knack for closing ranks against complaining children. Against such a front, the adaptive silence of victimized children should be seen as natural and inevitable.

DELAYED, CONFLICTED, AND UNCONVINCING DISCLOSURE

The negative response to complaint comprises the fourth category of the CSAAS: delayed, conflicted, and unconvincing disclosure. If the syndrome were a list of the most typical behaviors of molested children it would stop at category 3, entrapment and accommodation. Only a minority of children manage to disclose their abuse. Many adult survivors, one in three in a respected national sample (Timnick, 1985), have never told anyone before about their childhood sexual victimization. Still others know of nothing to disclose, unless or until they emerge from trauma-induced amnesia. The fourth category reflects on the dysphoric consequences for a select minority of survivors—those who expose themselves through disclosure.

In the original formulation of the CSAAS, Summit drew on clinical observations that most disclosures were prompted by adolescent authority conflicts, when a child seized emerging autonomy and indignation to complain of ongoing abuse. The clinical sample presenting in the seventies was comprised largely of adolescent and preadolescent incest victims, mostly girls. By 1980 it was more apparent that both boys and girls are subject to sexual abuse both within and outside of family relationships, and that the conflicts or opportunities which can lead to disclosure take different forms throughout childhood.

Hollingsworth (1986) noted that Summit (1983) suggests that child victims maintain a constant stew of fearful ambivalence; on the one hand wishing that they could somehow prompt rescue and at the same time desperate to keep the secret. The strongest internal cues threaten disaster, so the hope for escape rests on finding someone they regard as gentle and safe, who will understand without being told, or someone very strong who can overpower the dangers of telling. To escape the pain of uncertainty children may seek distraction, trying not to think about the abuse, or even succeeding in imagining it away through dissociation.

The ability to verbalize a complaint depends on a shifting window of disclosure, when a child is prompted to think about the abuse in the presence of someone who is regarded as safe and capable of understanding the dilemma of entrapment and providing opportunity for escape. Children typically test the waters of acceptance, questioning a potential listener's capacity to understand, then advancing and withdrawing tentative hints of personal involvement. Or a child may demonstrate some wordless charade that begs for relief. A young girl who was habitually molested by her father on her mother's shopping day later complained bitterly, "What did you think it meant when I hid your car keys in the dishpan?" The remorseful mother never had a clue.

The window of disclosure may open a little if a child is directly questioned, though research shows that most children deny their abuse when first asked about it, only to advance tentatively through a series of hints and self-contradictions with further questioning (Sorensen and Snow, 1991). It is little wonder, then, that interviewers are blamed for creating false notions of abuse in previously noncomplaining children, and that those who would protect the civil rights of defendants condemn the use of multiple interviews.

A corollary view of the disclosure process was framed by Seligman in 1975, long before the waters became muddied in adversarial dispute. According to Seligman's safety signal hypothesis, opportunities for disclosure are limited to experiences which form within the realm of a "safety signal." All human beings will be fearful all the time except in the reassuring presence of a safety signal, most often seen as a person who can provide an opportunity for the victimized individual to disclose the victimization. Seligman postulated as early as 1975 that most sexually abused and traumatized persons, including children, are terrified by the consequences of disclosure and may present as confused and ambivalent.

Most children will simply remain in hiding and not take the risk of talking candidly about the traumatizing experience. When a child does take a risk in the presence of the safety signal and when the family, clinical, medical, or legal system fails to provide a sense of safety and security to the victim, the child may simply return to the treacherous security of the secret, as noted in the fifth category of the CSAAS, retraction.

RETRACTION

It is unusual for a child to achieve lasting emotional comfort through disclosure. The child perceives the shock and dismay reflected by those who are willing to listen to such a complaint as fulfilling the prophecy of disaster. That point is driven home by the intrafamily and interagency conflict that typically follows. Acrimony between a mother and father and a de facto punishment of the disclosing child are not limited to incest. Typically parents are also mutually estranged and embattled in their reception of complaints against outsiders. Even if parents and agencies are mutually accepting and reassuring, the child may be haunted by the persisting inner voice of the disclosure/doom prediction. And in the victim's ambivalent feelings of mixed affection for the offender and apprehension of him, coupled sometimes with reinforcing cues from the accused, a child may feel more guilty and fearful for the plight of the offender than relieved. For whatever complex of variables, it is not unusual for a child to follow an inherently conflicted and unconvincing disclosure with a very convincing retraction.

As with each category of the CSAAS, behavioral correlation does not infer diagnostic confirmation of abuse. If a child's disclosure were false, then retracting it would assert the truth. A disclosure of sexual assault is not more or less true according to whether it is immediate or delayed, consistent or inconsistent, durable or reversible. The reason for including retraction in the syndrome was to show that denial of a prior assertion is not the final word but just another self-impeaching option which can be taken by legitimate victims. Retraction does not enhance the fact or the reliability of previous claims, but neither can it be assumed to nullify them.

Retraction is included also as the prime example of how society has traditionally picked and chosen what is "believable" about child sexual abuse, and how societal prejudice can shape the options available to a child. It is the convincing believability of offender bluff and alibi, coupled by the wishful idealism of adult-affiliated onlookers, that prejudices and makes unconvincing any child's best efforts at disclosure. And it is the child's willingness to accede to adult prejudice that encourages retraction. Ironically, it is the child's best effort to appease adults that elicits the most emphatic adult distrust. The welcome, self-evident truth of the retraction brands the child as a liar for the prior "false" complaint. The adult who might have felt compassion for a victim feels betrayed and humiliated by the child's "deceit," vowing never to be taken in again by a manipulative kid. Over time, the tradition of dismissing disclosures of abuse as fantasies or lies and assigning to children as a class an easy facility for making false accusations has been buttressed by the ease with which we have forced children to declare their real experience as false.

Thus the Child Sexual Abuse Accommodation Syndrome, consisting of (1) Secrecy, (2) Helplessness, (3) Entrapment and Accommodation, (4) Delayed, Conflicted, and Unconvincing Disclosure, and (5) Retraction, represents a coherent map to the entrenched myths which have produced a gulf of mistrust and disbelief toward children who complain of child sexual abuse. The same myths have dug a chasm of deliberate disinterest in identifying those victims who are unable to disclose the abuse. While the CSAAS allows for a more empathic understanding of a child's entrapment into undisclosed abuse, and while such empathy is vital for shepherding a victim or survivor out of self-deprecating isolation, the syndrome is not intended either to measure the accuracy of a disclosure or to identify symptomatically the legion of child victims and survivors who remain silent. Those urgent and worthy agendas must rely on other directions of clinical experience and research.

Syndrome Validity Issues

After 10 years of increasing recognition of the validity of CSAAS, some clinicians, defense attorneys, judges, and legal analysts have come to question its validity. Negative arguments assert that the CSAAS has caused sexual abuse to be overreported, that it urges mental health professionals to believe all allegations that are made by children, that the CSAAS is only a theoretical construct that attempts to prove that abuse took place, and that it was invented merely to provide an opportunity for mental health experts to testify against defendants. Such attacks compromise the availability of accommodation concepts for consideration by a jury. Some courts prohibit any reference to the CSAAS in expert testimony. Convictions have been reversed on appeal because CSAAS-related testimony had been allowed at trial. Exclusion rests on the argument that the CSAAS is not an authenticated diagnosis and that it does not meet the courtroom standard for scientific evidence to prove that a given child was molested.

These arguments and decisions reflect a misunderstanding or a misuse of the CSAAS and a confusion over the label, *syndrome.* Contrary to the definition assumed by legal analysts, a clinical syndrome is not necessarily a list of signs and symptoms or a diagnostic label for an established disorder. It can be, as legal scholar John Myers (1993) has defined it, a "non-diagnostic syndrome" which can alert clinicians to the possibility of undiscovered illness or describe a pattern of anomalies without established cause. A set of symptoms which would prove that a child had suffered abuse, and therefore was a genuine victim of crime, could not be presented in court without first proving its diagnostic reliability. If a nondiagnostic syndrome such as the Rape Trauma Syndrome or the CSAAS is not offered as a diagnostic fingerprint, it need not be subject to the test of scientific reliability required for a diagnostic instrument.

Summit (1992) has explained that his observations were derived not from medical research but from social and community clinical experience, and that the CSAAS was not tested, constructed, or worded to imply any diagnostic utility. Furthermore, the behaviors and clinical correlations which were mentioned in the text were selected not as diagnostic symptoms but as examples of the gulf between child and adult views of accommodation. It is adult societal denial and not the coping behavior of children which the CSAAS defines as disordered behavior. Any testimony drawing appropriately on the CSAAS should be judged therefore not as novel scientific evidence implying an offer of proof but merely as a distillation of clinical observation and opinion. Admissibility of CSAAS-related testimony hinges on a fine point of judgment about the relative impact of an expert witness on the role of the jury as the exclusive factfinder of the ultimate truth. A jury might be taken in by an expert touting an unreliable diagnostic instrument, but there is no such gullibility for the personal opinions of mental health professionals who are asked to provide expert testimony.

The tendency in most courts, defined by a number of state appeals and Supreme Court decisions, is to allow testimony based on the CSAAS if it can educate the jury against prejudicial myths; if it is offered to rebut specific inferences made by opposing counsel that a child's delay or inconsistency in disclosure is indicative of deceit; and if such testimony is directed not toward the behavior of the specific child in question but only toward children as a class. Further, any such testimony must not be worded to suggest that such behavior is *consistent with* abuse, an approach which might imply to the jury that the child who complains at once of abuse is necessarily a legitimate victim. Rather, the expert must be restricted to concluding that such things as nondisclosure, paradoxical behavior, inconsistent statements, and retractions are *not inconsistent* with a history of sexual victimization.

Even if the CSAAS is not presented as an attempt at diagnosis, does it then address issues that are valid and relevant for the education of a jury? Research over the intervening 10 years has validated the basic assertions of the CSAAS, often far beyond the original observations. The study of 116 confirmed victims by Sorensen and Snow (1991) shows that not only is spontaneous disclosure rare, but most boys and girls convincingly deny being molested if they are questioned about suspected sexual abuse; almost three fourths (72%) denied abuse when first questioned. Only 7 percent of those who initially denied abuse were able to follow with a convincing and unwavering *active disclosure*. The rest tested the water with the advances and retreats of *tentative disclosure,* often vacillating from acknowledgment to denial. The time required to move from tentative to active disclosure varied from a single session to several months of therapy. Some 22 percent of the sample retracted their previously active disclosure. Those who retracted often blamed parents or therapists for promoting their "false" allegation, until they were able to acknowledge, once and for all, that they were really abused.

Critics of child protection efforts also blame parents and therapists for "not taking *no* for an answer" in their "relentless grilling" of suspected victims. Defense arguments claim that mental health professionals have taken the CSAAS as an instrument of inquisition. The same arguments claim that children are so impressionable that they can be led even by unspoken gestures and cues from overzealous investigators to jump on the bandwagon of incriminating their own parents, teachers, and friends of the family. Far from being helpless to avoid posing as false victims in the wake of questioning, the real victims prove resourceful and tenacious in maintaining a posture of denial. Such reticence will defeat any investigation based on tentative questioning in one-time-only interviews.

Rather than impeaching the testimony of children who have developed disclosures only in the process of investigation, and rather than discarding such disclosures because questions were asked even in the face of a child's poor denial or retraction, a jury and the public at large must have some means of understanding the perplexing ambiguities of a child's natural process of disclosure. The CSAAS provides an accurate textbook for that understanding.

Critics may concede that the CSAAS had a place when children were never believed, but that it is now obsolete and inflammatory. The public is all too alert to child sexual abuse now, they say. People are willing to believe any allegation, no matter how preposterous. It is alleged that the commonly held myths and misperceptions that were once prejudicial against children have been blown away by the CSAAS mentality. The prejudice now goes against defendants, these experts claim, so they produce syndromes to identify false allegations and the adults who inspire them.

The fact that such victim-impeaching syndromes have emerged and the fact that they have been received so enthusiastically by judges, journalists, and the general public provides the most emphatic proof of the CSAAS position: adult society continues to reinforce mythic attitudes and ideas that keep child sexual abuse out of sight through suppression and repudiation of victim complaints.

These new syndromes produce the Parental Alienation Syndrome (Gardner, 1987), and come not from clinical experience with abused children but from court-generated objections to believing children who complain. Unlike the CSAAS, which is non-diagnostic, these syndromes are conceived and named to designate a disorder with obvious symptoms and specific cause. The disorders supposedly leave individuals unable to distinguish their own reality because they have been coached by powerful inquisitors to believe they have been sexually abused. Individuals afflicted with these syndromes make false accusations against innocent people, often those they have loved and depended upon, because they have been seduced into slavish loyalty toward their inquisitors, who exploit the victims' naiveté. Although such illnesses might seem unlikely unless proven through research and until recognized in diagnostic manuals, each is already being written into high court decisions which discredit victim claims without any test of scientific reliability.

Children are said to suffer from "Parental Alienation Syndrome" (PAS) (Gardner, 1987) when they claim they have been sexually assaulted by one parent who is no longer living with the custodial parent. Family Court judges have been known to assign full custody to the parent accused (usually the father), and to require monitoring of the limited visits allowed to the other parent (usually the mother) to prevent further parent-alienating brainwashing. A parent who protests such decisions or, worse, seeks alternate examinations or expert testimony to verify sexual victimization, only proves his or her malicious intention to use the child as a pawn against the alienated spouse (Gardner, 1987). The judicial reliance on PAS as the standard for custody disputes has forced some parents to go to jail for contempt of court for hiding their children. The hope that justice could not be so impossibly blind is belied by the appalling documentation of so many such cases (Armstrong, 1994).

The adult equivalent of the false accusation disease is the False Memory Syndrome (FMS). While the PAS is at least promulgated by a child psychiatrist, the FMS was conceived without benefit of clinic. The False Memory Syndrome is the invention of a burgeoning group of once-quiet families suddenly torn apart by the disclosure of an adult child claiming recovered memory of sexual abuse in childhood. Such memories are defined as false by the parents, who have no memory of molesting their children. They find some comfort in concluding that their children have been enticed to testify against them through the ministrations of a therapy cult. The syndrome is diagnosed if a young woman without previous complaint either reads a survivor self-help book and/or consults a therapist, also a young woman, who insists that the client's nondescript symptoms are a sure clue to a forgotten history of sexual abuse, most likely by her father. Members of the rapidly expanding FMS Foundation promote arguments that such "robust repression" is impossible and that there is no basis for concepts of posttraumatic amnesia (FMSF literature and lecturers seem to dodge discussion of well-documented observations of dissociation in favor of a straw man attack on Freud and theories of repression). The Foundation calls for lawsuits and professional practice restrictions against therapists who do "memory work." A related effort is pushing for laws that would make suspect even the taking of a routine history of childhood stressors.

This upstart group and its flagship syndrome would not merit profound concern even with its enormous popular support if it did not also attract such prestigious clinical and academic endorsement. The large and dedicated "Scientific and Professional Advirosy (sic) Board" (FMS Foundation Newsletter, 1993, p. 10) lists some 25 M.D. and Ph.D. members with senior academic credentials in major universities and hospitals. These professors and scientific researchers are willing to agree that therapists younger and less qualified than they have created a dangerous virus capable of destroying the very institution of the family.

There is reason for responsible concern (Brooks and Milchman, 1991; Elterman and Ehrenberg, 1991) that the acrimony of divorce or the missionary zeal of some segment of therapists might engender false allegations of sexual abuse. But these syndromes define the problem, the cause, and the cure with no research into alternative explanations. In both the parental alienation and the false memory syndromes, the one who claims to have been sexually abused is said to be suffering from a mental illness characterized by false accusations. Both syndromes lionize the accused as victims proved innocent by the characteristics of the syndrome. Both syndromes rely on authoritarian pretence to trivialize the reliability of the younger individual who claims to be abused. And both syndromes identify the same infectious agents and mode of transmission: the agents are those who question young people in concern for the possibility of undisclosed sexual abuse. The mode of transmission is communication through books, seminars, and collegial word of mouth that such questions deserve to be asked and that the answers deserve respectful attention. Both syndromes can be cured by the same remedy: kill the messenger.

The Child Sexual Abuse Accommodation Syndrome does not attempt to describe the symptoms of a child who is really abused. It only tries to illustrate that society maintains a reluctance to believe what victims are trying to say. These new syndromes of false allegations can't honestly prove a child wasn't molested, but they do generate the reasonable doubt so vital to the balance of justice and so cherished by those who don't want to believe. What the adherents of PAS and FMS do prove, beyond reasonable doubt, is that we are an adult society which cannot yet allow a fair and balanced view of the specter of child sexual abuse. As long as children and adult survivors are stifled by such prejudice there is a rightful place in the courts and in public consciousness for their rehabilitation through the Child Sexual Abuse Accommodation Syndrome.

REFERENCES

Akiskal, H. S. (1989), The classification of mental disorders. In: *The Comprehensive Textbook of Psychiatry*, 5th ed., ed. H. I. Kaplan & B. J. Sadock. Baltimore: Williams and Wilkins, pp. 538–598.

Armstrong, L. (1994), *Rocking the Cradle of Sexual Politics*. Reading, MA: Addison-Wesley.

Berliner, L., & Wheeler, J. R. (1987), Treating the effects of sexual abuse on children. *J. Interpers. Violence*, 2:415–434.

Brooks, C. N., & Milchman, M. S. (1991), Child sexual abuse allegations during custody litigations: Conflicts between mental health expert witnesses and the law. *Behav. Sci. & the Law*, 9:21–32.

Burgess, A., Holmstrom, L., & McCausland, M. (1978), Counseling young victims and their families. In: *Sexual Assault of Children and Adolescents*, ed. A. W. Burgess, A. N. Groth, & L. L. Holmstrom. Lexington, MA: D. C. Heath, pp. 147–156.

Elterman, M., & Ehrenberg, M. F. (1991), Sexual abuse allegations in child custody disputes. *Internat. J. Law & Psychiatry*, 14:269–286.

Finkelhor, D. (1979), What's wrong with sex between adults and children? Ethics and the problem of sexual abuse. *Amer. J. Orthopsychiatry*, 49:692–697.

FMS Foundation Newsletter (1993), (FMS Foundation, 3401 Market Street, Suite 130, Philadelphia, PA 19104-3315). April 6.

Gardner, R. A. (1987), *The Parental Alienation Syndrome and the Differentiation between Fabricated and Genuine Abuse*. Cresskill, NJ: Creative Therapeutics.

Hardt, G., & Stoller, R. J. (1990), *Intimate Communications: Erotics and the Study of Culture*. New York: Columbia University Press.

Hollingsworth, J. (1986), *Unspeakable Acts*. New York: Congdon & Weed.

Myers, J. E. B. (1993), Expert testimony describing psychological syndromes. *Pacific Law J.*, 24:1449–1464.

Seligman, M. E. P. (1975), *Helplessness: On Depression, Development and Death*. San Francisco: W. H. Freeman.

Selye, H. (1967), *The Stress of Life*. New York: McGraw-Hill.

Sorensen, T., & Snow, B. (1991), How children tell: The process of disclosure in child sexual abuse. *Child Welfare*, 70:3–15.

Summit, R. C. (1983), The child sexual abuse accommodation syndrome. *Child Abuse & Neglect*, 7:177–193.

—— (1992), Abuse of the child sexual abuse accommodation syndrome. *J. Child Sex. Abuse*, 1:153–163.

Timnick, L. (1985), 22% in survey were child abuse victims. *Los Angeles Times*, August 25:1.

Van Derbur Atler, M. (1991), The darkest secret. *People*, 35:88–94.

Whitcomb, D. (1992), *When the Victim Is a Child*. Washington, DC: U.S. Department of Justice.

Chapter 4
The Trauma of Family Violence

THOMAS W. MILLER, PH.D., A.B.P.P.,
LANE J. VELTKAMP, M.S.W., B.C.D.,
AND PAULA RAINES, J.D., PH.D.

The impact of prolonged and repeated traumatization as seen with survivors of domestic violence and child abuse is now considered as a more complex type of stress reaction than previously realized within the overall concept of posttraumatic stress disorder (PTSD). Survivors of multigenerational domestic violence and physical and sexual abuse are now recognized as suffering from a myriad of symptoms including complicated chronic depression with dissociative symptoms, substance abuse, impulsivity, suicide, and self-mutilation (Army Family Advocacy Program, 1985; Matsakis, 1987; MacLennan, 1995). Also recognized within the complexity of this disorder are characterological changes seen through personality disorders, difficulties in social and interpersonal relations, and identity confusion.

Considerable attention has been given to survivors of prolonged and repeated traumatization as evidenced in domestic

Acknowledgments. Appreciation is extended to Deborah Kessler and Katrina Scott, Library Service; Erling Eng, Psychology Service, VAMC, Lexington; Tag Heister, Virginia Lynn Morehouse, Robin Lynn Oakley, Sylvia Sparks, and Cathy L. Smith, Department of Psychiatry, University of Kentucky, for their assistance in the preparation of this manuscript.

violence and physical and sexual abuse (NCCAN, 1982, 1991; Fin-kelhor, 1984; USA Today, 1987; Conte, Berliner, and Schuerman, 1987). The area of adult nonsurvivors (Stark and Flitcraft, 1982) of such abuse and the multitude of symptoms which seem to cluster into three broad categories, including somatic, affective, and dissociative sequelae of prolonged trauma, have received much less attention.

The presence of depression in traumatized victims of abuse is well documented (Frayberg, 1980; Rosenhack and Nathan, 1985). Protracted depression is reported most commonly with symptoms including aggravated depressive symptoms, hyperarousal, intrusive thoughts, insomnia, psychosomatic symptomatology, and dissociation frequently associated with a posttraumatization period following the last incident of abuse. In addition, paralysis, apathy, and helplessness, then intense internalized anger, debased self-image, and ruminations of guilt, all are recognized to be part of a cluster of depressive symptoms frequently recognized in victims of prolonged abuse. These symptom clusters are found in persons regardless of whether they have been victims of domestic violence, prisoners of war, hostages, or otherwise tortured by strangers. Many victims of domestic battery can match the stories of abuse told by prisoners who have been brutally tortured.

Chronically traumatized individuals also exhibit anxiety, agitation, and hypervigilance recognizable not only in their insomnia and startle reactions, but in tension headaches, abdominal pain, gastrointestinal disturbances, and other forms of somatization. Prolonged victims of trauma frequently use a variety of altered consciousness states as a means of coping with memories of the stressful life event. Through dissociative experiences and voluntary thought suppression and denial, victims are able to survive the immediacy of the trauma. However, these psychologically adaptive mechanisms often come back to haunt the victims who can suffer later from disturbances of memory and concentration due to becoming conditioned to dissociation as a means of coping. Adult survivors of child sexual abuse and adult victims of domestic violence frequently use dissociative capacities in adapting and accommodating to stressful life experiences.

Survivors of domestic violence and sexual abuse often experience an extremely complex picture of psychopathology. They are, in fact, victims of a new diagnostic category labeled "Disorders of Extreme Stress." To qualify for such a diagnosis, an individual must have experienced repeated and prolonged trauma with a resultant impact on personality development outside the norm of what is usually exhibited in situations of a more acutely stressful nature. The term, *disorders of extreme stress not otherwise specified (DESNOS)*, represents an initial recognition by DSM-IV of the extensive work of Herman (1992a,b) which focuses on the significance of prolonged and repeated traumatization typified by extended domestic violence and physical and sexual abuse. Herman's findings should be carefully considered in the diagnosis and treatment of victims of such trauma.

Maltreated and abused children and spouses are finally becoming the focus of considerable concern (Polner, 1968). More than one million abused women and children seek medical attention for injuries caused by male spouses and parents each year. A number of studies have indicated that at least 20 percent, and perhaps as many as 33 percent, of the women seen in emergency rooms are there due to domestic violence (*JAMA*, 1990). Once in the emergency room, as many as one half the women requiring emergency surgery do so as a result of their battering (Stark and Flitcraft, 1981; *JAMA*, 1992). The frequency and violence of abuse, according to many studies, escalates when a woman becomes pregnant. It has been estimated that as many as 37 percent of pregnant women are assaulted and battered while they are pregnant. The results of the assault can be "placental separation, antepartum hemorrhage, fetal fractures, rupture of the uterus, liver or spleen, and preterm labor" (*JAMA*, 1992, p. 226). Shockingly, medical personnel are believed to identify only about one battered woman out of every 25 (Stark and Flitcraft, 1981, p. vii). Current estimates are that one-third of all married couples engage in spousal assault, and the number of women and children who are objects of such assault is close to 2 million per year (DeFazio, Rustin, and Diamond, 1975).

Two national epidemiological surveys (National Center for Child Abuse and Neglect, 1982, 1991; Russell, 1983; APA, 1987) have provided convincing evidence that abuse and maltreatment are occurring at an extraordinarily high rate. Most clinical researchers, as well as official military and other governmental resource agents, believe spouse and child abuse tends to be underreported. Furthermore, in some states when an abuser kills his partner and himself, there is no report or record of the crime since the perpetrator is dead and there is no one to charge with the murder. Therefore, the data on spouse and child abuse remain incomplete. This chapter will address the difficulties and complexities in understanding and diagnosing family violence. While the majority of PTSD cases reported in the literature arise from veterans exposed to combat experience, there is a growing recognition of the need for inclusion of family violence, involving child and spouse abuse within this population.

TRAUMATIC SRESS AND FAMILY VIOLENCE

Frayberg (1980) has focused on the children of survivors of the Nazi concentration camps, and notes that the impact of this experience on children led to separation and individuation, in addition to pathological identification with their traumatized parents' depression, guilt, and aggressiveness. It is clear that frequent repeated traumatization results in high levels of anxiety, depression, guilt, aggressiveness, and conscious and unconscious preoccupation with specific events that having affected the children of survivors has permeated two generations in the same family.

Horowitz and Solomon (1978) and others (Polner, 1968) have suggested that people who suffer long-term adaptive disability, complicated by memories of guilt and anxiety resulting from atrocities, both of a military and civilian nature, often exhibit signs of delayed stress. Polner (1968) cites numerous cases in

TABLE 4.1
Diagnostic Criteria for DSM-IV 309.89 Posttraumatic Stress Disorder

A.	Exposed to a traumatic event in which *both* of the following have been present:
	1. the person has experienced, witnessed, or been confronted with an event or events that involve actual or threatened death or serious injury, or a threat to the physical integrity of oneself or others
	2. the person's response involved intense fear, helplessness, or horror
B.	The traumatic event is persistently reexperienced in at least one of the following ways:
	1. recurrent and intrusive distressing recollections of the event
	2. recurrent distressing dreams of the event
	3. acting or feeling as if the traumatic event were recurring
	4. intense psychological distress at exposure to internal or external cues that symbolize or resemble an aspect of the traumatic event
	5. physiologic reactivity upon exposure to internal or external cues that symbolize or resemble an aspect of the traumatic event
C.	Persistent avoidance of stimuli associated with the trauma and numbing of general responsiveness (not present before the trauma)
D.	Persistent symptoms of increased arousal (not present before the trauma), as indicated by at least two of the following:
	1. difficulty falling or staying asleep
	2. irritability or outbursts of anger
	3. difficulty concentrating
	4. hypervigilance
	5. exaggerated startle response

which combat experiences have disturbed individuals long after return to civilian life. In most instances, the difficulties appear to center around guilt feelings, but may also contain the potential for the individual acting out.

DSM-IV (APA, 1994) defines PTSD (Table 4.1) as involving the development of characteristic symptoms following a psychologically distressing event that is outside the range of usual human experience and which would be markedly distressing to almost anyone. The traumatic event(s) are often reexperienced in a variety of ways, including recurrent and intrusive recollections of the event(s), distressing dreams, or dissociative states. While an individual is in a dissociative state there may be some form of acting out. In addition, some patients express an exaggerated startle response, have difficulty concentrating, and experience changes in impulse control and aggression, all of which have a dramatic impact upon an individual's ability to be adaptive and flexible to the demands of everyday work, family, and other relationships.

"AT RISK" FACTORS

Families at risk for violence appear to frequently have two elements in their history: (1) a multigenerational pattern of abuse, and (2) a particular family constellation. A multigenerational pattern of abuse is perpetuated by individuals witnessing and learning violence as a model of behavior and passing such learning on to subsequent generations, thereby continuing the "cycle of violence." Research has shown that persons most prone to violent behavior may share certain common experiences including witnessing parental violence during childhood, low self-esteem, impulsive behavior, a reserve of anger, isolation from others, and little social or familial support that leads to family violence. Efforts to recognize high-risk individuals and to provide early intervention in the form of prevention education may be of considerable benefit in reducing spouse and child abuse in all segments of the population.

There are several important ingredients in a model for identifying families with at-risk factors, which include:

1. One parent who may be extremely passive, dependent, or reluctant to assert him- or herself for fear of destroying the family unit;
2. A poor marital relationship, little constructive communication, or poor interpersonal relationships;
3. The perpetrator turning to the spouse or the child to relieve and displace emotional tension and stress;

4. Child victims of sexual abuse who feel emotionally deprived and may turn toward the perpetrator for support and emotional nurturance;
5. Generational boundaries are often unclear between the perpetrator and victim due to enmeshment;
6. A lack of social contacts outside the family;
7. Parents who have inadequate coping skills, particularly under stress;
8. Family problems becoming family secrets, therefore not allowing for change or intervention within the cycle of violence.

In addition, there are specific behavioral indicators of familial abuse. Victims of abuse frequently exhibit behaviors which may be the victim's way of communicating that something is wrong, that he or she is being abused. Unfortunately, physicians and health care providers frequently view these behaviors as "the problem," rather than symptoms of a far greater family problem: family violence. The most prominent physical and behavioral indicators for children and spouses are summarized in Table 4.2. (See chapter 3 for trauma accommodation syndrome.)

TREATMENT AND LEGAL CONSIDERATIONS

Treatment of the victim and the perpetrator is a complex process which may involve several professionals. Amongst professionals, collaboration, cooperation, mutual respect, and understanding of each other's roles are essential to the success of the treatment process (Russell, 1983; Miller and Veltkamp, 1990a). Reporting laws have been adopted in most states to recognize the need for open communication in the area of abuse. These laws recognize no privileged relationships beyond the attorney–client relationship. In physical and sexual abuse cases, siblings may also have been exposed to similar family themes as the victim and may also

TABLE 4.2

TABLE 4.2
Physical and Behavioral Indicators of Family Violence, Sexual Abuse, and Spouse Abuse

Family Violence

Physical Indicators
Unexplained bruises and welts
Unexplained burns, especially on soles, palms, back, or buttocks
Immersion burns
Rope burns on arms, legs, neck, or torso
Unexplained fractures to skull, nose, or facial structure; in various stages of healing; multiple or spiral fractures
Unexplained lacerations or abrasions to mouth, lips, gums, eyes, or external genitalia

Behavioral Indicators
Emotional constriction and blunted affect
Fear of adult contacts
Extreme withdrawal or aggressiveness
Extreme rejection or dependence on caretakers
Apprehension, fearfulness
Afraid to go home
Depression
Phobias, anxiety
Sleep disturbance
Withdrawn, inhibited behavior
Obsessive–compulsive behavior

Sexual Abuse

Physical Indicators
Difficulty in walking or sitting
Torn, stained, or bloody underclothing
Bruises or bleeding in external genitalia, vaginal or anal areas
Venereal disease, especially in preteens
Pregnancy

Behavioral Indicators
Sleep disturbances
Withdrawn or regressed behavior
Secondary enuresis or encopresis
Bizarre, sophisticated, or unusual sexual behavior or knowledge

(continued)

TABLE 4.2 (continued)

Poor interpersonal skills
Sexual promiscuity
Self-report of abuse
Anorexia
Extreme self-blame
Extreme fears

Neglect

Physical Indicators
Poor hygiene, consistent hunger, inappropriate dress
Consistent lack of supervision
Unattended physical problems or medical needs
Failure to thrive

Behavioral Indicators
Begging, stealing food
Constant fatigue, listlessness
Delinquency (e.g., thefts, vandalism)
Victim reports that there is no parent, guardian, or caretaker

---

have been abused. Siblings may feel guilt that they did not try to intervene and stop the abuse. The following are important areas for consideration when working with siblings (Burgess, Holmstrom, and McCausland, 1978):

1. Preserve the psychological bond the siblings have with their parents and each other.
2. Preserve continuity of relationships and place.
3. Reduce risk for siblings by providing supervision (i.e., monitor relationship with abusing parent).
4. Evaluate to determine if siblings are showing symptoms.
5. If siblings cannot be protected in their home, they should be removed.

It is equally, if not more, important that the perpetrator also be the focus of treatment. Historically, communities have upheld the perpetrator's continuance of the abusive patterns by asking the wrong questions about the abuse. The most frequently asked question has been, "Why doesn't she leave?" Increasingly, communities, social service agencies, prosecutors, and researchers are asking very different questions such as, "What's wrong with the abuser? Will the perpetrator go to jail? How do we protect and provide for the women and children? How do we stop the abuse from continuing? Is the family treatable and can its members be rehabilitated or reunited?"

Recently developed programs for intervening with families to stop the cycle of abuse require coordinated efforts between law enforcement, the courts, and social agencies. The most successful programs require that abusers understand that there are consequences for their actions, including arrest and incarceration. The focus of abuser treatment programs is to assist abusers in breaking through denial and taking responsibility for their actions, to help them examine and change sexist beliefs that men hold all the power within a household, to analyze and understand their cultural conditioning which views violence as an acceptable way of dominating their victims, and to learn healthy and nonviolent ways to respond to conflict (Paymer, 1994).

CLINICAL ISSUES IN FAMILY VIOLENCE

What emerges from the clinical research reported to date is the presence of various forms of abuse, from emotional abuse to physical battering. The number of unreported or underreported cases needs immediate attention and action by all health care professionals. Clearly, spouse and child abuse is not limited to any particular population of individuals, but has been found to be more prevalent among families experiencing financial pressures, frequent moves, alcohol and drug use, high stress, and isolation from peer groups and family support systems.

Child and spouse abuse is hypothesized to be more prevalent among men who have received military training during which they have learned a quick action response in combat, or who have been exposed to or participated in rape and abuse of women during their military experiences (e.g., during the Vietnam War). In certain situations, veterans may experience unresolved grief which may underlie the symptoms of PTSD and contribute to maltreatment and abuse of both spouse and children. Many military and former military personnel believe that military personnel may tend to react in hostile and aggressive ways when they encounter frustration with bureaucracy, patriotic holidays, or when flexibility and sensitivity are needed in the process of working through life stresses in the family.

The complexities and mixed reactions experienced by postmilitary personnel may make it more difficult for the veteran to integrate the memories of combat and wartime and its meaning into a broader civilian life pattern. Clinical observations suggest that the veteran may utilize a number of defense mechanisms to wall off these memories from everyday life situations; but, as with most stress response syndromes, the breakdown in these defenses generally occurs only after the termination of the real environmental stress event, a latency period of apparent relief, and then specific daily life stress providing factors which may lead to the violent impulsive outbursts seen in family violence.

Horowitz and Solomon (1978) note that in PTSD patients, there is often difficulty in distinguishing between the sadistic aspects of combat aggressiveness and the age-appropriate competitiveness of the child or spouse who wishes to be more autonomous. Veterans in such situations know that sadistic violence or torture is not only possible, since they have committed it under military rules and guidelines, but that violence can reduce tension at the same time it invokes guilt. What results may be a shortening of the conceptual distance between impulse and act, and as Horowitz and Solomon argued, fantasy and reality.

Another increasingly noted concern among Veterans Outreach Programs is that many veterans who are still mourning the death of close friends or who have unresolved survivor guilt related to their wartime experiences may have difficulty in interpersonal relationships where issues surrounding intimacy, marriage, and child rearing may precipitate violent outbursts (Mrazak, 1981a). Furthermore, veterans who have killed or fear they have killed women and children during combat may find it more difficult to make the transition to the role of husband and nurturing parent in postmilitary life.

Child rearing has been described as a stressful life experience in and of itself. Many veterans who are still working through the difficult transition from war to peacetime may have increasing difficulties in being nurturing parents and behaving appropriately to their families as they continue to be cut off from their own feelings, are insensitive to the feelings of others, afraid of closeness, and may have problems with impulse control. Titchner (1985) suggests that essential to the successful readjustment of a veteran following a combat experience is the individual's ability to make the transition from the "reflex" of combat aggressiveness to the adaptive, nondestructive aggression in civilian life, which includes care, compassion, empathy, and control toward spouse and children.

Community Resources
for Addressing Family Violence

The use of community resources in all cases involving family violence is a necessary part of a comprehensive treatment plan. Veltkamp and Miller (1990b) have summarized community resources available to the physician and other health care professionals. These include the following:

1. *Safe shelter and 24-hour crisis line:* This service provides a place where victims and abusers call anytime, day or night, to receive counseling, information, referrals, and screening for shelter.
2. *Criminal justice response:* Many communities make domestic violence a top priority for police, sheriff, and court response.

The police or sheriff can arrest and incarcerate perpetrators, the courts may jail offenders and require them to attend counseling or groups for perpetrators of abuse, and may issue emergency protective orders, restraining orders, or domestic violence orders for victims.

3. *Counseling and casework services:* These services are designed to facilitate the victim's exploration of alternatives and her eventual return to the community. Problem specific counseling must be available for offenders, as well as children.

4. *Legal advocacy program:* This service provides a legal advocate to act as a liaison between the victim of domestic violence, whether residing at a shelter or not, and the court system.

5. *Hospital advocacy program:* This service provides a hospital advocate who will meet a victim at the hospital to provide information, support and referrals.

6. *Perpetrator's group:* This service provides a forum for men to seek alternatives to violence, to break down the isolation they feel and provide alternatives to physically, psychologically, and sexually abusive behaviors.

7. *Community education:* This service provides programs on issues of domestic violence for public awareness.

8. Group for nonabusing parent.

9. Children's group.

SUMMARY

The role and function of the health care professional in the assessment of family violence is critically important. Health care providers are often the first to be able to identify possible abuse in assessing the health care of victims. The health care provider experienced in detecting physical and behavioral indicators of potential abuse can evaluate further the dynamics within the family and provide essential medical, health care, and referral to the abused patient. Furthermore, the physician can sensitize and alert other health care professionals and the protective services system of needed care for the abused victim.

REFERENCES

American Psychiatric Association (1987), *Diagnostic and Statistical Manual of Mental Disorders* (DSM-III-R), 3rd ed. rev. Washington, DC: American Psychiatric Press.

———— (1994), *Diagnostic and Statistical Manual of Mental Disorders* (DSM-IV), 4th ed. Washington, DC: American Psychiatric Press.

Army Family Advocacy Program (1985), *Analysis of Official Army Reports of Spouse Abuse.* Alexandria, VA: U.S. Army Community and Family Support Center.

Burgess, A. W., Holmstrom, L. L., & McCausland, M. P. (1978), Counseling young victims and their families. In: *Sexual Assault of Children and Adolescents,* ed. A. W. Burgess, A. N. Groth, & L. L. Holmstrom. Lexington, MA: D. C. Heath, pp. 147–156.

Conte, J. R., Berliner, L., & Schuerman, J. R. (1987), *The Impact of Sexual Abuse on Children.* Final Technical Report. Project No. MH 37133. Washington, DC: U.S. Government Printing Office. National Institute of Mental Health.

DeFazio, S., Rustin, S., & Diamond, A. (1975), Symptom development in Vietnam era veterans. *Amer. J. Orthopsychiatry,* 45:258–263.

DeJong, A. R. (1985), The medical evaluation of sexual abuse in children. *Hosp. & Commun. Psychiatry,* 36:503–509.

Finkelhor, D. (1984), *Sexually Victimized Children.* New York: Free Press.

Frayberg, J. T. (1980), Difficulties in separation-individuation as experienced by offspring of Holocaust survivors. *Amer. J. Orthopsychiatry,* 50:87–95.

Herman, J. L. (1992a), Complex PTSD: A syndrome in survivors of prolonged and repeated trauma. *J. Traum. Stress,* 5:377–391.

———— (1992b), *Trauma and Recovery.* New York: Basic Books.

Horowitz, M. J., & Solomon, G. F. (1978), Delayed stress response in Vietnam veterans. In: *Stress Disorders among Vietnam Veterans,* ed. C. R. Figley. New York: Brunner/Mazel, pp. 236–249.

Jones, A. (1994), *Next Time She'll Be Dead.* Boston, MA: Beacon Press.

Journal of the American Medical Association (1990), Editorial. Domestic violence intervention calls for more than treating the injuries. *JAMA,* 264:939.

———— (1992), Violence against women: Relevance for medical practitioners. *JAMA,* 267:3186.

MacLennan, B. W. (1995), *Problems in Estimating the Nature and Extent of Family Violence in the Armed Forces.* Research Report. Washington, DC: National Security Management, National Defense University.

Matsakis, A. (1987), *Wives and Children of Vietnam Veterans*. Silver Springs, MD: Vet Center Publication.

Miller, T. W., & Feibelman, N. D. (1989), Traumatic stress disorder: Diagnostic and clinical issues in psychiatry. In: *Stressful Life Events*, ed. T. W. Miller. Madison, CT: International Universities Press, pp. 553–571.

Mrazek, P. B. (1981a), *Group Psychotherapy with Sexually Abused Children and Their Families*. New York: Pergamon Press.

—— (1981b), Special problems in the treatment of child sexual abuse. In: *Sexually Abused Children and Their Families*, ed. P. B. Mrazek & C. H. Kempe. New York: Pergamon Press, pp. 117–125.

National Center for Child Abuse and Neglect (1982), *Executive Summary: National Study of the Incidence and Severity of Child Abuse and Neglect*. Washington, DC: U.S. Government Printing Office.

—— (1991), *Study Findings: National Study of the Incidence and Severity of Child Abuse and Neglect*. Washington, DC: U.S. Government Printing Office.

Paymer, M. (1994), *Violent No More*. Alameda, CA: Hunter House.

Polner, M. (1968), Vietnam war stories. *Transaction*, 6:8–21.

Rosenhack, R., & Nathan, P. (1985), Secondary traumatization in children of Vietnam veterans. *Hosp. & Commun. Psychiatry*, 36:538–540.

Russell, D. (1983), The incidence and prevalence of intrafamilial and extrafamilial sexual abuse of female children. *Child Abuse & Neg.*, 7:56–63.

Stark, E., & Flitcraft, E. (1981), *Wife Abuse in the Medical Setting: An Introduction for Health Personnel*. Domestic Violence Monograph, No. 7. Washington, DC: Office of Domestic Violence.

—— —— (1982), Medical therapy as repression: The case of the battered woman (data summary report, Minnesota Department of Corrections, St. Paul, Minnesota.) *Health & Med.*, 28(1):338–364.

Titchner, J. L. (1985), Post-traumatic decline. Paper presented at the Neuropsychiatric Institute, VA Medical Center, Coatsville, Pennsylvania.

USA Today (1987), News across the USA. August 21:p. 8A.

Veltkamp, L. J. & Miller, T. W. (1990a), Stages of trauma in abuse. *Internat. J. Fam. Psychiatry*, 9:259–275.

—— & Miller, T. W. (1990b), Clinical strategies in recognizing spouse abuse. *Psychiatric Quart.*, 61:181–189.

Chapter 5
Traumatization and Stress in Child and Adolescent Victims of Natural Disasters

ANAIT AZARIAN, PH.D., AND
VITALI SKRIPTCHENKO-GREGORIAN, PH.D.

Contemporary life is characterized by daily activities that are rapid, complex, and insecure, a way of life that has become the norm, typical of many societies. This staccato style varies in its impact on the health of individuals, families, and special populations. Our health is not only the result of our individual behavior, but is also the product of other environmental factors and conditions.

Mental health professionals have shown considerable interest in the problem of traumatization, particularly the trauma that is associated with stressful life events. For example, in a comprehensive volume (Miller, 1989), the following issues have been discussed as stressful events: life circumstances, medical illness, mental health, family stressors, abuse, combat stress. Even though

Acknowledgments. This study was supported by a special grant from Brown University, Providence, Rhode Island. We would like to acknowledge the support of Vartan Gregorian, President of Brown University. Appreciation is extended to Lewis P. Lipsitt, Ph.D., Brown University, and Anthony J. Palumbo, Ph.D., Institute of Puppet Therapy, Massachusetts, for their assistance and encouragement in the preparation of this manuscript.

77

these issues seem comprehensive, it is now time to extend our professional interest in stressors to those that occur as consequences of natural disaster.

The Earth is no longer seen as a static sphere, firmly held by Atlas: contemporary geophysics views the planet as an active, restless, dynamic, and often violent environment. In fact, natural violence, with its powerful and sudden impact, often results in great loss of human life, vast property damage, and profound distress to any survivors. Unfortunately, natural disasters arise everywhere, constantly, and without appointment. In the United States, during only a few months, there were devastating flooding in several states, fires, and an earthquake in California. In all, in the United States, during the 20-year period from 1965 to 1985, there were 531 federally declared disasters (Rubin, Yezer, Hussain, and Webb, 1986). Worldwide, between 1947 and 1973 there were 836 reported natural disasters, an average of 31 per year, in which 100 or more people were killed or injured or in which at least $1 million worth of damage was incurred (Gleser, Green, and Winget, 1981). This data does not include natural disaster phenomena from the former Soviet Union, Eastern Europe, and China; inclusion of these large areas could easily double the figures.

Natural disasters are a common, not incidental, aspect of life, an inevitable part of the cycle of destruction and renewal. Natural disasters warn us to understand and respect the great power of nature and to design our lives to accommodate these events. It is vital to study each disaster in terms of its impact and consequence, so we can minimize the resulting disruption of our lives.

Statistical information reveals that many children and adolescents have become victims of different types of natural disasters. Nevertheless, there are not many studies devoted to this area; most of the professional literature regarding disasters is about their impact on adults and property. In fact there is an extensive literature on the psychological consequences of traumatic experiences on adults, less on children. There is a special nomenclature used to describe the effects of trauma on adults: shell-shock, nervous shock, traumatic neurosis, survivor syndrome (Keppel-Benson and Ollendick, 1993). As early as the 1950s, the adult diagnosis of "gross stress reaction" appeared in the first edition of the *Diagnostic and Statistical Manual* (DSM-I; APA, 1952). This term was later modified to "posttraumatic stress disorder" (PTSD) in the third edition of the Manual (DSM-III; APA, 1980). It was only in the revised third edition of the Manual (DSM-III-R; APA, 1987) that a few posttraumatic symptoms specific to children were added.

We could easily speculate on the reasons for this obvious omission considering the voluminous visual documentation of war, political turmoil, and natural disaster, but Sugar (1989) has documented and commented on this in detail. Sugar points out that there are still many unsettled issues regarding the impact of trauma on children: What are specific children's reactions? Are they due to parental reactions or are they individualistic? Do children have similar responses regardless of sex, age, history, and developmental stage? Do children need special types of psychological treatment for PTSD?

This chapter is concerned with these questions, namely the impact of natural disaster on children and adolescents. It is based on the authors' experience with over 2500 young survivors of the great Armenian earthquake of 1988. We founded and led the Children's Psychotherapy Center, the first such institution in the former Soviet Union, which was devoted to the multifaceted treatment of children and adolescents who had survived the disaster. This work spanned about 3 years and has shaped our thinking and the framework within which we understand trauma and stress among children.

DISASTERS

The word *disaster* is made up of two parts: the Latin *dis* meaning against or reverse; and *astrum*, which means stars. Hence the word really signifies a *bad star* or *bad omen*. In the wider sense of the term, it implies a calamity, a catastrophe or cataclysm, an act of God or nature that is a great hardship to bear.

There are varying perspectives on disasters. Natural scientists concentrate on the physical agents and physical processes that lead to disasters. They link quakes and volcanoes to earth; floods and tsunami with water; hurricanes and tornadoes with the atmosphere (Ebert, 1988). From their vantage point, social scientists describe disasters as massive social disruptions, social crises, or changes in social patterns (Quarantelli and Dynes, 1977; Frederick, 1987). Among these changes may be wars, revolutions, riots, and acts of terrorism. Several researchers divide disasters into those that are natural and those that are manmade (Beigel and Berren, 1985; Baum, 1987). The latter group includes train accidents, plane crashes, explosions, and poisoning by pollutants. Further classifications have been made based overwhelmingly on stressful life events, such as physical and sexual abuse, rape, kidnapping, divorce, or death of parents and other significant figures (van der Kolk, 1987; Anthony, 1988; Miller, 1988).

In order to define natural disasters as stressful life events, we must extend our thinking and include characteristics which are related to the disaster's profound impact on the victims' mental health. Thus we can create a working definition of natural disasters as extraordinary, unexpected, and uncontrollable events that cause massive destruction of property, death or physical injury, loss of communality, terror, and serious threats which result in human stress because of the simultaneous impact of different environmental stressors breaking through personal defenses with such strength that an effective response is impossible.

Differences between Disaster Traumas

Working with over 2500 children, we had a very large database. We found that trauma from a natural disaster differs from that associated with other trauma such as rape or physical abuse.

The first distinctive characteristic of natural disaster trauma is the multiplicity of its effects. The limited professional literature in this area gives the impression that there are single traumas among the victims, and only a few authors have recognized the multifaceted aspects associated with the natural disaster experience (Sugar, 1988; Terr, 1990; Armstrong, O'Callaghan, and Marmar, 1991). Our own observations have clearly demonstrated this multiple aspect dimension, seen in hundreds of young victims of the quake (Azarian and Skriptchenko, 1992a). Consequently, it is critically important to expect several stressors to occur simultaneously during a natural disaster. These multifaceted stressors impact through all sense modalities; the terror comes from all sensory channels: sight, hearing, smell, touch, hunger and thirst, discomfort and cold. As a result of such interwoven stressors and such an overwhelming life experience, the survivors manifest a wide range of cognitive, emotional, and behavioral symptoms.

The second distinctive characteristic of natural disaster trauma is its long-term nature; this phenomenon has been labeled "secondary disaster" or "secondary injury" (Erikson, 1976; Symonds, 1980). It can best be described as a series of adverse events following the initial disaster impact that can have an even more traumatic influence than the initial impact on the survivor's well-being. According to Sugar (1988), a single disaster may set off a series of traumatic secondary events which will further enlarge the damage, akin to a domino effect. Consequently, to understand secondary injury from natural disaster, one has to keep this domino metaphor in mind because such a phenomenon is the rule rather than the exception. It is more likely that there will be sequential effects initiated by the first shock, then furthered by the chain of thoughts, sensations, feelings, and behavior triggered by these primary events.

The third distinctive characteristic of natural disaster trauma is mass victimization, both psychologically and physically. For example, the 1976 China quake, the worst in modern times, caused over 300,000 deaths (Ebert, 1988). This is an unthinkable amount of suffering. The scale of this mass trauma can be better appreciated from the works of Alexander (1985) and de Ville de Goyet

(1980) who estimated that for each 10 deaths due to earthquake disaster, 30 to 35 persons will require some medical attention, but 1 or 2 will require hospitalization. Gueri and Alzate (1984) write that children are most vulnerable to death and injury in natural disasters. No normal human being can "adjust" to terrifying disaster stressors without developing neurotic symptoms. When a disaster strikes entire families, groups, or populations they suffer from various psychotraumas (Lifton and Olson, 1976; Raphael, 1986). There is a great deal of evidence that rescue workers also suffer extreme psychological consequences as a result of a natural disaster (Armstrong et al., 1991; Clark, 1992). In fact, the spread effects of a disaster affect people at a distance, who may have only tangential relationships to the afflicted population, in terms of religious, national, and cultural affiliations (Yacoubian and Hacker, 1989).

Such a widespread disastrous effect complicates the recovery process of any member of a community or family, because recovering from psychological stress after trauma requires an active, dynamic exchange between the victims and their environment. Much positive interchange is needed and victims require continued and close social support. When there is mass victimization, such an interchange is drastically reduced. The flow of supportive transactions from the victims' environment runs slow and can have a debilitating influence. Normally, the community heals the victim, and the survivor in turn contributes to the health of the community; such a dynamic is destroyed along with the collapse of the infrastructure. The network that formerly cradled each social member is broken; for children, such a collapse is particularly traumatic. In developmental criteria, they are in greatest need of supportive environments, but when mass victimization occurs, this social buoyancy is wrecked. The children experience a true double jeopardy.

These three characteristics of natural disaster trauma differentiate this event from other more common types of traumas. Surprisingly these distinctions have been neglected in the stress literature. They should not be ignored because each of the characteristics described has an important impact on the survivors' health. With children and adolescents, for example, such refinements of treatment may make the difference between failure and successful recovery. We should make these events the focus of additional research efforts and look at the ways in which differences in the type of traumas experienced can be better understood to make rehabilitative efforts more appropriate and therefore more effective.

THE ARMENIAN EARTHQUAKE

Unfortunately, all the previously mentioned characteristics were present during the Armenian earthquake (Noji, 1989; Grigorova, Gasparian, and Manukian, 1990; Pomonis, 1990; Sudjian, 1990). On December 7, 1988, at 11:41 A.M., a devastating quake registering 6.9 on the Richter scale suddenly struck over 40 percent of the territory of Armenia, killing (during 41 seconds) over 25,000 people, injuring another 78,000, and leaving over 2000 amputees. More than 40,000 people who were buried under the ruins were saved and at least 53,000 families were left homeless. It was an incredible and almost instantaneous collapse of life and property.

Children suffered more than adults because they were in school at the time of the quake. The school buildings were inadequately designed and constructed; none was built to withstand such devastating force. In all, 83 schools and 90 kindergartens were destroyed. In the area of Leninakan, of the 18,000 reported deaths, 10,000 were children and adolescents; 3900 children lost 1 parent and 520 became orphans. After the quake, over 32,000 children were evacuated to different parts of the Soviet Union for between 2 and 6 months. In fact, 6000 children were lost in the postdisaster social chaos, and fortunately were later found and restored to their families. These figures are numbing because when one considers and imagines what this was in reality, the mind can only begin to grasp the widespread terror and loss that suddenly overwhelmed the population.

Adults and children simultaneously experienced an influence of multiple quake stressors:

- *Psychophysiological stressors:* strange and terrifying growling noises that came from underground, from the earth itself; screams of agony from all around; the sight of buildings collapsing and houses folding in on themselves like houses of cards; the odor of burning fires and dust.
- *Information stressors* that continued the terror: "How can I escape?" "Where are my relatives?" "What is going on?" The panic and implosion of information and missing information left most important questions unanswered.
- *Emotional stressors:* the omnipresent fear and confusion; the continued threat of death and damage; the fear for one's own survival and that of parents and relatives was for many simply unbearable.
- *Social stressors:* the loss of a community or neighborhood; the sudden realization that one has no school, or home, or street, or friends, was stunning and devasting to any sense of ego integrity.

Among some Armenian children, who were not visibly terrified by the earthquake itself, there was shock at witnessing their parents' and teachers' panic. Others suffered more after actual separation from parents and friends during the evacuation. We observed a number of these children upset when they finally realized they had lost a dear pet or had lost their toys and possessions.

Very often, ripple effects occurred psychologically as the secondary effects of the quake took effect. Being in school, many children initially experienced the physiological impact of the quake (pain, strange noise, terrible vibrations). Then, a little later, more emotional effects resulted; children became afraid of the school buildings (the emotional domino). Because there was no treatment for this fear, it continued to develop and created behavioral changes: children began to refuse to even attend school (the behavioral domino). And again adults paid no attention to these children, and as a result their behavioral troubles had a disastrous effect on their relations with teachers, parents, and classmates, creating different kinds of antisocial actions (the social domino). These emotional, social, and behavioral dominoes accumulated in impact and further burdened the children's well-being with diverse psychosomatic disturbances. The most frequent of these were nightmares, sleep disturbances, headaches, and loss of appetite (the psychosomatic domino). These in their turn, as a domino view suggests, additionally traumatized the children by adversely affecting their school performance and motivation to study (the cognitive domino).

TRAUMATIZATION IN DISASTER CHILDREN

What were the differences in terms of response between adult and child victims of disaster? The PTSD experienced by adults has been fairly well documented (Krystal, 1968; Hocking, 1970; Horowitz, 1976; Figley, 1978). Our practical experience with hundreds of child survivors has convinced us that the same kind of events that create PTSD in adults also can create it in children. Moreover, those events that may not seem too important or traumatic to adults, can adversely affect children. This has been corroborated by the recent researches by Keppel-Benson and Ollendick (1993), Garbarino and Kostelny (1993), and others who emphasize that children are more likely to experience simple events as traumatic because of their developmental level, their increased emotional reactivity, and their inability to influence an event—a kind of helplessness. So for many Armenian preschoolers, separation from parents and siblings during the mass evacuation was enough to result in symptoms of PTSD that did not seem to occur among adolescents and adults.

An additional support for this observation was our experience with young children who were dependent on parents or care providers. They seemed more adversely affected from "secondary disasters." For instance, after the quake parents and teachers were confused, in shock, or a state of panic. Their daily lives were so disrupted that many simply could not cope. This failure also damaged their ability to care for and manage the children, and this further exacerbated the children's trauma. The earthquake was accompanied by numerous traumatic secondary (domino) events which caused a powerful upheaval of family life and then deleterious effects on children's development and health. Many sensitive, empathic Armenian children developed PTSD symptoms as a secondary effect to the parents' symptoms, when each day they saw how the parents were struggling with the quake trauma.

There is another developmental consideration that points to the differential effects that disaster has on children. The children who do not have well-developed speech skills, or the experience of solving stressful situations in a family context, or who lack the traditional social support systems connected with adults, seem to be affected more powerfully by psychotraumas. Such children may not have well-founded religious beliefs, a network of intact family members and friends, and past experience with any tragedy, all of which shape how adults react to disaster. Most children need special assistance from adults after a disaster. Such children may suffer from PTSD for the rest of their lives if they do not receive complete and competent help from caring adults.

CASE VIGNETTE 1: CHILDREN 8 MONTHS AFTER THE QUAKE

We observed two brothers, 7 and 9, and a sister, 12, in the "Italian Village" near Spitak, a town of 20,000 inhabitants which was completely destroyed during the quake. The village was built near the town by the Italian government as humanitarian aid for Spitak's families, which had suffered many human losses. These children had lost their mother, grandparents, several cousins, aunts, uncles, and several friends. They lived in the new village with their father who worked in the cemetery every day preparing gravestones for his dead relatives. It is important to note that different cultures have particular rituals in regard to the timing of funerals, periods of prayer, and gravestone erection. For instance, according to ancient Christian Armenian tradition, all work on gravestones must be finished before the first anniversary of the victim's death, and requires the active participation of the living men of the extended family. Interestingly, such cultural rules saved the lives of many Armenian men because they could not commit suicide until these acts of ritual burial were completed. Male survivors had to go to the cemetery to complete these important cultural duties. In fact, this family activity had a calming effect on them; they had a physical and mental discharge of emotion while these lengthy rites were completed. When the year was over, very few of these greatly anguished men were still suicidal.

The children, however, had no such cultural responsibilities as an outlet. They lived without parental control and were forced to endure their trauma alone. The two brothers and sister experienced the initial quake trauma, and when they realized the tragic cause of their mother's absence and that of their relatives, their problems worsened. Then they moved from the destroyed town to a new place with a new neighborhood where everyone, adults and children, was very depressed. They were again shocked and lost. Their father spent less time with them due to his duties at the cemetery, so the older sister had to assume all the domestic responsibilities.

When we were observing them, the children clearly manifested both primary and secondary trauma symptoms; their facial expressions, physical movements, and responses to questions all demonstrated the impact of their recent lives. They feared strangers, lacked trust, did not want to communicate, felt helpless, and lacked direction and decisiveness. There was aggression on the part of the two boys toward their sister, while she was in a deep state of apathy. These children were unable to verbalize, explain, or understand their own feelings or emotions; they could not accept the legitimacy of their fears and nightmares. They could not even discuss what was happening with their father or friends. But, despite such overwhelming denial and reticence, they continued to play! Using black stones found on the ground, the brothers played at "cemetery." They used toy trucks to move play construction materials back and forth between several little gravestones they had created. A rare children's game indeed! It was in such a symbolic way that these young disaster victims tried to tell the adult world about their great misfortune. This somber, joyless play was a symptom of the PTSD these children endured.

This extreme, but unfortunately, typical case demonstrates that children cannot effectively cope with natural disasters without special adult assistance and intervention. We can also partially explain such traumatization from a neurological perspective as well.

Miller and Başoğlu (1992) recently suggested for consideration Chemtob, Roitblat, Hamada, Carlson, and Twentyman's (1988) model of PTSD based on hemispheric lateralization of cognition and affect. According to this model the right hemisphere in most individuals acts as an early warning system, starting the mobilization of the person's fight or flight response. The left hemisphere is responsible for analyzing the threatening aspects of a situation and for devising actions to cope with the external stressors. In some cases, according to this model, right brain activity may overwhelm the modulating influence of the left, thereby developing the symptoms of PTSD: anxiety, fear, irritability, physiological reactivity, and cognitive distortion.

In stressful situations, the right and left hemispheres of adults usually act in tandem, with simultaneous interaction, extensive exchange of information, and active access to past experience stored in memory (Gardner, 1982; Azarian, 1989). During stress, adult victims attempt to understand what is happening, to recode traumatic, sensory memories, and derive meaning from the series of stressful life events. They verbalize it and work to adjust each new negative experience into a safe, controllable form by fitting it into recalled past experience. Adult victims even formalize these experiences in order to find past schemas or cognitive patterns that will assist them in coping with the traumatic stresses.

But cognitive restructuring is not always easy; sometimes it is difficult for adults to gain access to past traumatic memories

(Johnston, 1988). Aspects of that event may be coded in flash-backs, dreams, nightmares, and fears. Gaining mental access to these mostly visual memories may even depend upon simple coincidence; that is, traumatic experience that is triggered by present sensory stimuli may become accessible by mere chance. Adult victims work on recoding each independent experience as a form of coping and attempt to reconstruct the whole event, and use common elements between the present and the past. These commonalities can be abstractions, associations, or speech. The second type of memory is more flexible, controllable, safe, and, of course, less painful. Usually, the right hemisphere involves the initial visual memories of the traumatic events and the left is responsible for the verbal recoding and recall.

So, for successful coping with the trauma victims need to use both sides of the brain, both forms of memory, own to their past experiences, and recall the experiences of others. This matrix of personal and social interactions is important for the best recovery from trauma. The victim's interaction with social environment, family, friends, and helpers, even his or her religious and philosophical beliefs, are helpful supports for improved health. Each of these elements helps the victim to reexperience, conceptualize, and transform traumatic memories into recollections that are less emotionally intense and better suited to successful living. For example, Sarkisian (1984) studied the coping process of Armenian women, who were survivors of the Armenian genocide of 1915. He concluded: "Their strong commitment to their religion and family helped them adapt to the adversities of the event, and continues to help them cope with life today in their old age" (p. 44).

The cognitive process is not the same with children, however. Because of their developmental level, children are often unable to carry out the same mental processes as adults. In early childhood, the assymetric hemispheric functioning is not sufficiently developed for children to produce necessary interactions and transactions between left and right sides of the brain, visual and verbal forms of memory. Their past experience is obviously less, and so they have a smaller supply of successful coping mechanisms to rely upon. This reduced schematic base limits their ability to find new ways of adjusting to the stressful circumstances. Children are also limited in their understanding of these events. They often use magical, not formal, operations to process experience. Some cannot abstract the force of natural disasters and therefore think of a disaster as a personified event. In addition to these intellectual limitations, children are unable to organize special relief discussions, rituals, or meetings with professionals as adult survivors do.

In the case of the three children in vignette 1, we found that they were still suffering trauma 8 months after the quake. Each of them faced life completely alone, and they lived in a frightening environment that was fragmenting and fragile. They were still unable to verbalize any of the disaster events, or the impact on their present lives. The children did not express any signs of an ongoing coping process. Everything seemed buried as well under a rubble of subconsciousness. Their traumatic memories were repressed under powerful defenses, and this caused serious psychological suffering when they suddenly broke through during nightmares or due to sensory stimuli. The next case vignette demonstrates that very significant parts of the disaster experience can be buried in children's memory. Children need adults' assistance in order to safely reexperience and recode traumatic memories into accessible and painless recollections.

Case Vignette 2: A Buried Boy

Souren, a 7-year-old boy, was trapped for about 5 hours under the ruins of his house. His father's hand was crushed by a stone as he lay under the rubble, but he was able to talk to Souren as they waited for rescue. The father's hand was unfortunately amputated, but they survived. Souren's grandmother and a family friend were killed as all of them sat around the same table. It was a typical story of some survivors who inexplicably escaped death while their relatives, who were often right next to them during the quake, did not.

Souren began to attend the Center about 6 months after the disaster. He presented as a depressed, fearful, reticent boy. He was very irritable and sensitive to any loud noise; even the TV, radio, or car sounds startled and upset him. He was unable to recall any details of being buried or rescued. During the initial treatment sessions he showed that his traumatic experience was stored mostly in figurative form. In art therapy sessions, he drew only a few colored spots. We repeatedly asked what these spots meant; finally he offered what was to be a significant meaning for him and the therapist: "In my pictures there are colors of our wallpaper . . . during the earthquake they were all torn . . . the guitar broke with a loud noise when I was standing on the balcony, then everything went black and I went to sleep." These disjointed, brief recollections meant that some coping process had begun; the boy was able to verbalize his traumatic experience using the detail of the colors of the wallpaper and the sound of the breaking guitar, visual and auditory stimuli that were becoming nonthreatening. These initial memories were the doorway we used to help Souren to recollect and verbalize his subconscious traumatic memories.

His progress was slow and deliberate. Souren was eventually able to recall how his father had consoled him as they lay buried, even how they were happily rescued by an uncle and other relatives. Nevertheless, even though his memories were gradually unfolding and his psychological state was improving, there was an important symbol of his trauma that he repressed. This boy had a recurrent nightmare that continued many months after the quake: a fish would appear in his dreams and bite him. This dream was relentless. Finding the source for such an atypical nightmare was the result of much hard work between his family, Souren, and the Center's team. It seemed that at the very moment the quake struck, Souren's father and the family friend were sitting around a table having a meal of dried fish and beer; Souren and his grandmother were in the same room. Unbelievably, the sharp, thorny fish fins were embedded in Souren's leg as he lay buried. He remembered only the pain of the fish fins; in fact, when he was rescued, his uncle saw the fish still embedded in the boy's leg! Obviously the boy had also seen the fins, but the recollection of that part of the painful day was so inaccessible to the child, that only the image of a biting fish in his dreams was available to his consciousness, but none of the details of the burial and rescue.

Souren's father, however, was able to remember and to describe the entire disaster experience in detail. Although he was severely traumatized, both physically and emotionally, his psychological recovery was complete 6 months after the quake.

Thus, traumatization in children and adults essentially differs. As part of a successful response to a disaster adults consciously and unconsciously use their regulatory thinking processes to work through the trauma to a level where it becomes relatively tolerable. Children are deficient in this respect, which may make it difficult for them to work through trauma.

Similar cases of children's traumatization have been observed in numerous young survivors of the earthquake. While distinguishing between various cases identifies important factors, such as age, sex, intensity of exposure to disaster stressors, and others, which differentiate the traumatization process, there are common reactions to the stressful event in children. However, the observations have shown that some children's responses to the disaster are positively constant across variables of the children's personality and the circumstances which had a traumatic impact.

COMMON STRESS REACTIONS TO DISASTER

The immediate reactions which usually may be evident in minutes or hours are confusion and shocklike states, disorganized behavior, crying and screaming, and then quiet apathy and hopelessness. This collapse of initiative is due to the suddenness of the disaster, the absence of any information about it, or lack of previous experience with a disaster. The children's reactions are often cued by the behavior of the adults they observe; the adults' panic and disorganization creates an environment for the children that is chaotic internally and externally. Children mirror the adult world, and when mass hysteria is pervasive, they too reflect such behavior. The next case demonstrates how this spread of emotions affected a young girl.

CASE VIGNETTE 3: A CHILD IN SCHOOL

This is the case of Armine, an 8-year-old girl. At the Center she repeatedly painted the moment of her stupor state, a moment she said she would remember forever. She was so confused during the earthquake that she could not escape from the school with her screaming teacher and classmates. She described the experience in this way: "I was at school, sitting at my desk and reading a book . . . suddenly it began. It was terrible and endless; the whole building was shaking crazily, the walls were cracking. My teacher became silly and acted like a clown, then went away, and I was dead. . . . My relative was also at the school, and so she came and helped me get downstairs so I could run into the schoolyard. . . . I thought that maybe it was a war . . . "

Denial

Denial is one of the most prevalent initial reactions to disaster. Children can persistently deny the death of their parents or siblings or the collapse of their home. It is an understandable reaction, something like saying, "This cannot be happening to me." Children who have experienced the death of loved ones often dissociate themselves from this event, preferring to believe that it is happening to someone else. Denial reactions are common to many traumatic events. Benedek (1985) noted that, "Adults and children both use denial as the initial method of coping with major disaster" (p. 168). Both denial and dissociation are primitive attempts by the victim to suppress any meaningful recollection of the initial traumatic event.

We found a difference, however, between the denial defense of children and that of adults. The latter customarily responded to the logic of the quake events, usually after several days, and began gradually to comprehend the situation and make adjustments. In the children we treated, we observed many cases where the denial lasted for many months, much longer than that of adults. Often children refused to accept the fact that their parents were dead or that a sibling had also died. They were very adept at rationalizing their denials, creating complex and interwoven cognitive assertions that supported their beliefs. Some children used primitive fantasies and magical thinking to further support their denial of the facts of their lives. In short, children extended the coping process needed to deal with postdisaster life; they clung to their existence before the disaster and persisted much longer in these irrational beliefs than adults did. Nevertheless, adults sometimes inadvertently enabled the children's adjustment fantasies because they were unable to answer questions about what had happened, particularly in regard to the deaths of loved ones. They avoided discussing the disaster because it was also painful for them to recall those terrible days.

Case Vignette 4: Denying Brothers

Two boys of 5 and 6 years old experienced their mother's death from the quake. After 3 days of this shock, they also witnessed their mother's coffin, surrounded by crying relatives. Despite these clear events, the children persistently denied her death and insisted that she had gone to Moscow on a business trip and that she would return after one year, bringing them presents and loving them for their good behavior. They avoided looking at any photographs of her, and would not touch any of her clothes or belongings. The maternal grandmother supported this denial and elaborate fantasy; she thought that it was best for their overall health. Nevertheless, 8 months after the quake they still suffered from several PTSD symptoms.

Anger

Anger is a frequently experienced emotion after a disaster, whether it is directed at the loss of loved ones, possessions, or a previous life-style (Gleser et al., 1981; Terr, 1990). We observed that among the quake survivors there were often disagreements with and hostility toward close family members. Adults were often angry at rescue organizers, medical care, local authority, the mass media, and so on. They were also angry at God who had failed to protect them from such an awful disaster. However, postquake children did not have as wide a range of hated objects; they tended to channel their anger to a scapegoat from their nearest friendship or neighborhood circle. They vented their anger mostly at teachers and parents who had controlled their prequake lives, and blamed them for not protecting them or preventing the disaster from happening. Many children were angry at their dead parents for leaving them alone. The children tended to be angry at those from whom they received care.

CASE VIGNETTE 5: THE MIRACLE SURVIVOR

This is the case of David, a young boy of 6 years old. He was one of only three children who miraculously came out alive from a kindergarten that had completely collapsed during the quake. As the quake began, his teacher asked him to call for one of the boys who was in the next room; she was confused and this request was illogical. Dutifully David ran to get the boy and saw that a large piece of wall had fallen on his friend. . . . The teacher and most of her pupils were also all killed. Later, David interpreted this request by the teacher as her wanting to kill him by sending him to the dangerous room. Each day David would very angrily repeat how his teacher wanted to kill him. He was extremely angry at her; his anger was typical, however, of many children who had experienced severe, multiple physical and emotional stressors of the disaster.

Guilt

Guilt was also very prevalent. It has been well documented that adult survivors often feel guilt that they survived and others did not (Rosenman, 1956; Lifton and Olson, 1976). They blamed themselves for not doing more to help those who died; they were filled with self-recrimination. With children, however, we did not expect a frequent guilt reaction, and we were surprised to find how widespread it was among children. The adolescents felt guilty that they had overslept on the day of the disaster and had missed seeing a parent who was later killed; some even felt guilt because they had refused some request from the parent the night before the quake or that they were surly, or that they had refused to talk to their parents the evening before the disaster. The younger children more frequently developed guilty feelings because they thought that their bad behavior had caused the quake.

Psychosomatics

Selye, the noted stress researcher, wrote extensively documenting the role of stress in illness. In particular, he pointed out (1956) that stress has a part in the development of every illness. We have sadly confirmed Selye's observations among young survivors of the earthquake. In the postquake period, we noticed that the children had physical symptoms that affected many parts or vital systems of their bodies. Most of the illnesses were gastrointestinal: nausea, vomiting, loss of appetite, stomachaches. They also suffered from various sleep disturbances: insomnia, nightmares, somnambulism, excessive sleepiness (narcolepsy). Headaches and dizziness were common, as well as skin irritation, allergic reactions, enuresis, even hearing and sight problems. In the same way that their minds were trying to deal with understanding and accepting the new realities, their bodies were also working out their changed circumstances. There was a total involvement of mind and body.

Anxiety

A parallel to somatic disturbance was the persistent problem of anxiety. This was often displayed by sudden panic attacks and a variety of fears. Panic attacks occurred most often in the first 2 months after the quake. The numerous aftershocks reinforced and helped maintain these fears. Many children for no apparent reason complained of chest pain, shortness of breath, accelerated heart rate, general discomfort, and intense fear of dying.

PSYCHOPATHOLOGY OF REACTIONS

We have described several reactions that represent common human responses to stressful events. These reactions are traditionally considered as signs of an individual's defense and coping mechanisms. Pavlov (1927) used the term *defensive reaction* for the reflexive responses to environmental stressors. Freud (1920) pointed out that an individual can activate "every possible measure" in response to external trauma, breaking his or her "protective shield" against stimuli. Further researchers have considerably developed our knowledge of defensive and coping mechanisms of those exposed to a wide range of stressful life events. Nevertheless, it must be asked in which circumstances human reactions can be considered as normal or as psychopathology.

CASE VIGNETTE 6: A BOY AND GOD

Levon, a boy of 10 years old, had been in school when the quake struck. He had experienced the destruction of buildings in the town of Kirovakan. After only a few hours of being a survivor of that destruction, his mother took him to check their relatives in the totally destroyed town of Spitak. These closely timed experiences had a profound effect on Levon's psychology. He felt guilty that he "could not do anything for his relatives"; that they had died and he was helpless to assist them. After 2 months this guilt was expanded to include all the Armenians who had suffered and died as a result of the quake, then he included all other victims of historical Armenian tragedies. He developed feelings of shame and self-blame. He became isolated. Seventeen months after the quake his mother brought him into the Center for treatment.

We can see from this case that the initial guilt reaction was prolonged for over 17 months and that it was accompanied by other psychological complications. Levon was not able to resolve the traumatic experience on his own. Having no relief and no satisfaction from his own attempts of coping, he began to display various reinforcements and modifications of the initial reaction, which in turn had a harmful effect on his personality.

Fear

A similar pattern was seen concerning the fear reaction. At first, quake children focused their fears on a new quake, darkness, loud noises, and vibrations. These were strong stimuli that occurred at the time of the catastrophe. However, if these children had little adult help or counseling, they began to fear everything; unrelated objects, people, animals, natural phenomena, places, personal thoughts and fantasies. The range of these fears was incredibly broad. In fact, completely unrelated fears developed, such as fear of being abducted by aliens and UFOs. For some children, these fears developed into specific phobias which further complicated their clinical picture and worsened their anxiety and depression.

There were other long-lasting reactions among the children who experienced the quake trauma. Signs of regression were often seen in children under 10. They were trying to increase their own safety by returning to an earlier stage of development. Some refused to sleep without their parents, or refused to let them out of their sight. This behavior gradually became a way to keep a parent involved with the child; by keeping his mother close to him a child could feel control over his environment, feel safe and protected. But such renewed dependency created additional problems. Highly dependent children were less interested in their usual activities, and some even lost skills they had acquired before the disaster. Such repression was a double-edged sword: on the one hand it appeared to offer relief for profound fears and on the other hand it delayed successful reintegration and resumption of development. This is one reason why long-lasting adverse reactions were especially harmful to the children who had to endure them.

Also, there were long-term abnormal games among the Armenian children traumatized by the quake. Mostly, they played at "earthquake" and "cemetery." According to Terr (1981) long-lasting destructive games can occur as an expression of children's postdisaster reactions to stress. Usually, play allows children a way of dissipating anxiety and helps them "to reexperience gratifying experiences from the past." Terr's well-documented study showed that psychically traumatized children attempt to use play, almost automatically, as a defense mechanism that has worked before. However, under specific posttraumatic circumstances, ones that overwhelm the children's coping capability, play does not alleviate the effects of the stress. If the children's play fails to reduce the stress discomfort, then more anxiety is created as a result of the defense failure. The child is lost in a world of joyless, monotonous, noncreative play that brings no relief, only more discomfort and anxiety. This protective environment of ennui keeps the child for months or even years in a formula of destructive play. Such ineffective postdisaster games can be viewed as part of PTSD in children (DSM-III-R; APA, 1987).

Of course, the nature of the trauma, the age of the young victims, their past experiences, and biological predispositions, personality and social environment all have an important influence on development of children's long-term, abnormal reactions to the disaster trauma. Most importantly, these reactions become indicators of children's coping disabilities and eventually symptoms of developing PTSD.

Armenian Children and PTSD Symptoms

Common Symptoms

Common symptoms which may indicate PTSD are as follows (DSM-III-R; APA, 1987):

- the trauma event is persistently reexperienced in many different ways;
- persistent avoidance of anything associated with the trauma;
- persistent psychosomatic symptoms which were not present before the event [p. 429].

Of course, such symptoms may appear in children and adolescents due to other unrelated disorders. This is why it is important when evaluating these young patients to carefully compare the appearance of the observed PTSD symptoms with the date of the traumatic event. Doing this is also important because the child may initially cope very well with the traumatic event, and not display any discomfort or symptoms until several months later. For this reason, we only used data from those children who personally experienced the 1988 quake, and restricted our sample to those who had begun to display emotional, behavioral, and psychosomatic symptoms afterwards.

Subjects

Subjects included 839 (N) children and adolescents from the cities of Kirovakan, Spitak, their suburbs, and adjacent villages. They were admitted to the Children's Psychotherapy Center in Kirovakan because they manifested unresolved posttraumatic stress. Usually, parents or guardians made the initial contact with the Center to ask for professional help. Their admission dates were between September 1989 and February 1990, or approximately one year after the quake date of December 7, 1988. The age and sex distributions are summarized in Table 5.1.

TABLE 5.1
Age and Sex Distribution among the Postquake Children Interviewed at The Children's Psychotherapy Center between September 1989 and February 1990

Age	Number of Children	%
3	26	3.1
4	68	8.1
5	75	8.9
6	91	10.9
7	83	9.9
8	74	8.8
9	58	6.9
10	71	8.5
11	65	7.7
12	75	8.9
13	51	6.1
14	52	6.2
15	24	2.9
16	16	1.9
17	10	1.2
Boys	461	55.0
Girls	378	45.0
Total (N)	839	100.0

RESEARCH INTERVIEWS

The research interviews were conducted at the Center by trained personnel. These informal sessions lasted from 1 to 2 hours and usually involved the child and their parent, or guardian if the child was orphaned. Due to the extreme trauma involved, we maintained a relaxed and nonthreatening atmosphere; sometimes, we had to compromise research protocol in order to realistically meet these children's great needs for security. These trade-offs were minimal but in some cases very real. We proceeded in a discussion manner, creating an atmosphere of familial talking and exchange of experience, rather than following a rigid line of questioning.

The subjects discussed in these interviews followed a general format which included: some general background information about the child and his or her family; detailed circumstances of the child's disaster experience. We inquired about the child's initial responses to the disaster, any behavior changes since the disaster, and any other information that the parent or child thought relevant to our inquiry. Often, these bits of information appeared inconsequential, but only later became significant the more we got to know the child. In some vague cases, we asked for additional interviews or for appointments with a psychiatrist, neuropathologist, or pediatrician to clarify some confusing information.

In addition to the interviews, personnel also used a structured questionnaire with 30 items indicating PTSD symptoms among the children. This special questionnaire has been created in order to take into account the common PTSD symptoms from the DSM-III-R as well as those most common among the Armenian post-quake children and adolescents.

Frequency of symptoms, which may indicate PTSD among children and adolescents, were recorded, and numbers of symptoms per child were estimated (Tables 5.2 to 5.4). Percentage distributions of the children and adolescents by age and sex also were obtained (Table 5.1).

RESULTS

The results of the interviews and material collected via the questionnaire revealed many different forms of reenactment by the children; each child had their own dynamic and form of reexperiencing the traumatic event.

The most frequent reenactment form was the nightmare or dream; for example, children often relived the collapse of their school and the panic of the attempted escapes. The faces of dead relatives and friends were also a common ideation.

Children also recalled the quake through their drawings, mostly of dark and gloomy scenes. Those who elected to draw their trauma seemed to prefer to pick a single traumatic event or object that encapsulated their general dread, panic, and fear. Falling stones, swinging chandeliers, corpses, tilting buildings, and other realistic objects of the disaster were frequently seen in these drawings (Azarian and Skriptchenko, 1992b).

One commonly observed phenomenon was the repetitive nature of the children's questions about the quake. They usually talked and talked about it, in a prattle of continuous anxious speech. Their questions were frequent and were for the most part unsatisfied by the answers their parents or other adults gave them. It was as if the questions were only an excuse to receive constant reassurance, not to get information.

There were also children who were taciturn and quiet; they were reluctant to discuss the quake or their experiences. However, they might play out themes about the disaster repeatedly, building up toy houses, destroying them, and then reconstructing and destroying them again and again. There were no played out rescue or saving events—or the traditional happy endings. No one was saved, only lost.

Our subjects also showed extreme avoidance behavior regarding anything connected with the quake: certain places, smells, sounds, memories, feelings, thoughts, even people who reminded them of the original traumatic events, were energetically avoided. They were also hyperalert and anxious about a new quake, or any danger. Some were extremely fearful to the point of panic.

Table 5.2 contains a summary of most of these fears. There were fears which were logically related to the earthquake: natural phenomena, loud noises, darkness, vibrations; fears related to the disaster location, like buildings, places, or even a new quake in the same location. Also we found the children had many fears relating to any thoughts or feelings that could be associated with the earthquake experience—ruminations about death and feelings of loneliness. We noticed there were fears about anything that could be construed as dangerous: animals, objects, or even strangers. Although the fears seemed to follow a comprehensible connection with the attributes of the original disaster, there was such variety in the range of the feared objects, that the fears can best be described as idiosyncratic.

TABLE 5.2
Distribution of Fears among the Postquake Children Interviewed at The Children's Psychotherapy Center between September 1989 and February 1990 (N = 839)

Fears of	Number of Children with the Fear	%
Vibrations	754	89.9
New Quake	681	81.1
Darkness	618	73.6
Loneliness	554	66.0
Death	551	65.7
Loud Noises	493	58.7
Buildings	415	49.5
Natural Phenomena	387	46.1
Strangers	194	23.1
Animals	190	22.6
Total (F)	4837	

Fears per Child = F/N = 4837/839 = 5.8
NOTE: N = Total number of children in the sample;
F = Total number of fears displayed by the sample children.

The emotional and behavior disturbances are shown in Table 5.3. In their wish to avoid traumatic places, the children, first of all, refused to attend their schools or kindergartens (26.5% of children), where most of them had experienced the initial quake. School is where young lives are socially organized, and such a reluctance further hampered children's recovery from the disaster trauma. Children also often refused any activities or contacts that could remind them of traumatic events. As a result many of them exhibited regression and self-isolation (20.6 and 27.2% respectively). The traumatized children had fewer personal goals and low levels of self-esteem. They expected bad events in their future, and even viewed the world as full of bad omens about their future lives. They had a belief in a foreshortened life, which is one of the salient characteristics of PTSD. There were children who had a pervasive sadness (41.6%), pessimism (31.8%), and those who had feelings of guilt (31.0%), and helplessness

TABLE 5.3
Distribution of Emotional and Behavioral Disturbances among the Postquake Children Interviewed at The Children's Psychotherapy Center between September 1989 and February 1990 (N = 839)

Disturbances	Number of Children with the Disturbance	%
Anxiety	653	77.8
Aggressiveness	380	45.3
Sadness	349	41.6
Pessimism	267	31.8
Sense of Guilt	260	31.0
Self-Isolation	228	27.2
Helplessness	228	27.2
School avoidance	222	26.5
Regression	173	20.6
Suicidal thoughts	130	15.5
Total (EB)	2890	

Emotional and Behavioral Disturbances per Child = EB/N = 2890/839 = 3.4
NOTE. N = Total number of children in the sample;
    EB = Total number of emotional and behavioral disturbances displayed by the sample children.

(27.2%). Surprisingly, there were only 15.5 percent who had recurrent suicidal thoughts. Considering some of the disastrous events the children had endured, we expected a higher percentage of them to harbor self-destructive ideation. In the light of Husain's research on normal U.S. high school students, where 25 percent "have thought about suicide to the point of having an actual plan in mind" (1990, p. 122), these quake subjects were astonishingly low in the incidence of reported suicidal thoughts.

We found that the postquake disturbances were mostly related to anxiety (77.8%), which was the symptom most frequently reported. This is, of course, understandable considering the type of disaster. The children were stressed to cope with overwhelming and sudden trauma. Trying to adjust to these new circumstances was so difficult that many of the children seemed angry and aggressive (45.3%). They were reacting not only to the new dangers and the further traumas, but also to demands that they accept these realities. They obviously protested and became aggressive.

Recent studies of the psychosomatic impact of trauma suggest that neurochemistry is involved in the symptoms of PTSD (Miller, 1988; Miller and Başoğlu, 1992). These models describe post-trauma psychosomatic involvement as due to "body chemistry." There were considerable numbers of the children in the sample with various physical problems that were not present before the quake. These symptoms persisted for a few months after the disaster and we considered them to be signs of true psychosomatic illnesses due to their initial onset and persistence.

Table 5.4 summarizes these disturbances, and one can see that nightmares were very common (57.1%). This level may be explained by the universal reexperiencing by the person of traumatic memories via the dreaming processes. The children's psychosomatic illnesses were also related to their increased sensory arousal and hypervigilance. They had difficulty getting to sleep and staying asleep. They would wake several times during the night. Many of them (31.1%) showed signs of insomnia.

TABLE 5.4
Distribution of Psychosomatic Disturbances among the Postquake Children Interviewed at The Children's Psychotherapy Center between September 1989 and February 1990 (N = 839)

Disturbances	Number of Children with the Disturbance	%
Loss of energy	569	67.8
Nightmares	479	57.1
Loss of appetite	439	52.3
Headaches	393	46.8
Concentration	344	41.0
Enuresis	300	35.7
Nausea	267	31.8
Insomnia	261	31.1
Stomachaches	159	18.9
Speech	143	17.0
Total (P)	3354	

Psychosomatic Disturbances per Child = P/N = 3354/839 = 4.0
NOTE: N = Total number of children in the sample;
    P = Total number of psychosomatic disturbances displayed by the sample children.

A markedly reduced ability to concentrate was another commonly observed behavior. We found that 41.0 percent of the children could not concentrate on a task; they were irritable and reacted with anger at any changes in their environment or routine. They developed headaches, nausea, stomachaches, and even speech disturbances in response to any uncomfortable sensory conditions.

Loss of energy in many children (67.8%) should be interpreted according to one of Freud's penetrating remarks: "An external trauma is bound to provoke a disturbance on a large scale in the functioning of the organism's energy . . . " (Freud, 1920, p. 35). So, straining every internal defensive mechanism to manage the postdisaster period markedly stresses the child's organism. Profound trauma can also produce neurochemical changes in regulation of normal feeding behavior (Miller, 1988). Thus, among postquake children about half (52.3%) had a loss of appetite. These children were obviously straining every internal defense mechanism to cope with the trauma they had experienced to the degree that they became ill and suffered persistent physical discomfort.

Discussion and Conclusion

Were the disturbances observed in the children of the Armenian earthquake symptoms of PTSD? It should be noted that research into psychological and psychiatric aspects of disaster "generally is really bedevilled by studies of N < 100, using a wide range of different intake and outcome criteria, measures of basic phenomena, and timing of the assessment schedules" (Raphael, Lundin, and Weisaeth, 1989, p. 2). Our sample of 839 children and adolescents was sufficiently representative. Also, we did not first diagnose the children and then select our sample from that pool; our approach to sample choice was simple and natural. We interviewed the children who lived in the disaster zone and who experienced multiple impacts from the quake stressors. Our subjects were not invited to the Center, but were brought there by their families because they were symptomatic. In addition, the admissions were, on the average, one year after the disaster. This long delay in itself helps rule out and control for reactions that might have been considered within the normal range of postdisaster behavior. In other words, we were able to refine our sample due to the natural sequence of events concomitant with the trauma. The children we saw had a long history of difficulty, severe enough to be considered proper for clinical intervention and treatment.

Second, some PTSD symptoms seem to have close similarity to the symptoms of Conduct, Adjustment, and Attention Deficit Hyperactive Disorders. Children with these disorders are most frequently diagnosed incorrectly (Doyle and Bauer, 1989). However, if we carefully note the DSM-III-R criteria (APA, 1987) for these disorders, we can differentiate PTSD from those mentioned. For example, in cases of Adjustment Disorder the stressor is usually in the range of common human experience. That is why its impact is less severe than multiple disaster stressors causing PTSD. Also, Adjustment Disorder typically begins within 3 months of the onset of a stressor and lasts no longer than 6 months. Moreover, the critical PTSD symptom of reexperiencing the trauma is absent. The other important symptom of PTSD, the sense of guilt, is absent in cases of Conduct Disorder. These symptoms had a high frequency rate among the postquake children (Tables 5.2, 5.3). These differences between PTSD, Conduct, and Adjustment Disorders are further highlighted due to the one-year interval between the quake trauma and observation of the children's symptoms. These facts help us feel confident about our PTSD diagnosis.

Third, it has been pointed out (Burke, Borus, Burns, Millstein, and Beasley, 1982) that there is continued controversy about the severity of psychological impact on children of disasters. Some investigators even deny that any serious symptoms occur. According to a recent overview (Green, Korol, Grace, Vary, Leonard, Gleser, and Smithson-Cohen, 1991), children do experience at least some PTSD symptoms, and this is true over a wide age range and with a variety of disaster stressors. It must be concluded that children have variable abilities to adjust to trauma: some children cope better than others. These coping skills are related to their cognitive, psychosocial, and physical developmental status. Garmezy (1983) suggested that early childhood genetic history, strength of familial bonds, existence of support figures in the school and environment, even biological predisposition, interact to determine the success of stress-resilient children. In fact, sometimes children can show a remarkable resilience. For example, a girl of 7 lost her entire family in the quake but for her 76-year-old grandmother. We tried for several hours to talk to this child, who persisted in being mute. Finally, though, the girl turned to us and said, "Don't talk to me. The only reason I'm living is for the sake of my grandma."

Nevertheless, from our own experience of direct interviewing of the children and from the literature (Sugar, 1992a), it seems that when there is an individual evaluation the percentage of children with different PTSD symptoms following a serious disaster may come close to 100 percent. If the assessment of the children's symptoms is based only on a parent or teacher questionnaire the percentage of children classified as symptomatic drops dramatically (Blom, 1986). This smaller percentage depends on the adult's tendency to minimize the children's problems, to underestimate the level of suffering they are experiencing. Such underreporting of symptoms may be due to the fact that the adults are preoccupied with their own problems or to the often observed fact that adults are less sensitive to the emotional health of children than one might expect. Some investigators have noted that after natural disasters many adults deny that their children have psychological or psychosomatic disturbances (Crawshaw, 1963; Moore, 1958). Our technique of interviewing the children themselves, and allowing them to describe their problems, helped reduce this tendency to underestimate the amount of PTSD symptoms in the children traumatized by the quake.

Figure 5.3 graphically illustrates the distribution of the children admitted to the Center by age. It reinforces our observations regarding the general psychological impact of the disaster on them as well as different age groups' vulnerability:

- The quake disaster affected a broad age range of children and adolescents, from 3 to 17 (who were 2–16 at the time of the quake).
- The great part (78.6%) were children and adolescents from 3 to 11 at the time of the disaster—their percentages are more than the average.
- Children under the age of about 2.5 years and adolescents above the age of 12 or so during the quake appeared to be more resilient to the impact of the disaster and their percentages are below the average. It may be because the very young children had few speech skills, or physical and behavior ability to tell their parents about any symptoms they were experiencing. It may be that their young age precluded them from adequate self-awareness, so that they were unable to describe themselves as suffering. They were not yet reflective. The older adolescents perhaps had enough coping skills to protect themselves from trauma and may have been independent enough not to complain to parents or teachers about their feelings.
- However, we observed 26 children under 2.5 years of age at the time of the quake who displayed symptoms of postdisaster stress. This correlates with the observations of Sugar (1992b) and Terr (1988) who presented several cases of toddlers being able to recall trauma and even crudely verbalize traumatic memories.
- Being about 5 years old at the time of quake impact was the age of most serious vulnerability. This is the age when the child realizes the adverse consequences of the tragedy, but does not yet possess adequate coping skills to deal with that awareness.

There are conflicting reports about sex differences among disaster survivors. In general, boys seem to be more affected than girls. Rutter (1983) has labeled them as being "more vulnerable." We found a difference between boys and girls as well: Table 5.1 listed 55.0 percent (461) of our sample as boys, and 45.0 percent (378) girls, a difference of 10.0 percent. This difference might indicate more severe and more frequent abnormal reactions among boys, which in turn might have made parents more alert to boys' problems and more likely to refer them to the Center for assessment and treatment.

If we consider our data (Tables 5.2 to 5.4) from the average number of disturbances, we can separate these symptoms into three groups: fear was the most frequent, averaging 5.8 per child; next psychosomatic and sleep disturbances were 4.0 per child; third, emotional and behavioral disturbances averaged 3.4 per subject. In general, we found 13.2 disturbances per child, which underlines the level of severity that such a natural disaster can have upon children.

The high level of fears among the children represents the phobic behavior among these survivors. Being exposed for such a long time to the stimuli associated with the traumatic event, these children developed phobias that Arieti (1979) described as, "a stage of generalized and intangible fear." These children perceived danger where there was none and reacted emotionally to situations where there was no observable danger. This increased their general anxiety and aggravated their symptoms of postdisaster stress. Although some potential limitations of this study can be addressed, we have presented a natural picture of long-term disturbances, indicating PTSD in postquake children.

There was a fortunate possibility in our study to observe a large sample of the children and adolescents (N = 839) representing the natural flow of the young quake survivors to the mental health professionals.

A COMPLEX APPROACH TO THE TREATMENT OF POST-DISASTER CHILDREN

It is axiomatic that behavior is a complex of interrelated factors; no one doubts, for example, that children are polymorphous, not only in terms of their own dynamics but also in terms of the array of responses their behavior prompts in others. The treatment of children traumatized by a disaster is also polyphasic: there is the long-term effect of the disaster itself to consider; the children's personal reactions due to parental influence; and the degree of severity of their symptoms, not to mention the variety of these manifestations. Our treatment of such victims had to reflect this multiplicity of causation, of form, and duration. The following case describes such a symptomatic diversity.

CASE VIGNETTE 7: THE GIRL WITH MULTIPLE DISTURBANCES

Anna was a normal girl of 10, typical, that is, of the victims we encountered daily. She was terrified of any vibrations and lived in constant fear of a new earthquake and felt herself to be in personal danger. She was afraid of buildings, loud noises, darkness, animals, strangers, and even rain. All of nature was her enemy. She was depressed, self-isolated, and almost entirely mute. She had diminished appetite, severe and frequent headaches. In addition to these postquake sufferings, she was enuretic and had nightmares. She was unable to study so her school performance naturally declined; this slowing of academic achievement made matters worse because her parents had unrealistically high expectations of Anna. In fact, there were often arguments and loss of control over their frustrations regarding her declining school behavior.

We had to ask ourselves the obvious clinical questions: In what order should these disturbances be treated? How could we have a trusting talk with Anna to help her improve her behavior if she refused to talk or even play with us or the other children at the Center? We were also chagrined at the prospect of not being able to change her parents' attitude toward her. It was from these common multiple causes that we developed our complex mode of treatment. We naturally and logically concluded that multi-problem children need multifaceted interventions (Azarian, 1990).

Traditional psychotherapy is not the treatment of choice for disaster traumatized children. Joyner (1991) who worked with the children of Hurricane Hugo, September 1989, correctly pointed out: "Working with children following a natural disaster requires a multifaceted approach" (p. 400). This observation is echoed by Terr (1990) who studied kidnapped children from Chowchilla, California, 1976: "major personality shifts that come about as a result of childhood trauma require intensive treatment . . . " (p. 286–287); and "Much good treatment represents a combined program" (p. 307). We also discovered that the complexity of the trauma set demands a parallel complexity of interventions.

Our treatment plans were complex, eclectic, and most importantly, flexible. This is the watchword when any intervention is planned: the more adaptable the therapy the more likely it will meet the dynamic needs of the child. We selected different theoretical and practical methods: cognitive–behavioral therapy, client-centered approach, and rational–emotional therapy, and we reformulated these into an appropriate treatment strategy for our patients.

For example, to deal with fear, the most frequent problem, the treatment team used special physical games, the synthesis of relaxation and aromatherapy, drawing, and even animated cartoons to bring about systematic behavioral desensitization such as fading or immersion simultaneously through the children's sensory modalities (smell, touch, sight, hearing).

Many of the postquake children suffered from great shame, guilt, and low self-esteem. They were often unable to experience satisfaction or pleasure. Our Center team worked to convince these depressed children that they were valuable, worthwhile individuals, loved and entitled to live full lives of meaning, with a certain future. Such high demands required equally high treatment standards: our team used makeup activities, video portraits, talking and story-telling, expressive dance and drama therapies, even aspects of occupational therapy, to encourage these children to express their repressed feelings, thoughts, and spiritual selves.

We also organized special self-help groups as well as counseling sessions for parents and teachers. We found that if the parents, caretakers, and teachers were helped to reduce their own stress levels, the children were less likely to suffer the effects of secondary stress.

It must be continually kept in mind that because the whole area was a disaster, the usual amenities were often absent, or inadequate. Our Center was like an island in a sea of disorder and neglect: confusion and government contradictions were the order of the day. The center was the only psychological resource and was consequently overburdened with cases. For this reason, we chose group therapy as the primary mode of treatment, although not always the preferred mode. We were forced to make do in very difficult circumstances. Groups of 8 to 10 children of the same age came to therapy twice a week, for approximately one hour. Treatment length varied somewhat, but was generally from 4 to 6 months in duration.

Evaluating the efficiency of such a complex therapy is a subjective process, even though we attempted to regulate our judgment by using the reports of independent commissions, objective, repeated testing, and feedback from patients and parents about the results of therapy (Azarian and Skriptchenko, 1990). We found overall, that the Center helped 74.4 percent of cases; that is, this percentage showed marked improvement in the presenting symptom picture. Those children who did not improve were given more intense individual therapy.

REFERENCES

Alexander, D. (1985), Death and injury in earthquakes. *Disasters*, 9:57–60.
American Psychiatric Association (1952), *Diagnostic and Statistical Manual of Mental Disorders* (DSM-I). Washington, DC: American Psychiatric Association.
———(1980), *Diagnostic and Statistical Manual of Mental Disorders* (DSM-III), 3rd ed. Washington, DC: American Psychiatric Press.
———(1987), *Diagnostic and Statistical Manual of Mental Disorders* (DSM-III-R), 3rd ed. rev. Washington, DC: American Psychiatric Press.

Anthony, E. J. (1988), The response to overwhelming stress in children: Some introductory comments. In: *The Child in His Family*, Vol. 8, ed. E. J. Anthony & C. Chiland. New York: Wiley, pp. 3–16.

Arieti, S. (1979), New views on the psychodynamics of phobias. *Amer. J. Psychotherapy*, 33:82–95.

Armstrong, K., O'Callahan, W., & Marmar, C. R. (1991), Debriefing Red Cross disaster personnel: The multiple stressor debriefing model. *J. Traum. Stress*, 4:581–592.

Azarian, A. G. (1989), *The Regulatory Influence of Past Experience on the Individual's Creative Thinking*. Doctoral dissertation. Lomonosov State University, Moscow, USSR.

―――― (1990), A complex approach to the methods of psychological treatment of children and adolescents. In: *Psychological Treatment of Children and Adolescents*, ed. A. G. Azarian. Yerevan, Armenia: Research Institute of Pedagogics, pp. 42–68.

―――― Skriptchenko, V. G. (1990), A report about the evaluation of the psychological treatment effectiveness. In: *Psychological Treatment of Children and Adolescents*, ed. A. G. Azarian. Yerevan, Armenia: Research Institute of Pedagogics, pp. 139–142.

―――― ―――― (1992a), Natural disasters result in multifaceted PTSD that demand a complex approach to treatment. *Child & Adol. Behav. Letter*, Spec. Suppl., 8(11):7–12.

―――― ―――― (1992b), *Survivors of Disaster: Armenian Children Draw the Earthquake*. Providence, RI: Brown University.

Baum, A. (1987), Toxins, technology, and natural disasters. In: *Cataclysms, Crises, and Catastrophes: Psychology in Action*, ed. G. R. VandenBos & B. K. Bryant. Washington, DC: American Psychological Association, pp. 5–54.

Beigel, A., & Berren, M. R. (1985), Human-induced disasters. *Psychiatric Annals*, 15:143–150.

Benedek, E. P. (1985), Children and disaster: Emerging issues. *Psychiatric Annals*, 15:168–172.

Blom, G. E. (1986), A school disaster—Intervention and research aspects. *J. Amer. Acad. Child Psychiatry*, 25:336–345.

Burke, J. D., Borus, J. F., Burns, B. J., Millstein, K. H., & Beasley, M. C. (1982), Changes in children's behavior after a natural disaster. *Amer. J. Psychiatry*, 139:1010–1014.

Chemtob, C., Roitblat, H., Hamada, R., Carlson, J., & Twentyman, C. (1988), A cognitive action theory of posttraumatic stress disorder. *J. Anxiety Disorders*, 2:253–275.

Clark, M. J. (1992), Care of clients in disaster settings. In: *Nursing in the Community*, ed. M. J. Clark. Norwalk, CT: Appleton & Lance, pp. 696–725.

Crawshaw, R. (1963), Reaction to a disaster. *Arch. Gen. Psychiatry*, 9:157–162.

de Ville de Goyet, C. (1980), The health impact of earthquakes. *Biomed. Res. Latin Amer.*, NIH 80-2051:215–233.

Doyle, J. S., & Bauer, S. K. (1989), Post-traumatic stress disorder in children: Its identification and treatment in a residential setting for emotionally disturbed youth. *J. Traum. Stress*, 2:275–288.

Ebert, C. H. V. (1988), *Disasters: Violence of Nature and Threats by Man.* Dubuque, Iowa: Kendall/Hunt.

Erikson, K. T. (1976), *Everything in Its Path: Destruction of Community in the Buffalo Creek Flood.* New York: Simon & Schuster.

Figley, C. (1978), *Stress Disorders among Vietnam Veterans: Theory, Research and Treatment Implications.* New York: Brunner/Mazel.

Frederick, C. J. (1987), Psychic trauma in victims of crime, and terrorism. In: *Cataclysms, Crises, and Catastrophes: Psychology in Action,* ed. G.R. VandenBos, & B. K. Bryant. Washington, DC: American Psychological Association, pp. 85–108.

Freud, S. (1920), Beyond the Pleasure Principle. *Standard Edition,* 18:1–64. London: Hogarth Press, 1955.

Garbarino, J., & Kostelny, K. (1993), Children's response to war: What do we know. In: *Psychological Effects of War and Violence on Children,* ed. L. A. Leavitt & A. Fox. Hillsdale, NJ: Lawrence Erlbaum, pp. 23–39.

Gardner, H. (1982), *Art, Mind, and Brain.* New York: Basic Books.

Garmezy, N. (1983), Stressors of childhood. In: *Stress, Coping, and Development in Children,* ed. N. Garmezy & M. Rutter. New York: McGraw-Hill, pp. 43–84.

Gleser, G. C., Green, B. L., & Winget, C. (1981), *Prolonged Psychosocial Effects of Disaster: A Study of Buffalo Creek.* New York: Academic Press.

Green, B. L., Korol, M., Grace, M. C., Vary, M. G., Leonard, A. C., Gleser, G. C., & Smithson-Cohen, S. (1991), Children and disaster: Age, gender, and parental effects on PTSD symptoms. *J. Amer. Acad. Child & Adol. Psychiatry,* 30:945–951.

Grigorova, L. F., Gasparian, A. A., & Manukian, L. H. (1990), *Armenia, December, 1988.* Yerevan, Armenia: Haiastan.

Gueri, M., & Alzate, H. (1984), The Popayan earthquake: A preliminary report on its effects on health. *Disasters,* 8:18–20.

Hocking, F. (1970), Psychiatric aspects of extreme environmental stress. *Dis. Nerv. System,* 31:542–545.

Horowitz, M. J. (1976), *Stress Response Syndromes.* New York: Jason Aronson.

Husain, S. A. (1990), Current perspective on the role of psychosocial factors on adolescent suicide. *Psychiatric Annals,* 20:122–127.

Johnston, D. R. (1988), The role of the creative arts therapies in the diagnosis and treatment of psychological trauma. *The Arts in Psychother.,* 14:7–13.

Joyner, C. D. (1991), Individual, group, and family crisis counseling following a hurricane: Case of Heather, age 9. In: *Play Therapy with Children in Crisis: A Casebook for Practitioners,* ed. N. B. Webb. New York: Guilford Press, pp. 396–415.

Keppel-Benson, J. M., & Ollendick, T. H. (1993), Posttraumatic stress disorder in children and adolescents. In: *Children and Disasters,* ed. C. F. Saylor. New York: Plenum Press, pp. 29–43.

Krystal, H. (1968), *Massive Psychic Trauma.* New York: International Universities Press.

Lifton, R. J., & Olson, E. (1976), The human meaning of total disaster: The Buffalo Creek experience. *Psychiatry,* 39:1–18.

Miller, T. W. (1988), Advances in understanding the impact of stressful life events on health. *Hosp. & Commun. Psychiatry,* 39:615–622.

——— Ed. (1989), *Stressful Life Events*. Madison, CT: International Universities Press.

——— Başoğlu, M. (1992), Posttraumatic stress disorder: The impact of life stress events on adjustment. *Integr. Psychiatry*, 7 (3–4):207–215.

Moore, H. E (1958), Some emotional concomitants of disaster. *Ment. Hygiene*, 42:45–50.

Noji, E. K. (1989), The 1988 earthquake in Soviet Armenia: Implications for earthquake preparedness. *Disasters*, 13:255–262.

Pavlov, I. P. (1927), *Conditional Reflexes: An Investigation of the Physiological Activity of the Cerebral Cortex*, ed. G. V. Anrep. New York: Dover, 1960.

Pomonis, A. (1990), The Spitak (Armenia, USSR) earthquake: Residential building typology and seismic behavior. *Disasters*, 14:89–114.

Quarantelli, E. L., & Dynes, R. R. (1977), Response to social crisis and disaster. *Ann. Rev. Sociol.*, 3:23–49.

Raphael, B. (1986), *When Disaster Strikes. How Individuals and Communities Cope with Catastrophe*. New York: Basic Books.

———Lundin, T., & Weisaeth, L. (1989), A research method for the study of psychological and psychiatric aspects of disaster. *Acta Psychiatr. Scand.*, 80 (Suppl.):1–75.

Rosenman, S. (1956), The paradox of guilt in disaster victim populations. *Psychiatr. Quart.* 30 Suppl. (part 2):181–221.

Rubin, C. B., Yezer, A. M., Hussain, Q., & Webb, A. (1986), Summary of major natural disaster incidents in the US, 1965 85. Washington, DC: George Washington University.

Rutter, M. (1983), Stress, coping, and development: Some issues and some questions. In: *Stress, Coping, and Development in Children*, ed. N. Garmezy & M. Rutter. New York: McGraw-Hill, pp. 1–42.

Sarkisian, Z. (1984), Coping with a massive stressful life event: The impact of the Armenian genocide of 1915 on the present day health and morale of a group of women survivors. *Armenian Rev.*, 37:33–44.

Selye, H. (1956), *The Stress of Life*. New York: McGraw-Hill.

Sudjian, L. (1990), *A Report of the Kumairy Health Department: Impact of the 1988 Earthquake of the Kumairy (Leninakan) Population*. Providence, RI: Brown University.

Sugar, M. (1988), Children and multiple trauma in a disaster. In: *The Child in His Family*, ed. E. J. Anthony & C. Chiland. New York: Wiley, pp. 429–442.

——— (1989), Children in a disaster: An overview. *Child Psychiatry & Hum. Develop.*, 19:163–169.

——— (1992a), Disasters. In: *Developmental-Behavioral Pediatrics*, ed. M. D. Levine, W. B. Carey, & A. C. Crocker. Philadelphia: Saunders, pp. 178–181.

——— (1992b), Toddlers' traumatic memories. *Infant Ment. Health J.*, 13:245–251.

Symonds, M. (1980), The "second injury" to victims. *Eval. & Change* (Special issue) 23(4):36–38.

Terr, L. (1981), Forbidden games. *J. Amer. Acad. Child Psychiatry*, 20:741–760.

——— (1988), What happens to early memories of trauma? A study of twenty children under age five at the time of documented traumatic events. *J. Amer. Acad. Child Adol. Psychiatry*, 27:96–104.

——— (1990), *Too Scared to Cry. Psychic Trauma in Childhood.* New York: Basic Books.

van der Kolk, B. A. (1987), The psychological consequences of overwhelming life experiences. In: *Psychological Trauma,* ed. B. A. van der Kolk. Washington, DC: American Psychiatric Press, pp. 1–30.

Yacoubian, V. V., & Hacker, F. J. (1989), Reactions to disaster at a distance. *Bull. Menninger Clin.,* 53:331–339.

Chapter 6
War-Related Posttraumatic Stress Disorder among Children and Adolescents

Philip A. Saigh, Ph.D., John A. Fairbank, Ph.D., and
Anastasia E. Yasik, B.A.

History

As in most areas of psychopathology, the majority of the published literature regarding the effects of extreme stress has dealt with the symptomatology of adults (Saigh, 1992a). Medical reports during the First World War (e.g., Bury, 1918; Fraser and Wilson, 1918) comprehensively chronicled the neurological and psychological effects of war-related stressors. By way of example, Southard (1919) described the symptomatology of a French corporal who was buried alive after a shell hit his bunker. Although the man escaped without physical injury "his pulse was variable; at rest it stood at 60; if a table nearby was struck suddenly, it would go up to 120" (p. 309).

With the advent of the Second World War, mental health practitioners evaluated and treated thousands of psychiatric casualties. Although the majority of the published literature from this period also involved adults exposed to extreme events (Lewis,

119

1942; Raines and Kolb, 1943; Grinker and Spiegel, 1945), significant contributions were made by a number of child clinical investigators. Bodman (1941), for example, described the symptomatology of a sample of British schoolchildren (age range 5–14 years) who developed emotional problems after they were exposed to repeated air raids. These symptoms included nightmares, war-related fears, psychophysiological reactivity on exposure to war-related stimuli, avoidance, and aggressive behaviors. In a similar vein, Mercer and Despert (1943) documented the trauma-related recollections and nightmares as well as the avoidance behaviors, psychophysiological reactivity, concentration impairment, and academic difficulties of French children who were exposed to puissant war-related stressors. Likewise, Bradner (1943) chronicled the forced evacuation of Finnish civilians during the Russio-Finnish War. Finnish families were compelled to leave their homes, herded into unheated railroad carriages, transported to unspecified areas under cover of darkness, and strafed by Soviet bombers. It is of considerable relevance to note that Bradner made distinct reference to the children's posttraumatic fears, blunted affect, nightmares, avoidance, and psychophysiological reactivity to war-related stimuli. He also reported that "even a year after the war, the sight of ruins had a profoundly depressing effect upon the children . . . war films, saddening war pictures in illustrated magazines, reports of war of any kind, still caused such symptoms of wartime to return at any given moment" (p. 319).

Whereas these reports reflect a selected review of the literature, it is apparent that the psychiatric morbidity that was described herein is suggestive of the presenting symptoms and associated features of posttraumatic stress disorder (PTSD; American Psychiatric Association, 1980, 1987). It is also apparent that the symptoms that were chronicled among children who were exposed to war-related stressors closely resemble the symptoms that were observed among children and adolescents who experienced extreme stress through criminal victimization (Rowan and Foy, 1993) or natural disasters (Green, Grace, Vary, Kramer, Gleser, and Leonard, 1994).

Validity

A system of classification offers a number of advantages for research and practice (Morey, Skinner, and Blashfield, 1986; Saigh, 1992a,b). Initially, it may serve as a basis for accurate communication. Without this, clinicians and investigators would use different terms to describe the same condition and the same terms to represent different phenomena. In a similar vein, a nosology may serve to enhance theory formation and facilitate clinical practice as well-founded diagnoses should lead to the provision of a treatment of choice for a given condition. Examined within this context, Quay (1986) said that a psychiatric classification should be "empirically validated by determining its relation to other variables. Of particular concern is differential validity; two putatively separate disorders ought not to be related in the same way to the same variable" (p. 37). Likewise, Van Pragg (1990) indicated that "there is nothing wrong with basing the first draft of an operational taxonomy on expert opinion. However, once having postulated a taxonomy, experts should be honorably discharged and replaced by researchers to study the merits of the system" (p. 149).

It is of interest to recall that the DSM-III PTSD classification was intuitively established (Saigh, 1992a) and that systematic field trials were not effected until DSM-IV took up the task in 1988 (c.f., Kilpatrick, Resnick, and Freedy, 1993; Saigh, Green, and Korol, 1996). Despite an abundance of information about the psychological sequelae of trauma, the notion that people may develop significant and chronic impairments as a function of exposure to extreme events has not always been readily accepted. It is recalled that General George Patton issued a memorandum on August 5, 1944, wherein soldiers who were diagnosed as "nervously incapable of combat" were to be classified as "cowards." Four days after issuing the memorandum, General Patton slapped the face of a hospitalized enlisted man who was diagnosed by medical personnel as having that condition (c.f., Dreyer and Glass, 1973, p. 26). More recently, Goodwin and Guze (1984) represented that there was an "almost total lack of evidence that posttraumatic stress disorder, delayed type, exists as a clinical entity" (p. 82).

Given the overriding need to empirically validate the classification, it is relevant to observe that a number of comparative studies have examined the differential validity of the PTSD classification as indicated by psychometric self-report (Fairbank, Keane, and Malloy, 1983), psychophysiological (Blanchard, Kolb, Pallmeyer, and Gerardi, 1982; Blanchard, Kolb, Gerardi, Ryan, and Pallmeyer, 1986; Zimering, Caddell, Fairbank, and Keane, 1993); and biological (Blanchard, Kolb, Prins, Gates, and McCoy, 1991) ratings. Whereas these studies represent a selected review of an expanding literature base, it may be fair to say that a considerable amount of experimental data supports the validity of the PTSD classification. It may also be observed that the aforementioned studies involved adult subjects and that appreciably fewer studies have been pursued with traumatized children or adolescents.

Nevertheless, the question of validity has also been pursued (albeit to a far lesser extent) by child-clinical investigators. In an effort to test the validity of the classification as it applies to adolescents, Saigh (1988) administered the Revised Children's Manifest Anxiety Scale (RCMAS; Reynolds and Richmond, 1978), Children's Depression Inventory (CDI; Kovacs, 1981), Test Anxiety Inventory (TAI; Spielberger, 1980), and the Conners Teacher Rating Scale (CTRS; Conners, 1969) to three groups of Lebanese adolescents (age range 12–13 years). The first group consisted of subjects who met diagnostic criteria for PTSD as measured by the Children's PTSD Inventory (Saigh, 1989a) after they were exposed to extreme forms of war-related stress, the second group was made up of test phobics, and the third group consisted of nonclinical controls. As hypothesized, the test phobic group had significantly elevated scores on the test anxiety scale and the PTSD group evinced significantly higher scores on the omnibus anxiety, depression, and misconduct scales. In a related study, Saigh (1989a) administered the RCMAS, CDI, and CTRS to three groups of Lebanese children (i.e., PTSD, test phobic, and nonclinical controls) whose ages ranged from 9 to 12 years. As in the case of the older cohort, the PTSD subjects experienced extreme forms of war-related stress and evinced significantly greater scores on the anxiety, depression, and misconduct scales than did their counterparts. In addition to concluding that a preliminary level of support for the classification as it applies to children and adolescents had been established, Saigh and Mrouegh concluded that these results paralleled those reported by investigators who studied traumatized adults.

More recently, Saigh, Mrouegh, and Brenner (in press) administered the Vocabulary, Reading Comprehension, Mathematics, Spelling, Language, and Science subtests of the Metropolitan Achievement Test (MAT); (Prescott, Balow, Hogan, and Farr, 1986) as well as the Lebanese General Ability Scale to three groups of Lebanese adolescents (age range 16 to 18 years). The first group met diagnostic criteria for war-related PTSD as measured by the Children's PTSD Inventory, the second group had been exposed to qualitatively and quantitatively similar war stressors and did not meet diagnostic criteria for PTSD (i.e., traumatized PTSD negatives). The third group consisted of nontraumatized controls. Data analysis determined that the MAT scores of the PTSD subjects were significantly lower than the scores of the traumatized PTSD negatives and controls. No significant differences were observed when the MAT scores of the traumatized PTSD negatives and controls were compared. In addition to providing an avenue of support for the classification, it was suggested that the results also served to support the untested assumption that academic underachievement may be an associated feature of PTSD in adolescents. Saigh suggested that PTSD in adolescents may serve as a critical filter for entry into professional and technical careers that draw heavily on preexisting scholastic skills. Attention was also drawn to the fact that the observed results are convergent with the finding that Vietnam veterans with PTSD completed substantially fewer years of formal education than comparable veterans who did not develop the disorder (Kulka, Schlenger, Fairbank, Hough, Jordan, Marmar, and Weiss, 1990).

Whereas appreciably fewer studies have explored the validity of the classification as it applies to children and adolescents, the differential levels of morbidity that were reported provide an empirical basis of support for the classification for children and adolescents. Of course, more research is anticipated (and warranted across different forms of trauma) as the DSM-IV PTSD classification presents a number of significant changes in the diagnostic criteria (APA, 1994).

EPIDEMIOLOGY

According to Davidson and Fairbank (1993), epidemiology involves "the study of the distribution and detriments of health-related states and events" (p. 147). Within this context it may be represented that information about the prevalence of a disorder among the general population as well as at-risk populations is of value in understanding the nature and scope of a psychiatric disorder. Reliable quantification of the prevalence of a disorder is also of importance to investigators who are interested in issues involving the etiology of a condition. In addition, epidemiological estimates are used by policy makers who effect decisions regarding the allocation of resources for prevention and treatment (Saigh, 1992a). Whereas several adult studies have examined the prevalence of war-related psychopathology among traumatized war veterans (Kulka et al., 1990), comparable large-scale investigations have not been effected with school-age populations in areas that have experienced war-related hostilities. On the other hand, a good deal of information is available from studies that examined at risk clinical samples of children and adolescents who were exposed to extreme forms of war-related stress. In the main, these studies may be classified according to two categories. The first involves investigations that did not measure for PTSD and the second involves studies that determined morbidity on the bases of the DSM-III, DSM-III-R, or DSM-IV, PTSD classifications. Although a host of studies fall into the former category, they are of interest inasmuch as they provide interesting symptomological profiles and as a general basis for gauging the effects of war stress on children and adolescents.

Viewed from a historical perspective, A. Freud and Burlingham (1943) examined a number of British children who had been in bombed areas during the London Blitz and represented that "so far as we can notice, there were no signs of traumatic shock to be observed in these children. If these bombing incidents occur when small children are in the care of their own mothers or a familiar mother substitute, they do not seem to be particularly affected. . . ." (p. 21). A. Freud and Burlingham cautioned, however, that "it is a widely different matter, when children, during an experience of this kind are separated from or even lose their parents" (p. 21). Regrettably, Freud and Burlingham did not report quantifiable estimates of psychiatric morbidity or detailed descriptions of posttraumatic impairments beyond general accounts of hostility or etiological formulations about the nature of fear. Bodman (1941), on the other hand, provided survey data involving 8000 British schoolchildren (age range 5–14 years). His data indicated that 300 cases or about 8 percent of the selected sample presented with psychological symptoms (see above) that were attributable to the raids.

Following the Second World War, Carey-Trefzer (1949) reevaluated 1203 British schoolchildren who had been exposed to various forms of war stress (e.g., air raids and their effects) and determined that 212 children or 17.62 percent of the sample "showed disturbances caused or aggravated by war experiences" (p. 556). These disturbances involved war-related nightmares and fears, scholastic difficulties, irritability, concentration and memory impairment, sleep disturbance, and avoidance behaviors.

Somewhat later, Kristal (1978) compared 66 Israeli adolescents who lived along the 1972 Israeli–Jordanian frontier to 77 matched adolescents living in an inland area. The former group had lived from 1968 through 1972 in an atmosphere of "ubiquitous threat and danger in the form of indiscriminate shelling and terrorist attacks'' (p. 74). In contrast, the inland residents reportedly did not experience war-related stress. Eighteen to 20 months after the Arab–Israeli cease fire, the subjects received dental examinations and it was observed that the war-exposed adolescents had a higher incidence of bruxism (teeth grinding, a psychosomatic condition associated with stress). Kristal also administered the Children's Manifest Anxiety Scale (CMAS; Castaneda, McCandless, and Pallermo, 1956) to both groups and a nonsignificant difference was noted. Both groups subsequently viewed a 12-minute film that simulated an ambush of an Israeli patrol, shelling, and civilians in great turmoil. The subjects went on to mark the CMAS, and data analysis revealed that the postfilm CMAS scores of the war-exposed adolescents were significantly greater than the scores of the adolescents who resided in areas that had not been exposed to the traumas of war. Kristal concluded that war-related stimuli in the border children's environment were stressful enough to evoke recollections of past traumas, and this coupled with an uncertain security situation were sufficient to induce bruxism. Kristal also represented that the adolescents who lived near the border had developed a disposition to respond to war-related cues through elevated levels of self-reported anxiety.

War-related events on the other side of the Israeli frontier also led to a series of serendipitous studies. Viewed in this context, Saigh (1985a,b) examined the course of self-reported anxiety before and after the 1982 Israeli incursion into Lebanon. As part of a psychometric cross-validation study, Wolpe and Lang's Fear Survey Schedule (1964), Spielberger, Gorsuch, and Lushene's (1968) State Trait Anxiety Inventory, and Saigh's (1982) Lebanese Fear Inventory (an index of war-related fears) were administered to 77 junior high school students. Fifty-seven days after the assessment, Israel invaded Lebanon. Israeli units subsequently surrounded West Beirut (the area where the junior high school is located) and laid siege to the area in an effort to destroy Palestinian combatants. Although a considerable proportion of West Beirut's civilian population evacuated to safer areas, a substantial number of civilians remained in West Beirut. In addition to being exposed to intermittent shelling and strafing, these individuals experienced considerable hardships as water and electricity were cut off at the height of the summer heat and as food, medicine, and petrol were in very limited supply. Following the withdrawal of Syrian, Palestinian, and Israeli forces, the Lebanese government, with the military support of American, French, British, and Italian troops, was able to reassert its authority over the capital for the first time in 8 years. Although the government's authority was limited to a 15-month interval, the assertion of Lebanese authority was associated with a pronounced reduction in the level of hostilities that had raged in Beirut before the Israeli incursion (i.e., abductions, shelling, and the like ceased).

Against this background, 64 of these junior high school students were located and interviewed about their experiences during the invasion. Sixteen of these individuals represented that they remained in West Beirut throughout the Israeli invasion and subsequent siege of the city. The subjects went on to mark the self-report inventories 6 to 8 weeks after the withdrawal of Syrian, Palestinian, and Israeli forces. Six months later, the junior high school students (46 evacuees and 16 nonevacuees) were reexamined. Data analysis determined that there were no statistically significant differences between the preinvasion scores of the evacuees and nonevacuees. Interestingly, it was also observed that there were no significant differences between the postinvasion scores of the evacuees and nonevacuees. In addition, the combined Lebanese Fear Inventory ratings of the evacuees and nonevacuees revealed that the selected sample's postinvasion scores (relative to war-related fears) were appreciably lower after the invasion. Saigh (1985a) subsequently concluded that "prolonged exposures to stressful circumstances that are subsequently mollified may not be associated with higher levels of anxiety" (p. 313). Saigh also concluded that "situationally specific fears may decrease after the stimuli that mediated these fears are withdrawn" (pp. 213–214).

In a similar effort to examine the psychological effects of the Israeli invasion of Lebanon, Hourani, Armenia, Zurayk, and

Afifi (1986) conducted a household survey involving 5795 subjects (52% were under the age of 20). To the credit of the individuals who physically collected the data, the survey was conducted
from July to August, 1982 (i.e., during the Israeli siege of West
Beirut). Although Hourani and her colleagues did not measure
for PTSD or administer standardized measures of emotionality,
a psychological symptom checklist was developed and administered to the selected sample. The investigators subsequently observed that items suggestive of PTSD (i.e., sleep impairment,
nightmares, and irritability) were endorsed by only approximately
8 percent of the subjects. Hourani et al. (1986) went on to conclude that "the survey findings have shown an unremarkable proportion of the psychological distress reporters among the
residents of west Beirut during the invasion and siege of 1982"
(p. 274).

Clearly, discordant accounts of psychiatric morbidity have been
reported. Of course, the studies that were considered herein involved different ethnic groups, stressors, measures, and data collection methods and time intervals. Nevertheless, six of the seven
studies that were reviewed (i.e., Bodman, 1941; A. Freud and
Burlingham, 1943; Carey-Trefzer, 1949; Saigh, 1985a,b; Hourani
et al., 1986) reported that the majority of children and adolescents who were exposed to war-related stressors did not develop
long-term emotional impairments. It is of considerable interest
to recall that these observations parallel the conclusion that was
reached by Rachman (1978) following a comprehensive analysis
of the British World War II psychiatric literature involving civilian
reactions to the London blitz. More specifically, Rachman concluded that "the great majority of the people endured the air
raids extraordinarily well, contrary to the universal expectation
of mass panic. Exposure to repeated bombings did not produce
a significant increase in psychiatric disorders" (p. 182).

War-studies Reporting PTSD Rates

As part of a case-control study that examined the validity of the
PTSD classification as it applies to children, Saigh administered

the Children's PTSD Inventory (Saigh, 1989a) to 840 Lebanese children (age range 8–12 years). These cases were referred for assessment by physicians, Red Cross personnel, mental health practitioners, and educators after they were exposed to extreme forms of war-related stress (e.g., observing the execution of a parent or being in an apartment building when it was hit by an artillery shell). Although the data were collected from 1 to 2 years after the subject's stressful experiences, 230 (104 males and 126 females) subjects or 32.50 percent of the sample clearly met diagnostic criteria for PTSD. In a related study, Saigh (1991) reported that 25.21, 55.65, 5.65 and 13.48 percent of these cases had been exposed to extreme forms of stress through direct experience (e.g., being shot), observation (e.g., witnessing the execution of a parent or sibling), information transmission (e.g., learning about the traumatic experiences of a parent or sibling), or combinations thereof.

Also within the context of war-related PTSD in Lebanon, Saigh (1988) effected a prospective study involving 11 female students at the American University of Beirut (age range 18–22 years). The course of self-reported anxiety, depression, assertion, and PTSD (as based on a DSM-III based structured interview that the author developed) was charted 63 days before the subjects were exposed to a devastating artillery bombardment as well as 8, 37, and 316 days later. The selected subjects in this study reported that they (1) were forced to take shelter in stairwells or basements; (2) were deprived of sleep for 36 to 48 hours; and (3) had never experienced a more threatening situation in their lives. It was also established that artillery shells landed within 25 to 300 meters of their homes and that the windows of their apartments had been shattered by explosions. Although the majority of the students reported 20 elevated levels of anxiety and depression as well as lower levels of assertion after the bombardment, the estimates observed 37 and 316 days after the traumatic event were not significantly different from the estimates that were observed 63 days before the bombardment. Diagnostic assessments revealed that nine students (81.81% of the sample) warranted PTSD diagnoses within one month of the bombardment. On the other hand, only one of the students, or 9.09 percent of the sample remained symptomatic 316 days after the bombardment.

Kinzie and his colleagues (Kinzie, Sack, Angell, and Mason, 1986; Kinzie, Sack, Angell, Clarke, and Ben, 1989) described the psychiatric morbidity of a sample of Cambodian adolescents who emigrated to America after the fall of the violent Pol Pot regime (1975–1979). Between the ages of 8 to 12 years, the subjects suffered "catastrophic trauma caused by separation from their families, forced labor, starvation, personal injuries, and the witnessing of many deaths and executions" (Kinzie et al., 1986, p. 501). Kinzie et al. (1986) administered the Diagnostic Interview Schedule to 40 subjects (mean age = 17 years) approximately 2.5 years after their immigration to the United States and observed that 50 percent met criteria for PTSD. Three years later, Kinzie et al. (1989) located and reexamined 27 of the Cambodian subjects (mean age 20 years). Of these, 8 (29.6%) met criteria for PTSD as measured by the Diagnostic Interview Schedule. Eleven (40.8%) never met criteria, and 8 (29.6%) manifested a variable course; 3 (11.1%) subjects who initially met criteria did not do so at follow-up; and 5 (18.5%) subjects who initially met criteria failed to do so at follow-up.

In an effort to learn more about the effects of war stress from adolescence to early adulthood, Sack, Clark, Him, Dickason, Goff, Lanham, and Kinzie (1993) administered the Diagnostic Interview for Children and Adolescents (DICA; Welner, Reich, Herjanic, Jung, and Amado, 1987) to 19 of the 40 original Pol Pot survivors. Of the 19 subjects (mean age 23 years) who were examined across assessment dates, 11 (57.89%) had PTSD in 1984, 9 (47.37%) met criteria in 1987, and 6 (31.57%) were diagnosed as PTSD positives in 1990. Similar levels of morbidity were observed by Realmuto, Masten, Files, Hubbard, Grotelushen, and Burke (1992) who administered the Reaction Index (Fredrick, 1986; Pynoos, Frederick, Nader, Arroyo, Steinberg, Eth, Nunez, and Fairbanks, 1987) to an independent sample of Cambodian adolescents (age range 14–23 years). Based on the responses of 47 subjects, Realmuto and his colleagues estimated that 39 percent met criteria for PTSD.

In order to control for the intervening effects of resettlement stress, Savin, Sack, Clarke, Nee, and Richart (1993) administered a Khmer version of the DICA and the Schedule for Affective Disorders and Schizophrenia for School Age Children (K-SADS; Puig-Antich, Orvaschel, Tabrinzi, and Chambers, 1980) to 99 Khmer youth (age range 18–25 years). These individuals had fled Cambodia after experiencing the horrors of the Pol Pot regime as children. Whereas they resided in the relative safety of a refugee camp (i.e., the Site Two Camp) located in Thailand for 10 years, 26.3 percent of the subjects met diagnostic criteria for war-related PTSD and 31.3 percent had a lifetime prevalence of the disorder. Comorbidity in the form of major depression was currently diagnosed among 68.7 percent of the Site Two subjects. It is of considerable interest to note that Savin and his colleagues compared the prevalence rates of the Site Two Pol Pot related PTSD to those that were observed by Sack et al. (1993) among a matched cohort in the United States. Whereas the PTSD rates among the Pol Pot survivors who remained in Thailand were somewhat higher than the rates that were observed in the United States, the differences were not statistically significant. Savin and his colleagues went on to observe that the diagnosis of war-related PTSD is a direct product of the original trauma and not a byproduct of contextual or resettlement stress.

More recently, Sack, McSharry, Clarke, Kinney, Seeley, and Lewinsohn (1994) conducted an elegant investigation wherein the DICA and K-SADS were administered to an independent sample (age range 13–25) of Khmer survivors of the Pol Pot era (n = 209). In this instance, subjects were randomly selected and examined for PTSD as well as comorbid conditions. Whereas the subjects had resided in the United States from 9.0 to 3.1 years, a point prevalence of 18.2 percent was observed for PTSD. In a similar vein, a lifetime prevalence of 21.5 percent was also noted. Comorbidity in the form of major depression was observed with a point prevalence of 11.0 percent and a lifetime prevalence of 34.9 percent. Additional DSM-III-R diagnoses evinced extremely low prevalence rates (e.g., 1.0% and 1.9% for current and lifetime prevalence of conduct disorder and no cases of psychoactive substance use were identified).

Recent research following the Gulf War has also focused on child and adolescent PTSD. Five months after Iraqi forces were driven from Kuwait, Nader, Pynoos, Fairbanks, Al-Ajeel, and Al-Asfour (1993) administered an Arabic version of the Reaction Index to 51 subjects (age range 8–21 years) who were attending a Kuwati summer school. Nader and her colleagues reported that 70 percent of the subjects had PTSD. Also within the context of the Gulf War, Weisenberg, Schwarzwald, Waysman, Solomon, and Klingman (1993) administered a Hebrew version of the Reaction Index to 492 Israeli children who were enrolled in grades 5 through 10. The subjects in this case had remained with their families in hermetically sealed rooms and worn gas masks during Iraqi missile attacks. As based on the assessments that occurred 3 weeks after the war, it was estimated that 25.61 percent of the subjects had PTSD.

It is readily apparent that considerable variability was reported. Indeed, current prevalence ranged from 9.09 to 70.00 percent and the lifetime prevalence ranged from 21.50 percent to 90.90 percent. Table 6.1 presents the PTSD prevalence data as reviewed herein.

The variability may be associated in part with the diversity that was evident relative to the type, duration, and intensity of the stressors that were encountered as well as the interval of time that occurred between stress exposures and clinical assessments. The epidemiological dissynchrony may also be associated with differences in the subject samples (age, gender, SES, treatment-seeking vs. community samples) or the way in which PTSD was diagnosed. Frequently, instruments or methods used to formulate PTSD diagnosis have different or untested levels of sensitivity and specificity. It may also be fairly represented that the majority of the measures that were used did not go through independent peer reviews that were primarily based on psychometric considerations. As such, the differences in the overall quality of measurement may have significantly contributed to the epidemiological variance.

TABLE 6.1
Current and Lifetime PTSD Estimates

Investigations	Subjects & Age	Measure	PTSD %	
			Current	Lifetime
Saigh (1989a)	840 Lebanese students, age range 8–12	Children's PTSD Inventory	32.50	
Saigh (1988)	12 Lebanese university students, age range 18–22	Structured interview	9.09	90.90
Kinzie et al. (1986)	40 Cambodian refugees, mean age 17	DIS	50.00	
Kinzie et al. (1989)	27 Cambodian refugees residing in U.S.A., mean age 20	DIS	29.60	
Sack et al. (1993)	19 Cambodian refugees residing in U.S.A., mean age 23	DICA	31.57	
Realmuto et al. (1992)	47 Cambodian refugees residing in U.S.A., age range 14–23	Reaction Index	37.00	
Savin et al. (1993)	99 Cambodian refugees in Thailand, age range 18–25	DICA&K-SADS	26.30	31.3
Sack et al. (in press)	209 Cambodian refugees residing in U.S.A., age range 13–25	DICA&K-SADS	18.2	21.50
Nader et al. (in press)	51 Kuwati students, age range 18–21	Reaction Index	70.00	
Weisenberg et al. (1993)	492 Israeli students, grades 4–6	Reaction Index	25.61	

Despite these differences, it is clear that exposure to a psychologically distressing event that is beyond the realm of normal human experience was not sufficient to induce the PTSD in all of the subjects that were sampled. It is also of interest to observe that the prevalence of the disorder seemingly decreases over time (Milgram, Toubania, Klingman, Raviv, and Goldstein, 1988; Kinzie et al., 1989; Saigh, 1989a; Sack et al., 1993) and that females may have higher rates of PTSD than males (Saigh, 1988, 1989b). Whereas PTSD estimates were reported across developmental levels, a systematic analysis of the prevalence of the disorder by age has not been conducted. Moreover, epidemiological information involving preschool children has not been investigated and it would be of considerable interest to systematically determine the prevalence of PTSD among this population.

Whereas the issue of comorbidity presents a host of clinical and theoretical challenges, only two studies (Sack et al., in press; Savin, Sack, Clarke, Nee, and Richart, 1993) sought to examine for comorbid conditions. Interestingly, the 21.5 percent point prevalence for major depression that Sack and his colleagues observed among Cambodian survivors of the Pol Pot is comparable to the 15.7 percent point prevalence estimates that was observed among Vietnam veterans by Kulka and his colleagues. On the other hand, Savin and his colleagues reported an appreciably higher prevalence of major depression (68.7%) among the Cambodian Site Two subjects who were residing in a Thai refugee camp. Certainly, historical events common to the daily lives of the selected samples may have had an influence on the observed levels of depression. It is also worthy to note that Sack and his coinvestigators observed no cases of substance abuse and that this observation is in contrast to the 22.2 and 6.1 percent current estimates of alcohol and drug abuse that were observed among Vietnam veterans by Kulka and his colleagues. Here again, historical events as well as maturation and selection differences relative to age and ethnicity may have contributed to the observed differences.

A RESEARCH AGENDA FOR THE NEXT DECADE

Over the past decade a number of studies have examined the effects of exposure to traumatic war events on youth. Yet, for a variety of reasons, research on war trauma and youth has been more limited than that for adults in terms of the range of issues examined and the research methods employed. Building upon what is currently known from research on trauma and PTSD among youth, and cautiously generalizing from the more numerous empirical studies on adult war veterans and civilians, we next describe briefly what we think are some critical areas for focused research.

First, well-designed epidemiologic studies are needed to begin to answer questions about the prevalence of PTSD and other war-related psychological disorders and adverse outcomes among young victims and survivors of war. Population studies could provide much needed information on the etiology, risk-factors, protective mechanisms, and comorbid conditions associated with PTSD (Fairbank, Schlenger, Caddell, and Woods, 1993). For example, structured PTSD interviews conducted with probability samples of youth drawn from war-exposed populations can provide estimates of the prevalence of PTSD and its comorbid conditions that control for biases introduced by self-selected samples, such as occurs in studies that rely on volunteers or patients drawn from a clinical setting.

Second, longitudinal research is needed to examine how war-related traumatic stress reactions are expressed by youth at different chronological ages and across developmental stages. Currently, we know little about how PTSD symptoms and other sequelae of war are affected by the young person's age at time of exposure. Additionally, longitudinal studies of youth are needed to provide data on the course of PTSD symptoms, cooccurring problems, and coping over time.

Future research on war trauma and youth also should take into account the multidimensional nature of war stress, as well as the fact that exposures vary with respect to frequency and severity. A major next step in PTSD research should be the development and psychometric evaluation of instruments intended to assess exposure to the broad range of potentially traumatic conditions to which youth are exposed during war. These factors are likely to include, among others, exposure to specific aspects of combat (e.g., artillery barrage, bombing, small-arms fire, etc.); witnessing and suffering abusive violence; separation from and loss of loved ones; destruction and loss of home and community; physical, social–cultural, and educational deprivations; and exposure to people who are wounded, dead, and dying. Delineation of the factors that define the traumatic nature of war for youth is unfortunately a necessary condition for understanding factors that contribute to adverse and resilient adjustment and coping. This kind of information is also necessary for the development of effective outreach, interventions, and treatments for those unfortunate youth exposed to the violence, chaos, and other ravages of war.

Research on war trauma and youth also needs to take into account the extent of exposure to other extreme life events, such as natural disasters, accidents, sexual abuse, and crime, as well as potential gender, developmental, and ethnocultural variations in the appraisal and meaning of extreme events and PTSD symptoms. Research protocols would also benefit from the inclusion of multisource information collection strategies that take into account the report of youth and important collaterals, such as parents, guardians, and teachers. In addition, research on war trauma and PTSD among youth could benefit greatly from the use of comparable measurement strategies across studies. Adoption of core measures and variables across studies would go a long way toward enhancing the communication and dissemination of findings to scientists and clinicians, as well as to those government and military officials whose policy decisions affect the waging of war.

Perhaps most importantly, developmentally and culturally appropriate interventions for the treatment of war-related PTSD among youth need to be developed and rigorously evaluated. There exists a need for research on more effective outreach and PTSD prevention strategies as well as for research on the efficacy of school- and clinic-based treatments, such as individual, group, and family; behavioral; cognitive behavioral; psychodynamic; brief; interpersonal; pharmacologic; and other therapies. While progress has been made in identifying some promising treatments for PTSD among youth, much work needs to be done in the area of therapy development and evaluation. For example, little is currently known about what treatment regimens are likely to be effective for youth exposed to specific aspects of war at particular developmental stages and with specific PTSD and comorbid symptoms and disorders.

Finally, investigators in the area of trauma and PTSD among youth should be fully aware that research with this vulnerable population brings with it special obligations to ensure protection against risks from research participation. Ethical research with traumatized youth requires strict assurance of informed consent, confidentiality, voluntary participation, and privacy, as well as the implementation of efforts to address the suffering of those youth identified as having war-related PTSD (e.g., referral for treatment).

REFERENCES

American Psychiatric Association (1980), *Diagnostic and Statistical Manual of Mental Disorders* (DSM-III), 3rd ed. Washington, DC: American Psychiatric Press.

——— (1987), *Diagnostic and Statistical Manual of Mental Disorders* (DSM-III-R), 3rd ed. rev. Washington, DC: American Psychiatric Press.

——— (1994). *Diagnostic and Statistical Manual of Mental Disorders* (DSM-IV), 4th ed., Washington, DC: American Psychiatric Press.

Blanchard, E. B., Kolb, L. C., Gerardi, R. J., Ryan, P., & Pallmeyer, T. P. (1986), Cardiac response to relevant stimuli as an adjunctive tool for diagnosing posttraumatic stress disorder in Vietnam veterans. *Behav. Ther.*, 17:592–606.

——— ——— Pallmeyer, T. P., & Gerardi, R. J. (1982), A psychological study of posttraumatic stress disorder in Vietnam veterans. *Psychiatric Quart.*, 54:220–229.

——— ——— Prins, A., Gates, S., & McCoy, G. C. (1991), Changes in plasma norepinephrine to combat-related stimuli among Vietnam veterans with posttraumatic stress disorder. *J. Nerv. & Ment. Dis.*, 179:371–373.

Bodman, F. (1941), War conditions and the mental health of the child. *Brit. Med. J.*, 11:486–488.

Bradner, T. (1943), Psychiatric observations among Finnish children during the Russo-Finnish War of 1939–1940. *Nerv. Child*, 2:313–319.

Bury, J. S. (1918), Pathology of war neuroses. *Lancet*, July 27:97–99.

Carey-Trefzer, C. J. (1949), The results of a clinical study of war-damaged children who attended a child guidance clinic. *J. Ment. Sci.*, 95:535–559.

Castaneda, R. M., McCandless, B. R., & Pallermo, D. S. (1956), The children's form of the Manifest Anxiety Scale. *Child Develop.*, 27:317–326.

Conners, C. (1969), A teacher rating scale for use in drug studies with children. *Amer. J. Psychiatry*, 126:884–888.

Davidson, J. R. T., & Fairbank, J. A. (1993), The epidemiology of posttraumatic stress disorder. In: *Posttraumatic Stress Disorder: DSM-IV and Beyond*, ed. J. R. T. Davidson & E. Foa. Washington, DC: American Psychiatric Press, pp. 147–169.

Dreyer, C. S., & Glass, A. J. (1973), Italian campaign (9 September 1943–1 March 1944). Psychiatry established at the Army level. In: *Neuropsychiatry in World War Two*, Vol. 2, ed. W. S. Mulling. Washington, DC: Office of the Surgeon General, Department of the Army, pp. 25–109.

Fairbank, J. A., Keane, T. M., & Malloy, P. F. (1983), Some preliminary characteristics of Vietnam veterans with posttraumatic stress disorder. *J. Consult. & Clin. Psychol.*, 51:912–919.

——— Schlenger, W. E., Caddell, J. M., & Woods, M. G. (1993), Post-traumatic stress disorder. In: *Comprehensive Handbook of Psychopathology*, 2nd. ed., ed. P. B. Sutker & H. E. Adams. New York: Plenum.

Fraser, F., & Wilson, R. M. (1918), The sympathetic nervous system and the irritable heart of soldiers. *Brit. Med. J.*, 2:27–29.

Frederick, C. J. (1986), Posttraumatic stress disorder and child molestation. In: *Sexual Exploitation of Patients by Mental Health Professionals*, ed. A. Burgess & C. Hartmann. New York: Praeger, pp. 133–142.

Freud, A., & Burlingham, D. T. (1943), *War and Children*. New York: Medical War Books.

Goodwin, D. W., & Guze, S. R. (1984), *Psychiatric Diagnosis*, 3rd ed. New York: Oxford University Press.

Green, B., Grace, M., Vary, M., Kramer, T., Gleser, G., & Leonard, A. (1994), Children of disaster in the second decade: A 17-year follow-up of Buffalo Creek Survivors. *J. Amer. Acad. Child & Adol. Psychiatry*, 33:71–79.

Grinker, R. R., & Spiegel, J. P. (1945), *War Neuroses*. Philadelphia: Blakiston.

Hourani, L. L., Armenian, H., Zurayk, H., & Afifi, L. (1986), A population-based survey of loss and psychological distress during war. *Soc. Sci. & Med.*, 23:269–275.

Kilpatrick, D. G., Resnick, H. S., & Freedy, J. R. (1993), *DSM-IV Posttraumatic Stress Disorder Field Trial: Criterion A and Other Stressor Event Histories Associated with PTSD in Clinical and Community Samples*. Crime Victims Center, Medical University of South Carolina, Charleston, SC.

Kinzie, J. D., Sack, W. H., Angell, R. H., Clarke, G., & Ben, R. (1989), A three year follow-up of Cambodian young people traumatized as children. *J. Amer. Acad. Child & Adol. Psychiatry*, 28:501–504.

——— ——— Angell, R. H., Mason, S. M., & Rath, B. (1986), The psychiatric effects of massive trauma on Cambodian children. *J. Amer. Acad. Child & Adol. Psychiatry*, 25:370–376.

Kovacs, M. (1981), *The Children's Depression Inventory*. Pittsburgh, PA: University of Pittsburgh Press.

Kristal, L. (1978), Bruxism: An anxiety response to environmental stress. In: *Stress and Anxiety*, Vol. 5, ed. C. D. Spielberger & I. G. Sarason. New York: Wiley, pp. 45–58.

Kulka, R., Schlenger, W. E., Fairbank, J. A., Hough, R. L., Jordan, B. K., Marmar, C. R., & Weiss, D. S. (1990), *Trauma and the Vietnam Generation: Report of*

Findings from the National Vietnam Veterans Readjustment. New York: Brunner/Mazel.

Lewis, A. (1942), Incidence of neurosis in England under war conditions. *Lancet,* 2:175–183.

Mercer, M. H., & Despert, J. M. (1942), Psychological effects of the war on French children. *Psychosom. Med.,* 5:266–272.

Milgram, N. A., Toubiana, Y. H., Klingman, A., Raviv, A., & Goldstein, I. (1988), Situational exposure and personal loss in children's acute and chronic stress reactions to a school bus disaster. *J. Traum. Stress,* 1:339–352.

Morey, L. C., Skinner, J., & Blashfield, R. K. (1986), Trends in the classification of behavior. In: *Handbook of Behavioral Assessments,* 2nd ed., ed. R. A. Ciminero, K. Calhoun, & H. Adams. New York: Wiley, pp. 47–78.

Nader, K., Pynoos, R., Fairbanks, L., Frederick, C., Al-Ajeel, M., & Al-Asfour, A. (1993), A preliminary study of PTSD and grief among the children of Kuwait following the Gulf crisis. *Brit. J. Clin. Psychol.,* 32:407–416.

Prescott, G. A., Balow, I. H., Hogan, T. P., & Farr, R. C. (1986), *Metropolitan Achievement Tests MAT6 Survey Battery National Norms Booklet.* New York: Harcourt Brace Jovanovich.

Puig-Antich, J., Orvaschel, H., Tabrinzi, M. H., & Chambers, W. (1980), *The Schedule for Affective Disorders and Schizophrenia for School Age Children (Kiddie SADS).* New York Psychiatric Institute and Yale University School of Medicine.

Pynoos, R. S., Frederick, C., Nader, K., Arroyo, W., Steinberg, A., Eth, S., Nunez, F., & Fairbanks, L. (1987), Life threat and posttraumatic stress in school-age children. *Arch. Gen. Psychiatry,* 44:1057–1063.

Quay, H. C. (1986), Conduct disorders. In: *Psychopathological Disorders of Children,* 3rd ed., ed. H. C. Quay & J. S. Werry. New York: John Wiley.

Rachman, S. (1978), *Fear and Courage.* San Francisco, CA: W. H. Freeman.

Raines, G. N., & Kolb, L. C. (1943), Combat fatigue and war neurosis. *U. S. Navy Med. Bull.,* July: 923–926, 1299–1309.

Realmuto, G. M., Masten, A., Files, L., Hubbard, J., Grotelushen, A., & Burke, C. (1992), Adolescent survivors of massive childhood trauma in Cambodia: Life events and current symptoms. *J. Traum. Stress,* 5:589–599.

Reynolds, C., & Richmond, B. O. (1978), What I think and feel: A revised measure of children's manifest anxiety. *J. Abnorm. Child Psychology,* 6:272–280.

Robins, L. N., Helzer, J. E., Croughan, J., & Ratcliff, K. (1981), National Institute of Mental Health Interview Schedule. *Arch. Gen. Psychiatry,* 38:381–389.

Rowan, A. B., & Foy, D. W. (1993), Post-traumatic stress disorder in child sexual abuse survivors: A literature review. *J. Traum. Stress,* 6:3–20.

Sack, W. H., Clarke, G., Him, C., Dickason, D., Goff, B., Lanham, K., & Kinzie, J. D. (1993), A six year follow-up of Cambodian adolescents. *J. Amer. Acad. Child & Adol. Psychiatry,* 32:3–15.

———— McSharry, S., Clarke, G. N., Kinney, R., Seeley, J., & Lewinsohn, P. (1994), The Khmer adolescent project I: Epidemiological findings in two generations of Cambodian refugees. *J. Nerv. & Ment. Dis.,* 182:387–395.

Saigh, P. A. (1982), The Lebanese Fear Inventory: A normative report. *J. Clin. Psychol.,* 38:352–355.

——— (1985a), Adolescent anxiety following varying degrees of war stress in Lebanon. *J. Clin. Child Psychology*, 14:210–215.

——— (1985b), An experimental analysis of delayed posttraumatic stress among adolescents. *J. Gen. Psychol.*, 146:125–131.

——— (1986), The Lebanese General Ability Scale (Forms A., B., and C). Beirut: American University of Beirut, Office of Research and Development.

——— (1988), Anxiety, depression, and assertion across alternating intervals of stress. *J. Abnorm. Psychol.*, 97:338–342.

——— (1989a), The development and validation of the Children's Posttraumatic Stress Disorder Inventory. *Internat. J. Spec. Edu.*, 4:75–84.

——— (1989b), The validity of the *DSM-III* posttraumatic stress disorder classification as applied to children. *J. Abnorm. Psychol.*, 98:189–192.

——— (1991), On the development of posttraumatic stress disorder pursuant to different modes of traumatization. *Behav. Res. & Ther.*, 29:213–216.

——— (1992a), History, current nosology, and epidemiology. In: *Posttraumatic Stress Disorder: A Behavioral Approach to Assessment and Treatment*, ed. P. A. Saigh. Boston: Allyn & Bacon, pp. 1–27.

——— (1992b), Structured interviews and the inferential process. *J. School Psychol.*, 30:221–226.

——— Green, B., & Korol, M. (1996), The history and prevalence of posttraumatic stress disorder with special reference to children and adolescents. *J. School Psychol.*, 34(2):107–131.

——— Mrouegh, M., & Brenner, D. J. (in press), Academic impairments among traumatized adolescents. *Behav. Res. & Ther.*

Savin, D., Sack, W. H., Clarke, G. N., Nee, M., & Richart, I. (1993), *The Khmer Adolescent Project: 11. A Study of Trauma from Thailand's Site Two Refugee Camp*. Division of Child and Adolescent Psychiatry, University of Oregon School of Medicine. Typescript.

Southard, E. E. (1919), *Shell Shock and Neuropsychiatric Problems*. Boston: Leonard.

Spielberger, C. D. (1980), *Test Anxiety Inventory*. Palo Alto, CA: Consulting Psychologists Press.

——— Gorsuch, R. L., & Lushene, R. E. (1968), *Manual for the State Trait Anxiety Inventory*. Palo Alto, CA: Consulting Psychologists Press.

Van Pragg, H. M. (1990), The DSM-IV depression classification. To be or not to be. *J. Ment. & Nerv. Dis.*, 178:147–149.

Weisenberg, M., Schwarzwald, J., Waysman, M., Solomon, Z., & Klingman, A. (1993), Coping of school-age children in the sealed room during Scud missile bombardment and postwar stress reactions. *J. Consult. & Clin. Psychol.*, 61:462–467.

Welner, Z., Reich, W., Herjanic, B., Jung, K. G., & Amado, H. (1987), Reliability, validity, and parent–child agreement studies of the Diagnostic Interview for Children and Adolescents (DICA). *J. Amer. Acad. Child & Adol. Psychiatry*, 26:649–653.

Wolpe, J., & Lang, P. (1964), A fear survey schedule for use in behavior therapy. *Beh. Res. & Ther.*, 2:27–30.

Zimering, R., Caddell, J. A., Fairbank, J. A., & Keane, T. (1993), Posttraumatic stress disorder in Vietnam veterans: An experimental validation of the DSM-III diagnostic criteria. *J. Traum. Stress*, 6:327–342.

Chapter 7
Adolescent Pregnancy,
A Stressful Life Event:
Cause and Consequence

Catherine A. Martin, M.D., Kelly K. Hill, M.D.,
and Richard Welsh, M.S.W.

Scope of the Problem

Adolescent pregnancy is increasing as a national health priority. The United States has significantly higher rates of adolescent pregnancy, birth, and abortion than other developed countries (McArnarey and Hendee, 1989), with pregnancy rates twice those of England and Wales and more than four times the rate in the Netherlands (Jones, Forrest, Goldmen, Henshaw, Lincoln, Rossoff, Westoff, and Wulf, 1985). Approximately 13 percent of all babies born in the United States are born to adolescent mothers, with one million teens becoming pregnant each year. By age 18, 26 percent of black adolescents and 7 percent of white adolescents will have carried a pregnancy to term (Mulcahey, 1990). Although the pregnancy and birth rates for all adult ages have been decreasing, the birth rates for adolescents have decreased to a lesser extent, and actually are increasing among very young

141

adolescents (those under 16 years of age). These trends will expose health care providers to a larger proportion of adolescents among obstetrical patients (Hollingsworth and Kreuther, 1981).

The adolescent who becomes pregnant is vulnerable to long-term personal consequences. Adolescence is a period of time in which dramatic physical and psychological changes occur (McArnarey and Hendee, 1989). In this developmental stage, there is accelerated growth in most organ systems, particularly the reproductive system. Young people today reach reproductive maturity earlier than was the case at the beginning of this century (Tanner, 1962). The average age of which menses occurs has decreased 3 months per decade with the average age of menarche today being 12.8 to 13.2, and boys also mature earlier (Tanner, 1962). This younger age of physical maturation puts children in a riskier position for earlier sexual activity and its consequences.

Adolescence is not only characterized by dramatic physical growth, but is also a time of important psychological development. However, cognitive and psychosocial maturation lag behind the rapid physical growth. There does not appear to be any correlation between biological and cognitive maturation (Orr, Brack, and Ingersoll, 1988). Because of the widening asynchrony between physical and psychological development, pregnancy during these years places increased demands and stresses on the teenager. Pregnancy itself is a developmental process requiring the future parent to embrace a new order of responsibility. Sadler and Catrone have called adolescent pregnancy a "dual developmental crisis" (Sadler and Catrone, 1983) as the young future mother confronts the dramatic physical and psychological changes simultaneously, of both adolescence and pregnancy.

The psychological developmental issues the adolescent faces include forming a sense of individuality and psychological separateness from the family of origin, developing operational thinking, making a career choice, and planning for the future (McArnarey and Hendee, 1989). In early adolescence, the child is still very dependent upon her parents for nurturance and approval. The majority of young adolescents think concretely and do not have insight into long-term consequences of their actions.

As the adolescent struggles with separating from the family of origin, she becomes increasingly independent and frequently tests the family value systems. This has been referred to as a phase of "self-love." In middle adolescence, there may still be concrete thinking and difficulty dealing with abstract ideas. As adolescence progresses, there is increasing dependence on the peer group for support and identity formation. Formal thought processes begin to develop with the ability to think abstractly and have insight into future consequences of behavior (Mulcahey, 1990).

Like adolescence, pregnancy is a time of physical and psychological adjustment. Many of the physical changes occur rapidly and require adjusting to a new body image as well as physical discomfort. These changes may be frightening to the adolescent who is already dealing with puberty. She is faced with the responsibility of caring for an unseen person often at the price of her independence.

As the adolescent is in the midst of separating emotionally from her family, it may be difficult to turn to her family for support during the pregnancy. Often the grandparents take on the primary responsibility for the infant. This may stress both family relationships and the adolescent's developing self (Mulcahey, 1990).

Adolescent pregnancy does have a significant impact upon the family and generally is viewed as a crisis. Statistics reveal that anywhere from 50 to 80 percent of unmarried pregnant adolescents continue to live with their family of origin (Rich, 1991). Adolescent pregnancy may be an unresolved adolescent conflict to do with leaving the family or a postponement of normal striving for autonomy (Raines, 1991). The final consequence of teenage parenthood is a structural change of mother–daughter interactions and conflicts inherent in coresidence. Many mothers have feelings of guilt, shock, anger, and sorrow upon learning about their daughters' pregnancy. Mothers view their daughters' pregnancy as a sign of their own maternal inadequacy and a threat to their daughters' ability to achieve future goals (Wilkerson, 1991). More specific is the issue of who will be in charge, and who will mother whom. There is also the confusing task of relating to a daughter who has fulfilled an adult task, but yet is still an adolescent and still retains significant immaturities (Rich, 1991).

The pregnant teen's entry into society as a self-sufficient adult may be delayed. She is at increased risk of not completing high school. Fifty to 75 percent of females not graduating from high school do so because of an unplanned pregnancy (Mulcahey, 1990). Many mothers who wish to return to school are unable to do so because of economic and child care issues. Not completing secondary school places the young mother at a disadvantage when facing a competitive job market. Adolescent mothers are at increased risk for unemployment, poverty, dependence on welfare, job and marital instability, and greater number of children per mother than older women (Furstenberg, 1976; Zuckerman, Walker, Frank, Chase, and Hamburg, 1984). These factors can lead to a self-defeating, vicious circle.

In addition to the psychosocial sequelae resulting from adolescent parenthood, these births are associated with increased health risks for both the young mother and the infant (Mulcahey, 1990). The adolescent, when compared to a healthy adult, is at significant risk of pregnancy-induced hypertension, premature labor, anemia, maternal mortality, and cephalopelvic disproportion. There is greater chance of perinatal mortality, neonatal mortality, prematurity, intrauterine growth retardation, developmental delays, repeat pregnancies, childhood accidents and neglect, and childhood behavior disorders (Zuckerman et al., 1984; Mulcahey, 1990). However, whether the higher risk of adverse perinatal and neonatal complications are a direct result of young maternal age, or result from the complexities of low socioeconomic status, educational disadvantage, crowding, and lack of social support is difficult to determine (McArnarey and Hendee, 1989). Perhaps the young maternal age indicates that this individual is at risk for other factors that contribute to higher pregnancy morbidity, rather than being a significant independent risk factor for poor pregnancy outcome.

The psychiatric sequelae of the pregnant adolescent facing this "crisis of teenage pregnancy" has not been systematically studied, although mental health problems are commonly described by clinicians caring for this population (Zuckerman, Amaro, and Beardslee, 1987). The pregnant adolescent may be more vulnerable to depression. After puberty, the occurrence of depression significantly increases as well as the sex ratio changing from primarily male to female (Rutter, 1986). It has been proposed that hormonal, cognitive, and social factors play a role in these trends (Rutter, 1986). The combination of hormonal changes that occur during pregnancy and those occurring during adolescence may result in a greater impact on affective functioning. In adults, depression has been reported to be more prevalent in women with children compared to those with no children in the home (Zuckerman et al., 1987). Further, the younger the mother, the greater the risk she will develop depression, so children alone are a stress, inducing depression (McGee, Williams, Kashani, and Silva, 1983). The social consequences that are associated with adolescent pregnancy, such as unemployment, place the mother at additional risk for depression (Brown and Harris, 1978). Colletta reported that in a sample of 75 young mothers (ages 15–19), 59 percent had depressive symptoms. The younger, single, and least educated women had the highest rates (Colletta, 1983).

A longitudinal study by Brown, Adams, and Kellan (1981) followed 828 women who were interviewed when their children were 6 and then 10 years of age. The mothers who had become pregnant during adolescence reported more depressed symptomatology compared with women who became pregnant when at least 20 years old. The teenage mothers continued to experience distress when compared to the older mothers.

Experimental drug use is frequent among adolescents. The pregnant adolescent may be at increased risk to engage in this type of experimentation as there are overlapping antecedents for drug use and adolescent pregnancy that include isolation from peers, depression, conflict in the home, school problems, punitive parental discipline, and low self-esteem (Zuckerman et al., 1987). In addition, there are reports of increased sexual behavior among drug-using adolescents (Jessor and Jessor, 1977; Hundleby, Carpenter, Ross, and Mercer, 1982). Kandel reports in a longitudinal study of Caucasian high school students that 61 percent of students who used marijuana and 41 percent who drank alcohol were sexually active compared to 18 percent of nonusers and 4 percent of teetotalers. In addition, adolescent substance use is associated with depression (Paton, Kessler, and Kandel, 1977; Kaplan, Landau, Weinhold, and Shenken 1984).

Clearly, adolescent pregnancy is a complex phenomenon that leaves the young mother and baby vulnerable to serious physical and psychosocial complications. Increased insight into the adolescent's motivations and stressors leading to her becoming pregnant can help improve interventions to change this increasing public health problem.

PILOT STUDY

METHOD

A study was conducted to investigate feelings about pregnancy, family relations, mood, and impulsivity in pregnant adolescents. Thirty-six pregnant adolescents were seen by a child psychiatrist through a university-based teen pregnancy program. The majority were randomly selected from a primarily second and third trimester population (average gestational age 28 weeks). An interview was conducted on feelings about the pregnancy, family relations, and a history of loss. The adolescents also completed the Children's Depression Inventory (CDI; Kovacs, 1983), the Modified Personal History Questionnaire (MPHQ), with the following subscales: Nicotine, Alcohol, Drug Use, Sexual Activity, and Delinquency. A goal of this study was to investigate the impulsive and depressive feelings and behaviors in the pregnant adolescent, with particular attention to history of loss and how that related to depression, high-risk behaviors, and conception.

DATA

Thirty-six cases were seen. The age range was 13 to 18 years, with an average age of 17.1 years. Of the 36 cases, only 7 reported no major losses. In the remaining 29 cases, major losses included parental divorce; never having known their father (or minimal contact with the father); absent mother; having to leave or being separated from the primary caregiver; murder or death of a parent, close family member, or significant other; and spontaneous or induced abortions.

Table 7.1 illustrates the correlations between high-risk behaviors in pregnant adolescents. Sexual activity most powerfully correlates with delinquency ($p<0.001$) and alcohol use ($p<0.01$). It also correlates with nicotine and drug use ($p<0.05$). In addition, substance use (nicotine, alcohol, and drugs) covary in this population, with alcohol and drug use with the most powerful correlations ($p<0.01$), then nicotine and alcohol ($p<0.01$), and then nicotine and drug use ($p<0.05$).

TABLE 7.1
Correlations between High Risk Behaviors in Pregnant Adolescents

MPHQ	Nic	Alc	Drug	Sex
Alc	.46[b]			
Drug	.40[a]	.80[c]		
Sex	.34[a]	.44[b]	.34[a]	
Del	.40[a]	.53[c]	.74[c]	.51[c]

[a] = p<0.05
[b] = p<0.01
[c] = p<0.001

Table 7.2 illustrates correlations between high-risk behaviors and the CDI and losses in pregnant adolescents. The CDI correlates with increasing significance with sexual activity ($p<0.01$), alcohol ($p<0.01$), drug use ($p<0.001$), and delinquent behaviors ($p<0.001$). It also correlates with losses. In addition, the CDI correlates with losses ($p\leq0.05$). The losses also correlate with alcohol ($p\leq0.05$) and drug use ($p\leq0.05$).

DISCUSSION

There are clusters of high-risk behaviors that covary in this pregnant adolescent population. Specifically, substance use (nicotine,

TABLE 7.2
Correlations between High-Risk Behaviors and the CDI and Losses in Pregnant
Adolescents

MPHQ					
	Nic	Alc	Drug	Sex	Del
CDI	.22	.47[b]	.55[c]	.50[b]	.61[c]
Losses	−.05	.41[a]	.40[a]	.15	.30

[a] = p<0.05
[b] = p<0.01
[c] = p<0.001

alcohol, and drug use) covary in this population as has been reported by Amaro, Zuckerman, and Cabral (1989) and Kokotailo, Adger, Duggan, Repke, and Joffe (1992). This is particularly worrisome given the implications of substance use in regard to teratogenicity and furthering the already present risk of complicated pregnancy. In addition, sexual activity correlates with substance use, increasing the likelihood of reproductive morbidity. All of these high-risk behaviors, with the exception of nicotine, covary with depression. In addition, losses covary with alcohol and drug use in this population. Adolescents who experience major losses may engage in high-risk behaviors to compensate for depressive feelings. Amaro et al. (1992) also found negative life events to be associated with drug use in the pregnant teen population. In fact, sexual activity and resulting pregnancy may be an attempt to compensate for the loss. The clinician must become aware of the vulnerability of this population to high-risk behaviors and loss. Structured questionnaires may be an efficient way to identify these issues.

Pregnancy could be an ideal time to identify loss issues and high-risk behaviors (i.e., alcohol and drug use, and delinquent behaviors) in adolescents. Also pregnancy may be an ideal time to begin to mobilize constructive mechanisms to deal with loss. Interventions could include therapy, reentering school, and developing parenting skills.

The following case further highlights the association of adolescent pregnancy with loss, depression, and alcohol and drug use.

It also poignantly demonstrates the personal and family turmoil resulting from adolescent pregnancy. The pregnancy can be seen as one way the adolescent deals with major life stressors as well as being the source of stress.

This actual case was seen from evaluation, followed from immediately "prior to conception," to after the birth of her infant.

CASE REPORT

PRIOR TO CONCEPTION

Outpatient Evaluation

Chief complaint Mary is a 16-year-old, single, white female seen initially with her aunt who is her legal custodian. At the Youth Services Center at her high school she reported that she was having angry feelings directed toward her aunt, of wanting to punch or kill her, and that if given a chance, she would attempt this. She also reports intermittent feelings of suicidal ideation.

Present illness Mary does complain of episodes of depressed mood that are precipitated by stressors such as the 2-year anniversary of her mother's death. She recently has had dreams of her mother and her corpse, which have been quite upsetting to her. She describes herself as being very irritable, oftentimes smiling while hurting on the inside, sleeping too much, having a variable appetite, and having difficulty concentrating. She has also recently been truant from school and has been hanging out in the woods behind the school. She recently drank alcohol and become intoxicated on one occasion while skipping school. She does have a good relationship with a boyfriend, but she adds she does not want to "get close to anyone." She denies that she uses alcohol or drugs regularly but does admit to experimentation.

Her aunt reported that at home, Mary is very difficult. She seems to "want everything her way," does not respond well to limits, and often seems very irritable. She is described as being "boy crazy."

Psychiatric history Her mother abused alcohol and tobacco during her pregnancy with Mary. Her mother was an alcoholic and apparently physically and verbally abusive, and died of cirrhosis when Mary was age 14. Her father also died apparently of a heart attack when Mary was age 13. She was sexually abused at the age of 8 by her stepfather. Mary was apparently removed from the home and placed in foster care when she was age 9. She stayed with a nonrelative foster family until she was placed with her aunt and uncle. She reports that her aunt convinced her that it was her fault that her mother had died. Her aunt was emotionally and physically abusive toward her and apparently had a history of substance abuse and frequent incarcerations. She was taken out of that home six months ago and now resides with a cousin.

Mary was seen in a psychiatric outpatient clinic at age 10 for evaluation for sexual abuse. Review of the records reveal that at that time she was very defensive and pseudomature, and did not deal directly with many issues relating to her abuse. Further, at age 15, on the one-year anniversary of her mother's death she took some pills at night, went to sleep, woke up the next day, attended school, but had some "ringing in her ears." She was taken to the emergency room but was discharged to outpatient psychiatric treatment which was never obtained.

Interview She initially avoided eye contact and answering questions directly. She denied any suicidal ideation, any homicidal ideation. She was administered the Beck Depression Scale which was significantly elevated at 28. On structured questionnaires she confirmed using hard drugs and narcotics from age 14 to 15, marijuana at age 14, played hooky 21 items, ran away from home 4 or 5 times, was expelled or suspended from school. It was easy for her to do bad things without feeling guilty, and she reported she was running with a bad crowd.

Follow-up She was followed as an outpatient. Six weeks after she was initially seen she presented to school intoxicated and was admitted to a psychiatric hospital.

AFTER CONCEPTION

Psychiatric Hospitalization

Admission Mary was hospitalized for 6 weeks on an adolescent unit. On admission she stated, "I guess I wanted to kill myself." She reported having been depressed for years and having recurrent suicidal ideation. Since the beginning of school this year, her grades deteriorated and she was sleeping more than usual. She felt she was worthless and was having trouble concentrating. Mary stated that the recurrent thoughts of hurting herself had come to a head on the day of admission when she was questioned about her drinking at school. She then decided to tell people how she really felt instead of hiding it from them.

Mary said she has problems with drinking and gets drunk several times a month in order to blot out her feelings. She also reported self-mutilation including carving on herself as a way to cope with depression. She described how her stepfather sexually abused her when she was 8 years old and that although this was reported, nothing happened. She also reported that a boy at school attempted to rape her this year and that there were no consequences for this boy.

Routine labs included initial Serum HCG which was reported as being negative.

Hospital Course She immediately began to deny that she had any problems. She was manipulative and attempted to bargain in order to be discharged. She made plans with another peer to elope after several days.

Further allegations of sexual abuse by her stepfather were reported to Social Services during her hospitalization. In the hospital Mary carved on her arm with a piece of plastic which resulted in superficial lacerations. She also threatened other patients. A repeat pregnancy test at 4 weeks into the admission returned positive. Her discharge plans were changed to include referral to a program for chemically dependent pregnant women. After confirmation of her pregnancy, the patient became demonstrably less irritable and moody.

Outpatient follow-up Mary was seen again in psychiatric consultation through the program for substance abusing women. She was 8 months pregnant.

At this time Mary's primary concerns were around starting school, having a new job, having a new baby, and not knowing how she was going to juggle all of this. She stated that things were looking up. She had her own apartment and would be going back to high school. She will be repeating the 10th grade, but felt she was used to being older than other students and that she could handle it. She was concerned about her financial limitations and only had $100 after paying the rent with her social security check, and she could not afford a phone.

Mary further elaborated on her memory of her childhood. Her parents were divorced when she was 3 years of age, and she only saw her father once at age 4 before his death when she was 13. She remembered his funeral and remembers fighting with his girl friend at that time. His girl friend said, "Are you a tramp or one of his bastard children?" She remembers crying over the casket and hugging her father. Her mother died from alcoholic cirrhosis when Mary was 14. Mary had been in foster care since age 9 because of abandonment. She had been left at a baby-sitter and her mother had failed to pick her up. She felt angry at her mother only because mother chose alcohol over her. She was told that if her mother stopped drinking she could return to her mother but her mother did not do this. She did have visits with her mother, but about half the time mother would be drunk or not show up for the visit. When she was 11 years of age her mother would not allow her to be placed for adoption so she was taken into the guardianship of her maternal aunt and uncle. This aunt had been her favorite, but with custody, the aunt fought with Mary, hit her, and made it clear to her that she was not one of her children.

She also took Mary's social security money. Mary was used as a baby-sitter and actually missed school because she was baby-sitting the younger children. Several months before her pregnancy she moved in with her cousin. She was very close to her and her child. Her cousin's husband is terminally ill and he was intolerant of Mary's acting out.

After discharge from the adolescent psychiatric unit, Mary did not return to her alcohol use or any other drug use. She went back to school and to living with her cousin. Her cousin and her husband were very disappointed in her pregnancy and Mary will not be allowed to return to her cousin's home after the baby is born. Mary got her own apartment and she continued to skip school, knowing that she had failed and not seeing the point of going to school.

She stated that she wanted to be pregnant and the baby gives unconditional love. Everyone needs to be loved. She knows she is loved by her aunt. Her baby won't know her past and will only know that she loves the baby completely.

On repeat of the Beck she scored a 9 and denied suicidal ideation.

After the Birth

Her social worker at the program for substance abusing pregnant women stated that Mary did well during the pregnancy at which time she was going to work daily and was well motivated. She was in an apartment with her baby but had been evicted regarding "noise" and having too many visitors. Her new boyfriend had a history of acting out. She was sleeping a lot. Her social worker requested that Mary return for follow-up. Mary did not come in.

Clinical Issues with the Stressed Pregnant Teen

This case report highlights a multitude of critical issues relevant to stress and teen pregnancy which are outlined in Table 7.3.

TABLE 7.3
Critical Concerns in Adolescent Pregnancy

A.	Covariation with High Risk Behaviors
	1. Suicidality
	2. Truancy
	3. Alcohol use
	4. Marijuana use
	5. Self-mutilation
B.	Family Dysfunction
	1. Abuse
	2. Abandonment
	3. Multiple placements
	4. Uninvolved father figure
	5. Alcoholism
	6. Mother role "baby-sitter"
C.	Loss
D.	Psychiatric Disorders
	1. Depression
	2. Substance abuse
E.	Lack of Insight
F.	Sexual Trauma
	1. Rape
	2. Sexual abuse by stepfather
G.	Therapeutic Window of Pregnancy
H.	"Daily Living" Stresses of Adolescent Pregnancy
	1. Parenthood
	2. Job
	3. Finances
	4. Shelter
I.	Fantasies of What Baby Provides

The troubled pregnant teen may have to deal with a multitude of issues, some of which originate with their traumatic upbringing, their psychological makeup, and ongoing dysfunctional behaviors.

Family upbringing may involve themes of abuse, neglect, and loss. A father figure may be frequently absent and unavailable, or physically and sexually abusive. This absence undoes the more positive benefits of the adolescent mother's father being present, which has a positive influence on emotional security, vocational decisions, and peer relationships (Rich, 1991). However, the troubled teen may also have to deal with a mother figure who may be similarly absent, inadequate, and destructive. In fact a series of losses and abusive situations may occur. It is no wonder that these teens desperately seek out intimacy to address the void left by their childhoods. In addition to the hoped for intimacy sexual activity may bring, there is a promise of a baby to love and be loved by. Many adolescent girls see a natural bridge from pregnancy to establishment of a family with a commitment from the infant's father. In the first trimester, it is not uncommon for the teen's family and the baby's father to express anger and disowning the pregnant teen. This may be a particularly difficult time for the pregnant teen. As time progresses, loyalties may be declared, primarily from the pregnant teen's family. As the pregnancy progresses, the family can begin to identify and attach with "the child of their child." Increasing evidence suggests that this family and social support can positively influence the adolescent, her infant, and their interactions (Wilkerson, 1991). Further, adolescent mothers who remain at home are more likely to return to school and ultimately receive a high school diploma, and become less dependent on welfare (Furstenberg, 1976).

Regardless of the level of functioning of the family, Jemail and Nathanson (1987) have suggested that a family experiences three stages when confronted with an unwanted adolescent pregnancy: (1) a crisis stage, (2) a honeymoon stage, and (3) a reorganization phase. The crisis phase is experienced by the family as a stressful event where the family is forced to acknowledge the pregnancy, and debates options for resolution. Grandmothers, for the unmarried adolescent, assume a needed role model function. However, they can easily become a "substitute mother" which may impede normal parent–child development. Not all grandmothers, however, are eager to assume additional child care responsibilities often thrust upon them by their daughters. They may be gainfully employed with little spare time available for additional responsibilities of motherhood or be emotionally unprepared. Excessive grandmother involvement may lead to confusion regarding lines of authority and roles (Cooley and Unger, 1991). Grandmother's presence may also inadvertently encourage the teen mother to be less attentive to her child (Rich, 1991). However, it is interesting to note that pregnant adolescents using alcohol and other drugs were less likely to have their own mothers in their home (Kokotailo et al. 1992).

It is reported that siblings often feel displaced, and in turn, the adolescent mother and baby compete for parental recognition and acceptance.

Adolescent fathers have unrealistic expectations of their infants' capabilities, express strong positive desires for the women they impregnated, a desire to participate in the naming of the child, a willingness to meet financial responsibilities, and a desire to establish a positive relationship with the impregnated girl's family (Wilkerson, 1991). Even so, this attachment to the unborn child is more difficult for the male. His interest may be more in multiple conquests and less in commitment (Schofield, 1965). Cevera (1991) found unwed adolescent fathers were often rejected and looked upon with disfavor by the adolescent girls' parents, particularly by mother, who feared competing loyalties and perceived the family would more than likely have to assume financial obligations. The potential unavailability may counter the potential availability of the baby's father to enhance a teenage mother's self-worth, sense of maternal competency, and attachment to the baby (Thompson, 1986).

In addition to attempting to make a family, the adolescent female may try to use her sexuality in an "aggressive, masterful" way. Prior to the pregnancy she may have been a sexual victim. If she initiates a sexual contact she is no longer the victim but the master. Even if there is no abuse, but paternal loss, the female adolescent may attempt to use her sexuality to "secure" a male relationship.

The pregnant teen may have been forced into a mother role for much of her young life. Neglect by one or both parents may have mandated her to care for her siblings. A pregnancy may be seen as a more just continuation of that role or as a ticket out of being "child labor" with little realization of the work that lies ahead with her new infant and family.

The stressed pregnant teen may have accompanying psychiatric difficulties. Alcohol and substance abuse may covary with unplanned sexual behavior (Jessor and Jessor, 1977). Further alcohol and substance abuse may contribute to disinhibition of both sexual partners. In addition, the female may be less in control while intoxicated and less capable of deflecting sexual advances. Obviously the use of alcohol and drugs during pregnancy can complicate the course of the pregnancy and the outcome. These infants are at increased risk for many problems including Sudden Infant Death Syndrome (SIDS), infections, developmental delays, and speech pathologies. Central nervous system injuries may manifest as behavioral disorders, irritability, and hypersensitivity to stimuli in the environment, and long-term disorders, such as Attention Deficit Hyperactivity Disorder, learning disabilities, and aggressive behavioral tendencies (Chasnoff, Burns, Burns, and Schnoll, 1986; Lindo, 1987; Brown and Zuckerman, 1991). The prospects of a teen mother raising a behaviorally disturbed cocaine baby or a child with fetal alcohol syndrome is particularly distressing. Other deviant behaviors frequently accompany unplanned and frequent sexual behavior. Jessor and Jessor (1977) describe this cluster of high-risk behaviors as "problem behaviors" that can include drug and alcohol use, truancy and delinquent type behaviors.

In addition to frank psychiatric disorders, the pregnant teen may be sorely deficient in insight, mastery, and planning. When asked about whether a pregnancy was planned, the teen frequently pauses and almost seems taken aback with the idea of "planning." "I was going to go to family planning." "I tried the pill but I got a headache" are frequent comments. In addition, it is rare that an adolescent female will have any expectations that her partner should use birth control. Focus of control is external (Morrison, 1985). Things happen and there is no planning. This inability to plan and take charge can persist throughout pregnancy and into mothering.

There does appear to be some affective and impulsive stabilization for some pregnant mothers during midtrimester. A calmness with a view of the future can occur. Constructive plans and behavior with the new infant in mind can occur. A new motivation to give up drug and alcohol and even nicotine use can be seen. This change may come from a sense of wholeness that comes with the symbiotic love of the unborn child. The teen may be able to fight for a baby even though they could not fight for themselves. Instead of identifying with the aggressor, the teen can identify with the baby and decide to give to them in a way that she was never given to. Of course planning and implementing these changes can be miles apart. The teen with great plans and limited resources and ability can become terribly disheartened and revert to previous destructive behaviors.

This case demonstrates the layers of knowledge. It takes time and practice for the teen to begin to put her feelings into words and thoughts. The stressed teen may have had years of relationships that completely undermined the ability to trust. For the teen, to be able to first articulate, and then begin to share feelings, may be a monumental task. This pregnancy may provide a small window of opportunity with its decrease in acting out behavior and new cathexis to a developing relationship. During this time strategies to involve the pregnant adolescent in therapy, education and group support should receive maximum effort.

REFERENCES

Amaro, H., Zuckerman, B., & Cabral, H. (1989), Drug use among adolescent mothers: Profile at risk. *Pediatrics*, 84:144–151.

Beck, A. T., Ward, C. H., & Medelson, M., (1961), An inventory for measuring depression. *Arch. Gen. Psychiatry*, 4:561–571.

Brown, E. R., & Zuckerman, B. (1991), The infant of the drug-abusing mother. *Pediatric Ann.*, 20:555–563.

Brown, G. W., & Harris, T. (1978), *Social Origins of Depression*. London: Tavistock.

Brown, H., Adams, R. G., & Kellan, S. G. (1981), The longitudinal study of teenage motherhood and symptoms of distress: The Woodlawn community epidemiological project. *Res. & Commun. Ment. Health*, 2:183–213.

Cevera, N. (1991), Unwed teenage pregnancy: Family relationships with the father of the baby. *J. Contemp. Hum. Serv.*, 72:29–37.

Chasnoff, I. J., Burns, K. A., Burns, W. J., & Schnoll, S. H. (1986), Prenatal drug exposure: Effects on neonatal and infant growth and development. *Neurobehav. Toxicol. & Terat.*, 8:357–362.

Colletta, N. D. (1983), At risk for depression: A study of young mothers. *J. Genet. Psychol.*, 142:301–310.

Cooley, M., & Unger, D. (1991), The role of family support in determining developmental outcomes in children of teen mothers. *Child Psychiatry & Hum. Develop.*, 21:217–233.

Furstenberg, F. F., Jr. (1976), The social consequences of teenage parenthood. *Fam. Plan. Perspect.*, 8:148–164.

Hollingsworth, D. R., & Kreuther, A. K. (1981), Letter. Teenage pregnancy. *N. Eng. J. Med.*, 304:121.

Hundleby, J. D., Carpenter, R. A., Ross, R. A., & Mercer, G. W. (1982), Adolescent drug use and other behaviors. *J. Child. Psychol. Psychiatry*, 23:61–68.

Jemail, J., & Nathanson, M. (1987), Adolescent single parent families. *Fam. Ther. Coll.*, 23:61–71.

Jessor, R., & Jessor, S. L. (1977), *Problem Behavior and Psychological Development: A Longitudinal Study of Youth*. New York: Academic Press.

Jones, E. F., Forrest, J. D., Goldmen, N., Henshaw, S. K., Lincoln, R., Rossoff, J. I., & Wulf, D. (1985), Teenage pregnancy in developed countries: Determinants and policy implications. *Fam. Plan. Persp.*, 17:53–63.

Kaplan, S. L., Landau, B., Weinhold, C., & Shenken, I. R. (1984), Adverse health behaviors and depressive symptomatology in adolescents. *J. Amer. Acad. Child Psychiatry*, 233:595–601.

Kokotailo, P. K., Adger, H., Duggan, A. K., Repke, J., & Joffe, A. (1992), Cigarette, alcohol, and other drug use by school-age pregnant adolescents: Prevalence, detection, and associated risk factors. *Pediatrics*, 90:328–334.

Kovacs, M. (1983), *The Children's Depression Inventory: A Self-Rated Depression Scale for School-Aged Youngsters*. Typescript.

Lindo, M. (1987), Drug addiction: Its effects on mother and baby. *Midwifery*, 3:82–91.

McArnarey, E. R., & Hendee, W. R. (1989), Adolescent pregnancy and its consequences. *J. Amer. Med. Assn.*, 262:74–82.

McGee, R., Williams, S., Kashani, T. H., & Silva, P. A. (1983), Prevalence of self-reported depressive symptoms and associated social factors in mothers in Dunedin. *Brit. J. Psychiatry*, 143:473–479.

Morrison, D. M. (1985), Adolescent contraceptive behavior: A review. *Psycholog. Bull.*, 98:538–568.

Mulcahey, K. M. (1990), Adolescent pregnancy: Prevalence, health and psychosocial risks. In: *Nutritional Management of the Pregnant Adolescent*, ed. M. Story. Washington, DC: National Institute of Health, pp. 1–6.

Orr, D. P., Brack, C. J., & Ingersoll, G. (1988), Pubertal maturation and cognitive maturity in adolescents. *J. Adol. Health Care*, 4:273–279.

Paton, S., Kessler, R., & Kandel, D. (1977), Depressive mood and adolescent illicit drug use: A longitudinal analysis. *J. Genet. Psychol.,* 131:267–289.

Raines, T. (1991), Family-focused prevention of adolescent Pregnancy. *Birth Defects Original Article Series,* 21:87–103.

Rich, O. (1991), Family-focused prevention of adolescent pregnancy. *Birth Defects Original Article Series,* 21:137–154.

Rutter, M. (1986), The developmental psychopathology of depression: Issues and perspectives. In: *Depression in Young People: Developmental and Clinical Perspectives,* ed. M. Rutter, C. Izard, & P. Read. New York: Guilford Press, pp. 3–32.

Sadler, L. S., & Catrone, J. C. (1983), The adolescent parent: A dual developmental crisis. *J. Adol. Health Care,* 4:100–105.

Schofield, M. (1965), *The Sexual Behavior of Young People.* London: Longmans Green.

Tanner, J. M. (1962), *Growth at Adolescence.* Boston, MA: Blackwell.

——— (1978), *Fetus Into Man: Physical Growth from Conception to Maturity.* Cambridge, MA: Harvard University Press.

Thompson, M. (1986), The influence of supportive relations on the psychological well-being of teenage mothers. *Soc. Forces,* 64:1006–1024.

Wilkerson, N. N. (1991), Family focused secondary prevention with the pregnant adolescent and adolescent father. *Birth Defects Original Article Series,* 27:116–130.

Zuckerman, B. S., Walker, D. K., Frank,, D. A., Chase, C., & Hamburg, B. (1984), Adolescent pregnancy: Biobehavioral determinants of outcomes. *J. Pediatrics,* 105:857–863.

——— Amaro, H., & Beardslee, W. (1987), Mental health of adolescent mothers: The implications of depression and drug use. *JDBP,* 8:111–116.

Chapter 8
Life Events and Adolescent Suicidal Behavior

ERIK J. DE WILDE, PH.D.,
AND INEKE C. W. M. KIENHORST, PH.D.

Although suicides in adolescence occur less often than in older age groups, taking all causes of death the proportion of suicides is higher among adolescents than among older groups. In the World Health Organization *Annual* (WHO, 1989), suicide ranked among the two or three leading causes of death for those 15 to 24 years of age in the 39 member states of the United Nations that report data on mortality. In these countries, 9 to 21 percent of all deaths among adolescent males aged 15 to 24 are caused by suicides, 6 to 28 percent for females.

Also, even more than actual suicides, efforts in clinical practice and research deal with nonfatal suicide attempts. Several studies have shown that many suicides are the last in a series of suicide attempts, making previous suicidal behavior the most powerful predictor of future suicide (Van Egmond and Diekstra, 1989). In follow-up studies among adults, it was estimated that 10 to 14 percent of those who attempted suicide will eventually die because of suicide (Diekstra and Moritz, 1987), a percentage that will certainly be lower in adolescence given the attempted suicide rates in this group. A frequency study in the Netherlands (Kienhorst, De Wilde, Van den Bout, Broese van Groenou, Diekstra,

161

and Wolters, 1990) demonstrated that in the group aged 14 to 21 the attempted suicide rates are unmistakably high: approximately 1 out of 50 Dutch adolescents was ever engaged in this behavior. Most of these adolescents are female (boy:girl ratio is about 2:3). Anonymous surveys in the United States have estimated the prevalence rate of attempted suicides to be significantly higher: 8.4 percent (Smith and Crawford, 1986) and 9 percent (Harkavy-Friedman, Asnis, Boeck, and DiFiore, 1987). Trends in the hospital discharge rates for attempted suicide (the only official source and thus an underestimate of attempted suicides) appear to be closely related to the suicide mortality statistics, which are rising (Diekstra, 1992; WHO, 1982).

Among other things, these figures raise the question of what characteristics distinguish young people who are at high risk for suicide. In his inspiring book *Adolescent Suicide,* Jacobs (1971) was among the first to recognize life events in this respect. He compared 50 adolescent suicide attempters with matched control subjects from schools and hypothesized that the first of four phases leading to a suicide attempt consists of a "longstanding history of problems (from childhood to the onset of adolescence)" and the second phase is a period of "escalation of problem" (since the onset of adolescence and in excess of those "normally" associated with adolescence) (Jacobs, 1971, p. 64). Jacobs' phases have important implications for prevention of adolescent suicidal behavior. First of all, they imply that those children who display a multitude of problems in their childhood are more at risk for attempting suicide during their adolescence. This would imply that the detection of risk of this behavior could start at a very young age. Second, the notion that attempted suicide is based on problems seems straightforward and logical, but is often not recognized as such. Suicide itself is often romanticized by making it appear as a logical, rational, well-thought choice to end one's life instead of a desperate and emotional method of solving one's problems. This would confirm the much believed idea that learning adequate problem-solving strategies would be effective in preventing suicide. Unfortunately, Jacobs did not find adequate support for his valuable hypotheses. There was no systematic, well-described comparison of his two groups and he could therefore not supply sufficient empirical support for his "escalation of problems." An even more substantial critique concerns the *specificity* of his results: by comparing with a "normal" control group, he did not account for the possibility that stressful life events may play a role in the etiology of *any* abnormal problematic behavior.

Since then, several studies have compared suicidal adolescents with heterogeneous psychiatric groups of nonsuicidal adolescents (Stober, 1981; Taylor and Stansfeld, 1984; Khan, 1987) or with other clinical groups (Deykin, Alpert, and McNamarra, 1985; Slap, Vorters, Chaudhuri, and Centor, 1989). Friedman, Corn, Aronoff, Hurt, and Clarkin (1984) compared suicidal depressed adolescents with nonsuicidal depressed adolescents, but restricted their research to family history of illness. Chronic psychiatric illness of a parent (especially depression) was more frequently found among suicide attempters. Cohen-Sandler, Berman, and King (1982) compared suicidal children and young adolescents (5–14 years old) with depressed and other psychiatric control groups regarding life events during different developmental periods. They found that more life events were related to suicidal behavior with increasing age.

Almost 20 years after Jacobs, Spirito, Brown, Overholzer, and Fritz (1989), in their impressive review of attempted suicide in adolescence, can safely conclude that "Presence of stressful life events . . . seems to have important implications for understanding suicide attempts in children and adolescents" (Spirito et al., 1989, p. 348).

In this chapter, we will evaluate the discriminative value of life events between a group of adolescent suicide attempters, a group of depressed adolescents who never attempted suicide, as well as a group of nondepressed, nonsuicidal adolescents. To get an even finer description of the relation between the experience of life events and adolescent suicidal behavior, we will discuss the relation between the occurrence of events in our suicide attempter group and the *suicidal intent* with which the attempt was made.

METHOD

SUBJECTS

Three groups of subjects were asked to cooperate with this study. The first group was comprised of 41 girls and seven boys 14 to 21 years old (mean ± SD age = 17.5 ± 1.5 years) who attempted suicide 1 to 52 weeks before the measurement date. The second group consisted of 52 girls and 14 boys 14 to 21 years old (mean = 17.9 ± 1.6) who suffered from a depressed mood at the time of assessment and had never attempted suicide (the adolescents who suffered from a depressed mood will be referred to as "depressed adolescents" in the remainder of the text). The third group comprised 31 girls and 12 boys 14 to 21 years old (mean = 17.5 ± 1.3), randomly selected from a "normal" school population. The three groups were not matched, but there were no significant differences among them in relevant sociodemographic features such as age (F = 1.45, df = 2, 154, p = 0.24), sex (χ^2 = 2.43, df = 2, p = .30), and current type of school (χ^2 = 7.22, df = 4, p = 0.12).

Two methods were used to recruit subjects for this study. First, institutions for mental health care were asked for referrals, and second, 9393 secondary school students were screened (Kienhorst, De Wilde, Van den Bout, Diekstra, and Wolters, 1990). Approximately half of the suicide attempters and half of the depressed adolescents were recruited through the institutions of mental health care. The rest of the suicide attempters and depressed adolescents, as well as the entire group of normal adolescents, were recruited from among the 9393 secondary school students. The suicide attempters and the depressed adolescents did not differ significantly in this recruitment procedure (χ^2 = 3.0, df = 2, p = 0.08).

Almost two-thirds of the suicide attempters took an overdose of medicine or some toxic substance, one-quarter injured themselves, and the rest threw themselves in front of a moving vehicle, tried to hang themselves, or jumped from a height. The mean ±

SD score of the suicide attempters on the Suicide Intent Scale (Beck, Schuyler, and Herman, 1974), 6.8 ± 3.4, was comparable to that of 50 British adolescents who attempted suicide (Hawton, O'Grady, Osborn, and Cole, 1982). Three suicide attempters had scores of 13, indicative of a strong suicide intent. The mean risk score of all 48 suicide attempters on the Risk–Rescue Rating (Weisman and Worden, 1972) was 8.1 ± 2.1, indicative of a moderately low risk, and their rescue score on this scale was 11.6 ± 2.3, indicative of a moderately high rescue level.

The 66 depressed adolescents were tested for depression at two separate times. First, at the time of the screening procedure preceding the interview, they were selected randomly if they appeared to have a score of 46 or higher on the Zung Self-Rating Depression Scale (Zung, 1965) and had a score of at least 16 on the Depression Adjective Checklist (Lubin, 1967). The depressed adolescents referred from the institutions of mental health care met research diagnostic criteria (Spitzer, Endicott, and Robins, 1978) for major depressive disorder. The second assessment took place at the time of the interview. Subjects who had a score of 46 or higher on the Zung scale at that time were included in this study. Their mean score on the Zung scale was 51.9 ± 5.2, compared with 49.4 ± 11.7 for the suicide attempters and 33.5 ± 5.6 for the normal subjects.

For the normal comparison group, 45 students were initially selected at random for interview from among the secondary school students screened. The criteria for selection were that these students reported they had never made a suicide attempt and that they did not score higher than 46 on the Zung scale or 16 on the Depression Adjective Checklist. Nevertheless, at the time of interview, two students met the criteria for depression and were removed from the study, leaving 43 adolescents in the normal comparison group.

Measures

A semistructured interview including several self-report questionnaires was conducted with each subject by a graduate psychology student or a psychologist who was especially trained for this purpose. Before the actual data collection, a pilot study was carried out with eight adolescents; the interview was modified on the basis of the findings of this pilot study.

The *Life Event Time Schedule,* a part of the *Life History Interview* (Kienhorst, De Wilde, Diekstra, and Wolters, 1991), was developed for this study. The main objective of this instrument is to assess the occurrence of life events as well as when they took place. The Life Event Time Schedule consists of 77 items, chosen for their known importance regarding suicidal behavior. Nineteen of these items were examined for this study: serious illness, accident; change in living situation (e.g., a change from living with one's biological family to living with a foster family); change in caretaker (e.g., from two biological parents to one); separation of parents (parents living apart or divorced); reunion of parents; change of residence; death of a family member; events concerning the physical health of a family member (serious illness, hospital admission, becoming an invalid); events concerning the mental health of a family member (psychiatric hospital admission, nervous breakdown, contact with mental health institute); unemployment of a family member; imprisonment of a family member; sibling leaving home; change of school or type of school; repeating a class; ending a relationship; physical abuse; sexual abuse; and criminal events (breaking the law, prosecution, fine, or imprisonment). Because our primary interest lay in the occurrence of specific events, no effort was made to assign weights to the individual items.

The Suicide Intent Scale was constructed in 1974 by Beck, Schuyler, and Herman. Suicidal intent is defined as the seriousness or intensity of an attempter to terminate his or her life with the attempt. It is operationalized by adding the ratings on items such as: whether precautions were made to prevent discovery or intervention, the degree of planning, the purpose of the attempt. High scores denote a strong wish to end one's life with the intent, low scores denote the opposite. The interrater reliability between two interviewers on 45 cases was found to be .95, the internal reliability .82 (Beck et al., 1974).

The Risk-Rescue Rating Scale was designed by Weisman and Worden (1972). It operationalizes roughly the same content as the previous instrument, but discriminates between two separate constructs: the risk of the attempt (e.g., the agent used, level of consciousness, lesions/toxicity), and the possibility of rescue (e.g., location, accessibility to rescue, delay until discovery), both described by five items. The scores significantly discriminated suicides from suicide attempts and showed an interrater reliability ranging from .78 to .94 (Weisman and Worden, 1974).

DATA ANALYSIS

The number of events reported was analyzed separately for three time periods: up to 12 years of age; from 12 years of age until the date of suicide attempt or the date of the interview; and the last year before the suicide attempt or date of interview. Univariate comparisons were made with the Kruskal–Wallis nonparametric analysis of variance (Kruskal and Wallis, 1952). The distribution of the attained statistic, H, which was corrected for ties, is approximately by χ^2. To determine which groups were different from each other, a Tukey Honestly Significant Difference procedure (Winer, 1971) was performed whenever H reached significance. In addition, for significant differences the percentage of subjects in each group who experienced the event in a given period is described in the text. This indicates the *person-rate* frequency of the events, as opposed to the *event-rate* data given in the tables.

To determine the relation between the occurrence of the events and suicidal intent, the data of the suicide attempter group were analyzed by multiple regression analysis, with the intent, risk, and rescue scores as dependent variables in three separate analyses. All events were analyzed simultaneously, resulting in the final Beta coefficients representing the impact in the multivariate model of each event, controlled for by all others.

TABLE 8.1
**Number of Life Events Experienced by Adolescents Who Attempted Suicide,
Depressed Adolescents, and Normal Adolescents (significant only)**

	Suicide Attempters (n = 48)	Depressed Adolescents (n = 66)	Normal Adolescents (n = 43)	H	Tukey's HSD
Childhood					
Separation of Parents	.23	.06	.09	7.81^a	s-d
Physical Abuse	.19	.14	.00	6.29^a	s-n
Adolescence					
Change in Living Situation	1.15	.35	.09	21.77^c	s-dn
Change in Caretaker	.60	.24	.12	12.57^b	s-dn
Separation of Parents	.31	.11	.05	10.82^b	s-dn
Physical Abuse	.23	.29	.07	7.56^a	d-n
Sexual Abuse	.44	.26	.05	11.87^b	s-n
Preceding Year					
Change in Living Situation	.33	.08	.00	19.71^c	s-dn
Change in Caretaker	.13	.02	.00	10.57^b	s-dn
Separation of Parents	.10	.03	.00	6.28^a	s-n
Change of Residence	.17	.06	.00	6.03^a	s-n
Physical Health Event of Family Member	.04	.36	.07	13.71^b	d-sn
Mental Health Event of Family Member	.46	.18	.07	5.97^a	s-n
Repeating a Class	.10	.02	.00	8.29^a	s-dn
Sexual Abuse	.10	.05	.00	6.17^a	s-n

^{a}: $p < .05$; ^{b}: $p < .01$; ^{c}: $p < .001$
Data in this table have been previously published in *American Journal of Psychiatry* (1992), 149:45–51.

RESULTS

Table 8.1 shows the significant results only for the three periods: childhood, adolescence, and the year preceding the attempt (for the suicide attempters) or interview (for the two other groups). The childhood results indicate that suicide attempters differed from depressed adolescents in that they experienced more events of separation of their parents before the age of 12. This occurred in 11 (23%) of the suicide attempters, compared with four (6%)

of the depressed adolescents and four (9%) of the normal adolescents. Suicide attempters also differed from normal adolescents in that they reported more events of physical abuse before the age of 12 than did normal adolescents. Seven (15%) of the suicide attempters, seven (11%) of the depressed adolescents, and none of the normal adolescents reported physical abuse in childhood.

There were more differences among the three groups during adolescence. Suicide attempters differed from depressed and normal adolescents in that they experienced more changes in living situation and in caretaker as well as parental divorce or separation (of course, these variables are correlated). Twenty-one (44%) of the suicide attempters experienced changes in living situation, compared with 12 (18%) of the depressed adolescents and two (5%) of the normal adolescents. Eighteen (38%) of the suicide attempters reported changes in caretaker, compared with nine (14%) of the depressed adolescents and five (12%) of the normal adolescents. Thirteen (27%) of the suicide attempters experienced parental separation, compared with seven (11%) of the depressed adolescents and two (5%) of the normal adolescents. Suicide attempters differed from normal adolescents in that they reported more sexual abuse. Sixteen (33%) of the suicide attempters reported sexual abuse during adolescence, compared with 14 (21%) of the depressed adolescents and two (5%) of the normal adolescents.

Depressed adolescents reported more physical abuse during adolescence than did normal adolescents. Nineteen (29%) of the depressed adolescents reported physical abuse during adolescence, compared with 11 (23%) of the suicide attempters and three (7%) of the normal adolescents.

In the year preceding the suicide attempt or the year preceding the interview, suicide attempters experienced more changes in living situation and caretaker and more repetitions of a class than both other groups. Thirteen (27%) of the suicide attempters reported changes in living situation during the last year, compared with four (5%) of the depressed adolescents and none of the normal adolescents. Six (13%) suicide attempters, compared with one (2%) depressed adolescent and none of the normal adolescents, reported changes in caretaker. Five (10%) suicide attempters, compared with one (2%) depressed adolescent and none of the normal adolescents, reported repeating a class. Five (10%) suicide attempters, compared with two (3%) depressed adolescents and none of the normal adolescents, reported separation of parents. Six (13%) suicide attempters, compared with four (6%) depressed adolescents and none of the normal adolescents, reported changes of residence. Nine (19%) suicide attempters, compared with nine (14%) depressed adolescents and one (2%) normal adolescent, reported mental health events involving family members. Five (10%) suicide attempters, compared with two (3%) depressed adolescents and none of the normal adolescents, reported sexual abuse.

Depressed adolescents differed from both other groups in that they reported more physical health events of family members during the preceding year. Sixteen (24%) of the depressed adolescents reported such an event, compared with two (4%) of the suicide attempters and two (5%) of the normal adolescents.

TOTAL NUMBER OF EVENTS

Figure 8.1 gives the mean number of total events experienced by the subjects in each group. As can be seen, the overall differences between the three groups become larger throughout the lifetime period, with the largest differences in the preceding year. In childhood as well as adolescence, the suicide attempters differ from the normal as well as from the depressed group.

SUICIDAL INTENT, RISK, AND POSSIBILITY FOR RESCUE

Individually, the events do not relate strongly to the scale scores: only 3 out of the (19 times 3 =) 57 correlations are significant at a .05 level. On chance alone one could expect 2.85 significant differences. Multivariately, it is possible to combine the events in such a way that together they have more relation. By the direct method of the multiple regression analysis, more insight is given

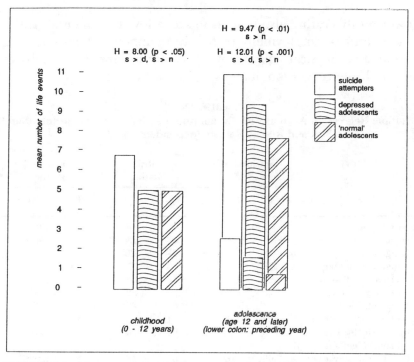

FIGURE 8.1. Mean number of life events during childhood, adolescence, and the year preceding the attempt/interview.

as regards the unique contribution of the variables. The overall predictability of the rescue ratings proved to be better (69% variance explained) than that of the suicidal intent (56% explained). A positive (that is, more events of this kind are related to a stronger intent to die with the suicide attempt) and significant influence is found by the leaving home of siblings and physical abuse. Accidents, imprisonment of family members, and sexual abuse show an opposite effect. It should be noted that these are "relative" descriptions: Virtually the entire group did not score high on the Suicide Intent Scale. Risk was significantly influenced only by the unemployment of family members and, negatively, by criminal events. The degree of rescueability was positively related to the report of illnesses and accidents, imprisonment of family members, and criminal events. Those attempters who scored lower on this rating also tended to score lower on mental health events and unemployment of family members, siblings leaving home, and physical abuse. Table 8.2 summarizes the results of the multiple regression analysis.

TABLE 8.2
Multiple Regression Analysis with Events (independent) on Suicide Intent and Risk and Rescue Ratings (dependent variables)

	Suicide Intent Scale		Risk Rating		Rescue Rating	
	β	t	β	t	β	t
Serious Illness	−.08	−.52	−.03	−.18	.27	2.06*
Accident	−.34	−2.10*	.03	.23	.30	2.49*
Change in Living Situation	.18	.74	−.27	−1.26	−.01	−.03
Change in Caretaker	−.03	−.12	.13	.55	.08	.42
Separation of Parents	−.29	−1.33	−.16	−.83	−.08	−.48
Reunion of Parents	.27	1.14	.27	1.32	−.32	−1.81
Change of Residence	.03	.18	.04	.23	.04	.29
Death of Family Member	−.20	−1.09	.01	.08	.12	.83
Physical Health Event of Family Member	−.03	−.21	.03	.20	.04	.35
Mental Health Event of Family Member	.00	.02	−.07	−.48	−.27	−2.08[a]
Unemployment of Family Member	.11	.53	.46	2.61[b]	−.36	−2.33[a]
Imprisonment of Family Member	−.44	−2.19[a]	−.21	−1.18	.69	4.37[c]
Sibling Leaving Home	.35	2.25[a]	.27	1.90	−.43	−3.45[c]
Change of School or Type of School	.10	.63	−.09	−.61	.12	.95
Repeating a Class	.33	1.84	.32	1.81	−.23	−1.49
Ending a Relationship	.14	.78	.24	1.50	−.01	−.05
Physical Abuse	.72	3.36[b]	.18	.98	−.77	−4.74[c]
Sexual Abuse	−.66	−2.88[b]	.25	1.22	.17	.96
Criminal Events	−.20	−1.14	−.43	−2.84[b]	.38	2.87[b]
Multiple correlation:	.75		.77		.83	

[a]: $p < .05$; [b]: $p < .01$; [c]: $p < .001$

Discussion

This study compared adolescent suicide attempters with both depressed and nondepressed adolescents who never made a suicide attempt with respect to the occurrence of life events during childhood, during adolescence, and during the year before the attempt or the year before the date of the interview. In all three time periods, suicide attempters reported more negative life events than did "normal" adolescents. Suicide attempters also reported more negative life events, especially in childhood and during the preceding year, than did depressed adolescents. The overall differences among groups in life events during childhood became larger during adolescence and still larger during the year before the attempt or interview.

In this respect our study seems to confirm the two cited hypotheses of Jacobs (1971), who compared adolescent suicide attempters with normal matched control subjects. Our study seems to confirm Jacobs' hypothesis that suicide attempters have a long-standing history of problems during childhood and adds the evidence that this is true not only when suicide attempters are compared with normal subjects but also when they are compared with depressed adolescents. The overall number of life events suggests that the risk of a suicide attempt during adolescence might be detected during childhood.

In our comparisons of suicide attempters with normal adolescents during adolescence and during the preceding year, our study confirms Jacobs' suggestion that suicidal adolescents experience a period of escalation of problems starting at the onset of puberty. With respect to life events in adolescence, however, our group of depressed adolescents were "in the middle" of the other two groups. During the preceding year, our suicide attempters experienced considerably more problematic life events than did both depressed and normal adolescents.

These results stand for the person-rate frequencies as well as the event-rate frequencies, excluding the possibility that certain statistics may be blurred by the fact that a few individuals in one group experienced an excessive amount of life events.

Looking at the type of events, one can observe that suicide attempters suffered from more turmoil in family life during all three time periods. In childhood this was characterized by separation or divorce of parents and unemployment of family members. Under these unstable familial circumstances, characterized by immoderate changes in living situation and caretaker during adolescence, the suicide attempter was characterized by more periods of sexual abuse. During the last year before the attempt, further social instability—changes in residence and repetition of a class—occurred.

Regarding the finding that adolescent suicide attempters experienced more abuse during adolescence, an extra remark may be appropriate. Our findings, plus those of Deykin et al. (1985), suggest that physical and sexual abuse is an important field of attention when dealing with adolescent suicide attempters.

The variables that discriminated between our three groups appeared not to be predictive of the suicidal intent with which the attempt was made. The results of those events that were related (within a multivariate model) to suicidal intent and risk and rescue ratings are difficult to interpret, as they do not tell us anything about the *motive* with which the attempt was made. One could summarize this as follows: The experience of negative life events may have an impact on the decision to attempt suicide but do not predispose an adolescent to a suicidal death. Given the substantial ratio between nonlethal and lethal suicide attempts, larger in this age group than in any other, this seems an important subject to investigate further.

To make a correct estimation of the value of our findings, methodological remarks should be kept in mind. For pragmatic reasons, studying a reasonably large group of adolescent suicide attempters almost requires the use of a retrospective method to investigate changes during childhood. Comments suggest that making use of semistructured interviews may be better than using self-report questionnaires (Paykel, 1983) and that predefined events may be more reliable than open-ended questions requiring spontaneous recall. In the present study, both preferable choices were made. In addition, each reported event was discussed in reasonable detail: the interviewer asked when exactly the event took place, how long it lasted, who was involved. This procedure, too, may very well increase reliability. However, adolescents who recently attempted suicide may have a different recollection of various life events, influenced by their mood, for example (Teasdale, 1983). Apart from the fact that this may apply to depressed adolescents as well, we think it unlikely that children easily forget events such as parental separation or divorce or repeating a class.

Another possible critique was formulated by Brown (1972), who described "retrospective contamination," which for this study suggests that the suicide attempters reported more problematic life events to account for their attempt. In the present study, this might have been the case for the suicide attempters as well as the depressed adolescents, who might have reported more events to account for their depressed mood.

The life events considered here were not studied as causes for suicidal behavior. They are possibly interrelated: one event may lead to another, and they may cluster and have cumulative effects. For example, the divorce of parents may be related to changes in living situation and caretaker and may precede the reunion of parents. Moreover, this study focused on the importance of life events alone regarding suicidal behavior. Of course, this implies a considerable simplification of processes that adolescents in general and suicidal adolescents in particular go through during childhood and adolescence. For instance, the present study did not investigate any constitutional or neurobiological factors. In addition, psychological variables, which probably have great importance in suicidal behavior (Spirito et al., 1989; Keinhorst, De Wilde, Van den Bout, Diekstra, and Wolters, 1990), were not investigated here. This should be kept in mind as well when assessing the importance of life events in suicidal behavior.

In spite of these methodological questions, we conclude from these results that adolescent suicide attempters are different from both normal and depressed adolescents with regard to life events. The suicide attempt seems embedded in a situation of not just the problems every adolescent has to deal with but turmoil in family life, already rooted in childhood and not stabilizing during adolescence, in combination with stressful life events during the period of adolescence and social instability in the year preceding the attempt.

References

Beck, A. T., Schuyler, D., & Herman, J. (1974), Development of suicidal intent scales. In: *The Prediction of Suicide,* ed. A. T. Beck, H. L. P. Resnick, & D. J. Lettieri. Baltimore, MD: Charles Press.

Brown, G. W. (1972), Life-events and pyschiatric illness: Some thoughts on methodology and causality. *J. Psychosom. Res.,* 16:311–320.

Cohen-Sandler, R., Berman, A. L., & King, R. A. (1982), Life stress and symptomatology: Determinants of suicidal behavior in children. *J. Amer. Acad. Child Psychiatry,* 21:178–186.

Deykin, W. Y., Alpert, J. J., & McNamara, J. J. (1985), A pilot study of the effect of exposure to child abuse or neglect on adolescent suicidal behavior. *Amer. J. Psychiatry,* 142:1299–1303.

Diekstra, R. F. W. (1992), *Suicide and Parasuicide among Adolescents and Young Adults.* Paper presented at the Academia Europaea Study Group on Problems of Youth, June.

——— Moritz, B. J. M. (1987), Suicidal behaviour among adolescents: An overview. In: *Suicide in Adolescence,* ed. R. F. W. Diekstra & K. Hawton. Dordrecht: Martinus Nijhoff, pp. 7–24.

Friedman, R. C., Corn, R., Aronoff, M. S., Hurt, S. W., & Clarkin, J. F. (1984), The seriously suicidal adolescent: Affective and character pathology. In: *Suicide in the Young,* ed. H. S. Sudak, A. B. Ford, & N. B. Rushforth. Boston: John Wright, pp. 209–226.

Gispert, M., Wheeler, K., Marsh, L., & Davis, M. S. (1985), Suicidal adolescents: Factors in evaluation. *Adol.,* 20:753–762.

Goodyer, I. M. (1990), Annotation: Recent life events and psychiatric disorder in school age children. *J. Child Psychol. Psychiatry,* 31:839–848.

——— Kolvin, I., & Gatzanis, S. (1985), Recent undesirable life events and psychiatric disorder in childhood and adolescence. *Brit. J. Psychiatry,* 147:517–523.

Harkavy-Friedman, J. M., Asnis, G. M., Boeck, M., & DiFiore, J. (1987), Prevalence of specific suicidal behaviors in a high school sample. *Amer. J. Psychiatry,* 144(9):1203–1206.

Hawton, K., O'Grady, J., Osborn, M., & Cole, D. (1982), Adolescents who take overdoses: Their characteristics, problems and contacts with helping agencies. *Brit. J. Psychiatry,* 140:118–123.

Jacobs, J. (1971), *Adolescent Suicide*. New York: Wiley-Interscience.

Khan, A. U. (1987), Heterogeneity of suicidal adolescents. *J. Amer. Acad. Child & Adol. Psychiatry*, 1:92–96.

Kienhorst, I. C. W. M. (1988), *Suïcidaal Gedrag bij Jongeren. Onderzoek naar Omvang en Kenmerken. (Suicidal Behavior among Children and Adolescents. A Study of the Frequencies and Characteristics*. Doctoral dissertation. Baarn: Ambo.

———— De Wilde, E. J., Diekstra, R. F. W., Wolters, W. H. G. (1991), Construction of an index for predicting suicide attempts in depressed adolescents. *Brit. J. Psychiatry*, 159:676–682.

———— ———— Van den Bout, J., Broese van Groenou, M. I., Diekstra, R. F. W., & Wolters, W. H. G. (1990), Self-reported suicidal behavior in Dutch secondary education students. *Suicide Life-Threat. Behav.*, 20:101–112.

———— ———— ———— Diekstra, R. F. W., & Wolters, W. H. G. (1990), Characteristics of suicide attempters in a population-based sample of Dutch adolescents. *Brit. J. Psychiatry*, 156:243–248.

Kruskal, W. H., & Wallis, W. A. (1952), Use of ranks in one-criterion variance analysis. *J. Amer. Stat. Assn.*, 47:583–621.

Lubin, B. (1967), *Depression Adjective Checklist: Manual*. San Diego, CA: Education and Industrial Service.

Paykel, E. S. (1983), Methodological aspects of life events research. *J. Psychosom. Res.*, 19:87–89.

Slap, G. B., Vorters, D. F., Chaudhuri, S., & Centor, R. M. (1989), Risk factors for attempted suicide during adolescence. *Pediatrics*, 84:762–772.

Smith, K., & Crawford, S. (1986), Suicidal behavior among "normal" high school students. *Suicide & Life-Threat. Behavior*, 16(3):313–325.

Spirito, A., Brown, L., Overholzer, J., & Fritz, G. (1989), Attempted suicide in adolescence: A review and critique of the literature. *Clin. Psychol. Rev.*, 9:335–363.

Spitzer, R. L., Endicott, J., & Robins, E. (1978), *Research Diagnostic Criteria (RDC) for a Selected Group of Functional Disorders*. New York: Clinical Research Branch of the NIMH.

Stober, B. (1981), Social environment and suicidal children and adolescents: A comparative study. In: *Depression et Suicide*, ed. J. P. Soubrier. Paris: Pergamon Press.

Taylor, E. A., & Stansfeld, S. A. (1984), Children who poison themselves: 1. A clinical comparison with psychiatric controls. *Brit. J. Psychiatry*, 145:127–135.

Teasdale, J. D. (1983), Negative thinking in depression: Cause, effect or reciprocal relationship? *Adv. Behav. Res. Ther.*, 5:3–25.

Van Egmond, M., & Diekstra, R. F. W. (1989), The predictability of suicidal behaviour: The results of a meta-analysis of published suicides. In: *Suicide Prevention: The Role of Attitude and Imitation*, ed. R. F. W. Diekstra, R. A. Maris, S. Platt, A. Schmidtke, & G. Sonneck. Leiden, Netherlands: Brill.

World Health Organization (1982), *WHO Reports and Studies No. 74: Changing Patterns in Suicide Behaviour*. Copenhagen: WHO/Euro.

———— (1989), *World Health Statistics Annual*. Geneva: World Health Organization.

Weisman, A. D., & Worden, J. W. (1974), Risk-rescue rating in suicide assessment. *Arch. Gen. Psychiatry*, 26:737–746.

Winer, B. J. (1971), *Statistical Principles in Experimental Design*, 2nd. ed. Tokyo: McGraw-Hill Koyakusha.

Zung, W. W. K. (1965), A selfrating depression scale. *Arch. Gen. Psychiatry*, 12:63–70.

Chapter 9
Life Events and Substance Abuse during Adolescence

PETER VIK, PH.D., AND SANDRA A. BROWN, PH.D.

Since Holmes and Rahe (1967) introduced the Life Change Inventory, many researchers have demonstrated a link between stressful life events and physical and mental health problems. In the early 1970s, alcohol researchers began documenting an association between life stress and alcohol use. Hore (1971a,b) found that relapses among abstinent alcoholics were often preceded by a stressful experience. Other researchers have demonstrated a higher incidence of negative life events among alcohol abusers who relapsed than among abusers who remained abstinent (e.g., Billings and Moos, 1983; Miller, Hedrick, and Taylor, 1983; Rosenberg, 1983; Brown, Vik, Patterson, Grant, and Schuckit, 1995).

Stressful life experiences have been implicated in adolescent substance use and abuse as well (Hendren, 1990). A number of studies have linked stressful life events and adolescent substance use (e.g., Bruns and Geist, 1984; Newcomb and Harlow, 1986; Wills, 1986; V. Johnson and Pandina, 1991). Stressful life experiences and adolescent substance use, however, must be understood in the context of adolescent development as developmental issues influence the nature of adolescent stress, teens' perceptions of stressors, and the manner in which teens react, cope, and adapt to their stressful life experiences.

Characteristics of Adolescent Life Stress

Adolescence is marked by a series of developmental stages with unique biological, psychological, and social changes. Conceptualization of psychosocial stress and stressful life events, in the context of rapid development during adolescence, raises questions regarding causality, severity, and chronicity of such life adversity. In addition to general stress issues, adolescence poses several unique concerns for the study of psychosocial stress, including normative versus nonnormative stressors, age and developmental factors, and gender issues. The following sections briefly review these key concerns regarding stressful life events among adolescents.

Causal Relationship

Stressful life events have been hypothesized to impact on mental and physical health. Mental and physical health outcomes attributed to stress may in turn generate further psychosocial stress. Stressful life events and alcohol use share a similar reciprocal relationship (Finney, Moos, and Mewborn, 1980; Allan and Cooke, 1985). Increased stress may provoke alcohol use, while drinking also produces negative life consequences (e.g., drunk driving arrests) which contribute to the experience of life adversity. Further, in some cases, cessation or reduction in alcohol or drug use may result in greater psychosocial demands than failing to change substance abuse patterns (Brown, 1993).

To demonstrate an etiological role for stressful life events in substance abuse, researchers must attend to two key methodological issues. First, a temporal relationship in which stress precedes substance use must be demonstrated. While retrospective and cross-sectional designs help us to learn the magnitude of association, they fail to adequately demonstrate temporal relationships and therefore limit causal inferences. Prospective designs are required to demonstrate a causal role for life stress in the limitation or exacerbation of substance use. The second issue which complicates causal interpretations is the inclusion of alcohol or drug related events in aggregate indices of stressful life events. Conservative attempts to demonstrate that substance use is in part a consequence of stress are weakened by the inclusion of life stresses occurring subsequent to or resulting from substance use. We have argued previously (Brown, Vik et al., 1990) that a conservative approach demarcating the temporal sequence of stress and substance use, and empirical connections between substance use and specific stressors, permits greater confidence that the observed relationship reflects an etiological relationship between stressful life events and substance use. Failure to address sequence and consequence issues complicates any demonstration of a meaningful causal relationship between stressful life events and substance use among teens.

SEVERITY OF STRESSFUL EVENTS

Life adversity can range in severity from benign daily hassles to acute events posing tremendous personal threat to an individual (Grant, Brown, Harris, McDonald, Patterson, and Trimble, 1989). Some formulations of life stress consider any event as contributing to an overall level of stress (i.e., adaptational demand), while other perspectives may emphasize only severe or protracted stressors as having a significant impact on psychosocial functioning (Dohrenwend and Dohrenwend, 1974). Such cutoff distinctions in life events will influence the type of relationships evaluated and the extent to which life events appear to be associated with adolescent substance use or abuse. For example, some studies have found no relationship between life stress and alcohol or drug use (e.g., Herman, Schuckit, Hineman, and Pugh, 1976; Morrissey and Schuckit, 1978). In contrast, among alcohol dependent adults, we (Brown, Vik, McQuaid, Patterson, Irwin, and Grant, 1990) demonstrated that highly threatening life stressors occurring posttreatment predicted subsequent addiction relapse. Less severe stressors (e.g., minor illness in family member) did not increase posttreatment relapse risk. This evidence suggests that stressful life experiences may vary in their addiction risk value, with severe or protracted stressors posing the greatest risk for problem drinking.

Stressful life events among adolescents will vary in severity as well. Daily hassles, such as homework assignments, may not challenge and tax a teen's coping resources to the same degree that a major event posing a threat to or change in life-style would (e.g., parental separation or divorce). Daily hassles, however, may have a greater impact on psychosocial functioning and behavioral outcomes when they occur in the context of more severe stress (Wagner, Compas, and Howell, 1988).

CHRONICITY OF STRESSFUL LIFE EVENTS

Some stressful experiences may be chronic, such as interparental conflict, while other forms of life adversity present as an acute crisis (e.g., an automobile accident). Previous experience with a stress can be conceptualized as either beneficial or detrimental to children (Emery, 1982; Grych and Fincham, 1990). Familiarity with a stressful event may desensitize a teen to the potential threat and facilitate the process of reacting and adapting to the event by establishing routine patterns of response. In contrast, chronic exposure of a child to a stressor may engender adaptive styles which become increasingly maladaptive as the child becomes older (Sroufe, 1989). Thus, prolonged exposure to a persistent psychosocial stressor may reduce opportunities to change adaptational efforts in a developmentally appropriate fashion. Consequently, protracted life adversity may impact negatively on social functioning (Maccoby and Martin, 1983), result in reduced availability or utilization of age appropriate coping techniques in response to life stressors, and increase the risk that the child will employ maladaptive coping techniques (including substance use) or demonstrate other negative behaviors. The negative effects on offspring who are raised with an alcoholic parent are similarly best understood from this conceptualization of adaptive versus maladaptive processes in children (Johnson and Rolf, 1990).

Developmental Level

The prevalence of life stress appears to vary with age and developmental stage. Further, the impact of each type of stressful experience will vary with developmental characteristics such as level of cognitive development (Burnside, Baer, McLaughlin, and Pokarny, 1986).

Adolescence can be viewed as a phase of both stage specific common life stressors and heightened vulnerability to uncommon stressors. For example, all teenagers face major developmental changes which create stress (Gore and Colten, 1991), such as transition through puberty, increased concern for peer relationships, and issues of autonomy (Hendren, 1990). Other common life events occur frequently but are not universally experienced by all teens (e.g., school changes, legal trouble, parental divorce). In contrast, catastrophic events may occur which pose unusual challenges to a teen (e.g., death of a parent, life-threatening illness in self). The developmentally related events implicate adolescence as a period of elevated stress. Severely threatening or catastrophic events occurring in the context of the elevated stress of the adolescent years may pose a greater challenge for the individual during adolescence than during other developmental periods (e.g., middle childhood).

Evidence suggests that certain types of events are most salient at one age while other events have their greatest impact at other developmental stages. Compas and Wagner (1991) found that family events (e.g., problems or arguments with parents, siblings, or family members) was the strongest predictor of psychological symptoms during junior high school. In high school, peer related events replaced family events as most predictive, and by college, academic events had the greatest impact on psychological symptoms. Likewise, Newcomb, Huba, and Bentler (1986) found that accident and illness events became less desirable with age, while sexual and autonomous experiences became more desirable.

Finally, the timing of normative events can prove stressful for an adolescent. A normal developmental change may be delayed or occur at an atypical time, thus rendering the change more stressful for the teen than if the experience had occurred when commonly anticipated (Gore and Colten, 1991). For example, delayed onset of puberty has been related to self-image, behavior problems (Nottelman, Susman, Inoff-Germain, Cutler, Lorianx, and Chrousos, 1987), and social popularity (Gross and Duke, 1980). These consequences may in turn increase risk for alcohol or other drug involvement. In contrast, substance use may delay pubertal development and further provoke these negative consequences.

GENDER

Consistent gender differences have been found in adolescent stress. Adolescent girls report more stressful experiences than boys (Bruns and Geist, 1984), particularly stress of an interpersonal nature (Wagner and Compas, 1990), and they perceive stressful events as more undesirable than boys do (Newcomb et al., 1986). Nevertheless, girls evidence no greater vulnerability than boys to develop psychosocial problems as a consequence of stressful experiences (Burke and Weir, 1978; Compas and Wagner, 1991). Reactions to stressful experiences may be influenced by stereotypic gender roles, especially by middle adolescence (Windle, 1992). Thus, girls respond more often than boys in an internalized manner while boys are more apt to act out. Externalized responses to stress evoke more negative consequences than internalized stress reactions, while internalized responses are less apparent and may go unnoticed. As a result, girls' vulnerability to stressful experiences may likewise be less apparent, leading to the possibility of overlooking or underestimating their level of distress.

STRESSFUL LIFE EVENTS
AND ADOLESCENT SUBSTANCE USE

Several studies have demonstrated a relationship between psychosocial stress and teen alcohol and drug use. Many of these studies use aggregate counts of stressful life events to estimate the level of stress a teen experiences. Several studies demonstrating a relationship between specific family stressors and teen substance use are reviewed. An adolescent's struggle to establish appropriate autonomy and independence is facilitated by a stable and supportive family. Consequently, family stress poses a dual threat to adolescents by both increasing a teen's stressful experiences and potentially limiting or restricting the capacity of family members to provide support and coping assistance.

STRESS AND ADOLESCENT SUBSTANCE USE

In two studies by Brown (1987, 1989), stressful life events varied according to adolescents' personal alcohol and drug use and the level of use by the teens' parents. She recruited samples of abusing teens from adolescent substance abuse treatment programs, and sociodemographically comparable nonabusing teens from the same communities. This sampling procedure produced demographically similar groups: abusing teens with and without substance abusing parents, and nonabusing teens with and without substance abusing parents. Teens who abused alcohol or drugs and nonabusing offspring of a substance abusing parent reported more negative life events than nonabusing teens without an abusing parent. Alcohol and drug abusing teens reported more deviant and emotionally distressing life experiences than nonabusing teens. Parental alcohol or drug abuse was associated with increased risk of parent and family problems reported by teen offspring. In particular, family stressors were most common among the nonabusing offspring of abusing parents. Teens evidencing no personal alcohol or drug abuse but with alcoholic parents also reported more uncontrollable and chronic stressors, and life stress independent of the teen's behavior. Finally, alcohol and drug use inconsistencies across generations (i.e., parent abuses but teen does not; teen abuses but parent does not) was associated with more emotionally distressing life events for adolescents than when abuse (or no abuse) was consistent across parent and offspring generations.

Alcohol use among adolescents has been linked to greater stress associated with social and personal competence. V. Johnson and Pandina (1991) sampled 1380 teenagers, aged 12, 15, and 18, via random telephone calls, and recontacted these teens 3 and 6 years later for follow-up interviews. Teenagers who used alcohol evidenced difficulty getting along with others, poor relationships with parents, and decreased self-efficacy and goal-directedness. Similarly, adolescents with a family history of alcohol dependence reported more stressful interpersonal relations than teens without a family history of alcoholism. These findings held regardless of adolescent age or time of contact.

Elevated life stress has been hypothesized to lead to drug use. Bruns and Geist (1984) found support for this hypothesis when they surveyed 566 high school students and 55 adolescents in residential treatment for drug abuse. They found that increased intensity of adolescent drug use was associated with higher levels of stress within the past 2 years and stressful experiences occurring more than 2 years earlier. Unfortunately, these findings are based on retrospective data with no control for alcohol and drug use. Age of initial alcohol and drug use, age at progression to regular use, and stress consequent to substance use, were not clearly delineated. These methodological limitations preclude causal interpretations based on these data regarding stressful life experiences and substance use.

A recent longitudinal study by Windle (1992) permitted for testing of cross-sectional and prospective designs. Windle found that the relationship between stressful life events and problem behaviors among high school sophomores and juniors depended on the type of research design employed. In terms of alcohol use, he found that as stressful life events increased, concurrent alcohol use and alcohol related problems increased. When examined prospectively, however, few reliable associations were found between stress and alcohol use. Stressful life events interacted with perceived social support by friends to predict alcohol consumption 6 months later among boys. Among girls, alcohol related problems reliably predicted the number of stressful life events 6 months later. Nevertheless, as Windle noted, these prospective analyses tested the degree to which stressful experiences predicted alcohol use at least 6 months after the event occurred. Stress may exert an immediate influence on adolescent substance use, and with the passage of time, various events may intervene to weaken or intensify the impact of stress on substance use.

Substance use appears to increase when teenagers feel a need to control their emotions. Labouvie (1986) identified 617 adolescents via random telephone calls, who admitted to current alcohol and/or marijuana use. He found that most teens did not use alcohol and marijuana as a means of coping; however, teens who did use substances for emotional self-regulation (i.e., use in response to problems and hassles) drank more alcohol and smoked more marijuana than teens who did not use substances as a means of coping. Additionally, teens reporting more frequent use of alcohol and marijuana as a means to cope also reported more social and life stress than those whose substance use was not related to coping attempts.

Life stressors have been found to predict substance abuse via mediating cognitive constructs. Newcomb and Harlow (1986) tested path models including stress as a predictor of substance abuse on two separate groups of young adults and adolescents. One sample included 376 high school and college students surveyed via random telephone sampling. The second sample included 640 undergraduate students. In both studies, a meaningless and perceived loss of control over one's life mediated the relationship between stress and substance use. Among college students, however, there was a direct relationship as well between stress and substance use. These findings suggest that the impact of psychosocial stress on substance use is in part indirect, operating via cognitive interpretations. It is important, therefore, to identify and clarify the mediational mechanisms for the relationship between psychosocial stress and adolescent substance use.

In a prospective study of 901 seventh, eighth, and ninth grade students, Wills (1986) found that higher levels of stress at the beginning of the school year predicted greater tobacco and alcohol use at the end of the school year. These results held whether stress was measured according to subjective ratings, recent events (i.e., daily events including interpersonal relationships, physical well-being, and praise versus criticism from others), or major events (identified from adolescent life event inventories by J. H. Johnson and McCutcheon [1980] and Newcomb, Huba, and Bentler [1981]. In addition, Wills found that negative events moderated the relationship between positive events and substance use; the inverse relationship between positive events and substance use was strongest at high levels of negative events. Finally, under high stress, substance abuse was more likely among teens without behavioral or cognitive coping skills or supportive adults available than teens with adequate coping and support resources. Furthermore, teens who responded aggressively to high levels of stress were more likely to use alcohol and tobacco than nonaggressive teens. These findings support a causal role of stress on alcohol and tobacco use, and indicate that negative events increase use while positive life experiences reduce this risk, and highlight the importance of coping and support resources as mediators of the stress/substance use relationship.

FAMILY STRESS AND ADOLESCENT SUBSTANCE ABUSE

In a prospective study by Pandina and V. Johnson (1989), adolescents from families with a history of alcoholism, heavy parental alcohol use, but no history of family alcoholism; highly stressed nonalcohol using families; and nonalcoholic nonstressed families were compared. The authors found that adolescents exposed to family stress (i.e., due to ulcers, nervous breakdown, or depression among family members) did not develop intensive or problematic drinking at a greater rate than adolescents exposed to parental alcohol use or teens from nonstressed, nonalcoholic families. Adolescents whose parents either abused alcohol or drank heavily did report more consequences related to their own alcohol use and more episodes of intoxication. Therefore, it appears that stress alone does not account for teen substance use, but that other factors, including modeling of drinking, availability of alcohol, and biological risk factors, may increase the likelihood of substance use in response to stress.

Family disruption has been associated with greater alcohol drinking among teens. Data gathered from 2595 seventh and tenth grade students demonstrated that teens from nondivorced families drink alcohol less often and in lower quantities than teens from divorced families (Burnside, Baer, McLaughlin, and Pokarny, 1986). Teens at greatest risk for use were those from nonintact families in which a parent drank alcohol.

In a prospective study of 508 families over a 5-year period, boys were found to increase their alcohol and drug use shortly after a parental divorce (Doherty and Needle, 1991). Boys from divorced families increased their substance use at a greater rate than girls following parental divorce and an age matched comparison sample of adolescents from nondivorced families.

SUMMARY

These studies provide support for an association between stressful life events and adolescent substance use among both clinical (i.e., substance abusing) and nonclinical samples. This relationship is complex and clearly bidirectional: stressful life events influence alcohol and drug use, and substance use in turn generates stressful life experiences. There is support for a causal relationship between stressful life events and the emergence of teen substance use. Results from a few prospective studies demonstrated that stressors predicted later increases in alcohol and drug use.

Severity of stressful life events appears to vary with substance use levels among adolescents, with severe or negative events producing the greatest risk for teen substance use (Wills, 1986). Teens who abuse alcohol differ from nonabusing teens in the number of negative, but not positive, life events (Brown, 1987, 1989). Furthermore, positive life experiences appear to provide a protective influence by reducing the influence of negative life events on later substance use.

Only two studies have reported gender differences in substance use in response to stress. One study (Doherty and Needle, 1991) reported evidence that boys were more likely than girls to initiate substance use following family disruption. Similarly, while girls typically reported higher levels of stress than boys, Bruns and Geist (1984) found that polysubstance abusing boys reported more stressful life events than girls. Given the few studies that have examined gender issues with regard to stress and adolescent substance abuse, no definitive conclusions should be drawn regarding differential gender effects until additional studies have clarified gender differences and the theoretical mechanisms explaining them.

To date, studies typically fail to adequately report on issues regarding the chronicity of stressful life experiences, age and developmental stages, or gender differences. This is unfortunate given that current developmental perspectives emphasize the reciprocal influence between context and individual (Sroufe, 1989). Developmental factors determine a child's understanding of and reaction to stress, and early stressful experiences will influence later appraisals and responses to stress (Newcomb et al., 1986). Therefore, developmentally sensitive models are called for that address cognitive and historical factors which influence stress appraisals and highlight age and gender appropriate resources for responding to stress.

MECHANISMS OF STRESS

The studies reviewed demonstrate a clear relationship between stress and substance use among adolescents. Mere associations between stressful life events and substance use, however, fail to capture the nature of this relationship in a way which permits meaningful understanding and prediction of behavior. Life adversity appears to impact upon adolescent substance use directly and via mediating or moderating variables (Newcomb and Harlow, 1986; Wills, 1986). Several mechanisms which may mediate a causal relationship between stressful life experiences and adolescent substance abuse have been proposed. Important among these mechanisms are coping strategies, social resources, and family environment and relationships.

COPING

Coping has received considerable attention as a mediator explaining the impact of stress on various health and psychosocial outcomes. Cognitive formulations of coping typically recognize two phases in response to stress during which an individual understands and prepares to act in response to a stressful experience. First, each life stressor is perceived with a personal degree of salience or significance (Lazarus and Folkman, 1984). This primary processing or appraisal utilizes cognitive factors which include attributions of cause and locus of control (Chwalisz, Altmaier, and Russell, 1992) as well as an evaluation of the negativity of an event (Grych and Fincham, 1990) and its personal relevance. Based on these factors, the individual evaluates the situation as either an actual loss or harm, a threat, or a challenge (Chwalisz et al., 1992). During secondary processing and appraisal, several interpretations are made including reason for an event (causal attribution), who is responsible for it, and whether the individual has sufficient skills and resources to cope with the circumstances (Grych and Fincham, 1990). The goal at this second stage is to evaluate and select potential coping options consistent with the individual's understanding of the event. Perception of one's ability to successfully deal with a specific situation (self-efficacy) and beliefs about the effects of a given behavior or response (outcome expectancies) are important cognitive features which influence responses.

This coping framework appears to apply easily to the adolescent substance use arena. For example, the "Drinking to Cope" perspective (Crutchfield and Grove, 1984) characterizes substance use as a means of coping with stressful situations. Individuals with few coping options are at elevated risk for using alcohol and drugs as a means of dealing with stress. Consistent with this perspective, Litman, Eiser, Rawson, and Oppenheim (1979) found that abstinent alcoholics with a larger repertoire of coping skills were less likely to relapse in response to stress compared to alcoholics with fewer coping options. Wills (1986) has reported that severely stressed teens possessing few cognitive and behavioral coping skills were more likely to use alcohol and tobacco than severely stressed teens with adequate coping skills. Furthermore, stressed teens who relied on avoidant coping styles reported greater alcohol use than stressed teens evidencing active coping skills and nonstressed teens. Other research on adolescent substance abuse indicates that teenagers with little self-efficacy and those who hold positive outcome expectancies of substance use (e.g., increased social facilitation) may utilize psychoactive substances to reduce the threat or distress of an event (Myers and Brown, 1990a; Brown, 1993).

Application of coping theories to the addiction arena has traditionally been among adults. Recently, however, Myers and Brown (1990a,b) demonstrated differences in self-reported coping efforts among substance abusing teens. Adolescents completing residential treatment for drug and alcohol abuse were presented with a high-risk scenario for substance abuse relapse. Teens who later returned to substance abuse following treatment appraised the scenario as less important and difficult than teens with more successful outcomes. Furthermore, the adolescents who later had more severe relapses endorsed fewer problem-focused coping strategies than the improved group of teens. These studies, including the findings by Wills (1986), are important initial investigations of how coping mediates the association between stressful life experiences and substance use among adolescents.

SOCIAL RESOURCES

Long viewed as a buffer to stress (e.g., Rook and Dooley, 1985) and an aid to coping (Thoits, 1986), social support is one mechanism through which stressful life events and substance abuse are linked. Social support has been demonstrated to impact drinking and drug use decisions among adults (e.g., Billings and Moos, 1983; Brown, 1985). Among adolescents experiencing high levels of stress, substance use increased when few supportive adults were

available (Wills, 1986). Although peer relations increase in importance during adolescence (Compas and Wagner, 1991), the supportive and protective role of friendships has not traditionally
been addressed by developmental research (Gore and Colten,
1991). During early adolescence, social interaction skills with
same and opposite sex peers are less refined, and there is pressure
to conform and be included in social groups. Social relations
become an integral part of a teen's sense of identity (Kegan,
1982), and girls in particular develop their self-image and self-
esteem in part through intimate friendships (Gore and Colten,
1991). Adolescent social networks, therefore, may prove as much
a source of stress as a source of support with regard to substance
use (Grizzle, 1988).

It is not surprising, therefore, that social relations among adolescents play a significant role in the initiation of substance use
(Newcomb and Bentler, 1988a), as well as relapse following adolescent substance abuse treatment (Brown, Vik, and Creamer,
1989). Peer relationships are one of the most consistent and
strongest factors found to influence initial use of substances
(Newcomb and Bentler, 1988a). Thus, while social relations may
support an individual during stressful situations, these resources
may also provide direct modeling of substance use, increased
availability of substances, and pressure to use alcohol and drugs.

We have studied the role of social resources in the clinical
course of adolescent substance abuse and in relation to other risk
factors for teen alcohol and drug use. General measures of social
support (number of supports and satisfaction with supports) were
found to be unrelated to adolescent posttreatment substance use
(Richter, Brown, and Mott, 1991). More refined measures of social resources have, however, been consistently linked to teen
alcohol and drug use. For example, a higher proportion of substance abusing individuals in adolescents' social resource network
has been consistently related to greater substance use after treatment (e.g., Myers and Brown, 1990b; Richter et al., 1991; Vik,
Grizzle, and Brown, 1992). Likewise, teens who identified themselves as similar to their social resources and who perceived
higher levels of support from their social resources were less likely

to relapse or took longer to relapse than teens who perceived themselves as less similar to their social supports (Vik et al., 1992). Among adolescents, therefore, drug and alcohol use within one's primary social resource network is important to substance use and abuse as well as resistance to use whereas generic measures such as perceived support may be inconsistently related.

FAMILY ENVIRONMENT AND RELATIONS

Family characteristics are related to adolescent life adversity and teen alcohol and drug use in a variety of ways. Several studies have demonstrated negative effects of family relationships and disruption on adolescent alcohol and drug use (Burnside et al., 1986; Pandina and V. Johnson, 1989; Doherty and Needle, 1991). In contrast, family environment can serve protective functions to help adolescents manage stressful life experiences, buffer their impact, and directly and indirectly influence substance use. For example, family stress may threaten teens by generating life adversity for the teen, and by disrupting or limiting the protective capacity of the family.

Family disruption is related to an increased rate of initial substance use and abuse among boys (Doherty and Needle, 1991). In particular, the process of marital dissolution, including separation, divorce, and interparental conflict, increases offspring risk for both immediate and delayed externalizing and internalizing problems (Emery, 1982; Hetherington, 1979; Grych and Fincham, 1990; Hodges, 1991). Similar parental problems have been associated with increased substance abuse among adolescents (Werner, 1986). Family disruption, therefore, may directly increase teen substance use in response to stress, decrease the protective role of the family in substance use initiation, or produce other problems which increase the risk for teen substance use.

In addition to family disruption, there is clear evidence that substance use among family members increases a teen's likelihood of using drugs and alcohol (Newcomb and Bentler, 1988b). The increased risk in offspring use has been attributed to genetic influences, environmental factors, and gene–environment inter-actions or covariations. Alcohol and drug use by family members may impact teen use via modeling influences, increased availabil-ity, and by contributing to the development of positive alcohol related outcome expectancies. Environments in which a family member uses or abuses alcohol or drugs may influence offspring substance use indirectly via increased stress for the adolescent. Offspring of alcohol abusing parents report more stressful family experiences relative to nonabusing teens of nonabusing parents (Brown, 1989). Thus, family disruption and parental substance abuse contribute to increased experience of stress and, therefore, contribute to risk for adolescent substance use.

Considerable attention has been given to children who flourish despite growing-up in difficult situations (Masten, 1989). One protective factor of resilient children is the quality of the par-ent–child relationship. Parental support has been demonstrated to mediate the impact of interparental conflict on children (Tschann, Johnston, Kline, and Wallerstein, 1989; Forehand, Thomas, Wierson, Brody, and Fauber, 1990; Grych and Fincham, 1990; Vik, 1991). Unfortunately, this relationship often suffers in disruptive family contexts, reducing child resiliency while increas-ing experienced stress. Nevertheless, a warm and supportive rela-tionship between a child and parent may reduce the impact of family disruption and parental alcohol abuse on teen substance use and abuse (Brody and Forehand, 1992).

STRESS–VULNERABILITY MODEL

Life stress and adolescent substance abuse intertwine in a com-plex pattern of reciprocal relations. Adolescent substance abuse is accompanied by and provokes a variety of negative consequences which further add to the adaptational demands of youth. Con-versely, life adversity has been identified as a risk factor for both the onset of substance use among adolescents and perpetuation of adolescent substance abuse. With regard to the latter, we have reviewed several mechanisms believed to contribute to adolescent vulnerability to use substances in response to life adversity. No single mechanism, however, thoroughly explains the relationship between stressful life events and subsequent substance abuse. The stress-vulnerability perspective for addictive disorders (Brown, Vik et al., 1990, 1995) incorporates several aspects of psychosocial functioning to estimate an individual's likelihood of using alcohol or drugs in response to significant life adversity. A stress-vulnerability conceptualization may be particularly helpful in clarifying the causal role life stress plays in the progression of adolescent addictive disorders. Adolescent psychosocial vulnerability to the negative impact of stressful life experiences is determined by the presence or absence of various risk and protective factors. Teens with greater vulnerability to the negative impact of stress are considered most likely to use alcohol or drugs as a means of coping with stressful life experiences.

Experiences posing the greatest threat are determined in part by developmental tasks confronting the teen, the degree of personal threat posed by such events (e.g., threat to self-esteem, self-image, or social role), and the demand such experiences place on adaptational processes. The major developmental task of adolescence is the process of separation from family and individuation of one's sense of self. Significant stressful experiences of adolescence would include events which either impede or escalate this process. For example, early onset of puberty can lead others to treat a young teen as a mature individual before that teen is psychologically and emotionally prepared for such treatment. In contrast, others in the environment may treat the late maturing teen in such a way as to prevent or inhibit her or his efforts to be recognized as a mature individual. Some experiences may challenge the way a teen perceives him- or herself (e.g., rejection by a member of the opposite sex, teasing by a classmate, failure on an exam). Still other experiences may place adaptational demands on an individual (e.g., serious illness in self or important other; change in family structure; valued friend moves away).

Adolescent vulnerability to substance use in response to stressors can be understood as a function of intrapersonal and environmental variables and their interaction. Psychological factors contribute to vulnerability via stress appraisals and coping decisions in response to stressful events. Reduced sense of personal control over an event (locus of control and self-efficacy) will lead to generation and utilization of fewer coping responses and employment of less effective coping options, including substance use. Teens who believe that substance use will alleviate negative feelings or enhance functioning (especially social interaction) are seen as more likely to use alcohol or other drugs in response to significant stress.

With the stress-vulnerability model, emotional factors, in particular psychiatric symptoms, are viewed as contributing to adolescents' vulnerability for alcohol and drug use in response to stress. Emotional factors are particularly salient given the sometimes extreme range and fluctuation in mood and problem behaviors common among adolescents. Most prevalent cooccurring psychiatric disorders among adolescent substance abusers are conduct, mood (depression and anxiety), and eating disorders, although conduct problems are best known to cooccur with substance abuse in adolescents. Impulse control problems, behavioral undercontrol, and lack of personal restraint among adolescents have been linked to substance use with limited anticipation of consequences of use. To the extent that alcohol and other drugs are viewed as producing improved affect or stress–tension reduction (Goldman, Brown, Christiansen, and Smith, 1991) they may be appraised by teens as viable coping options. Among adults, such beliefs have in fact been linked to the perpetuation of substance use problems.

Finally, environmental conditions impact on adolescent vulnerability to substance use. Modeling of substance use by family members, peer encouragement of use, and availability and accessibility of substances all increase a teen's risk for alcohol and drug use. Furthermore, environmental characteristics may influence other risk factors. For example, family disruption and stress may reduce parental supervision, interfere with parenting behaviors, and re-strict availability of family members to provide support or assis-tance with stressful experiences. Family disruption has been associated with increased delinquent, internalizing, and exter-nalizing behaviors in adolescents. Environmental influences may also protect an adolescent from substance use. For example, a supportive relationship with at least one parent, educational pro-grams, peer disapproval of substance use, and limited access to alcohol and drugs can reduce a teen's vulnerability to using alco-hol and drugs while fostering alternative cognitive and behavioral strategies for dealing with stressful situations.

In summary, the stress-vulnerability model represents a means for describing the relationship between stressful life experiences and substance abuse observed among adolescents. Several age specific conditions apply to this model, however, including the nature and relevance of a stressful experience to a teen, develop-mental factors, a teen's understanding and reaction to an event, the importance of mood and behavior in influencing teen reac-tion to stress, and the increased salience of environment as a source of stress and resource for coping. Considerable research has yet to be conducted in order to fully understand how best to apply this model to adolescent alcohol and drug use.

CONCLUSIONS

Research has verified a relationship between stressful life experi-ences and adolescent substance abuse, and begun to identify im-portant mechanisms which drive this bidirectional relationship. While conceptualizations of stress among adolescents must ad-dress traditional life event related issues such as severity and cau-sality, developmental factors take on greater importance when evaluating the stress-substance abuse relationship among teens. In particular, teens are at risk of experiencing a variety of norma-tive as well as major or atypical stressors. Second, given the neuro-cognitive developmental level, teens may be vulnerable to distal events occurring during childhood as well as chronic, ongoing distressing situations. Finally, parents in stressed families may be less able to offer support to teenage family members. Therefore, adolescence is a period of increased risk for greater environmental stress, especially family and social stress, as well as less perceived control over stressful experiences. At the same time, increased environmental stress can reduce the availability of family members to provide support, coping resources, and general help to buffer stress.

There is support as well for conceptualizing stressful life events as serving a causal role in initiating adolescent substance use and perpetuating or exacerbating use. We have emphasized throughout this chapter that the relationship between stress and substance use is bidirectional. Causal formulations, however, contribute to the development of theoretical models of adolescent vulnerability to alcohol and drug use which may have both prevention and intervention implications. We advocate the use of research designs which control for temporal relations and alcohol or other drug influence on life experiences. These theoretical and methodological considerations may yield more refined analyses of the relationship between stressful life events and teen substance use and facilitate partialling out components of the stress/substance abuse relationship among adolescents.

Finally, a number of mechanisms appear to contribute to an adolescent's overall vulnerability to use alcohol in response to stress. Intrapersonal and environmental risk and protective factors combine to either increase or decrease a teenager's likelihood of using drugs or alcohol. Several studies have demonstrated how coping, social support, and family relationships and environment contribute to the association between stressful life events and adolescent substance use. Future research is needed to explore how these factors combine to impact the psychosocial vulnerability of adolescents to use alcohol or drugs in response to stressful life events.

This review raises several important research issues related to the clinical understanding of adolescent substance abuse. The stress-vulnerability model proposed offers a general framework for conceptualizing the link between psychosocial stress and adolescent substance abuse. Specifics of the model, however, require clarification, such as which risk and protective factors contribute to psychosocial vulnerability, the relative importance of different factors which contribute to the psychosocial vulnerability for an adolescent, and the impact of developmental changes and environmental changes (e.g., transitions to new schools) on adolescent perceptions of and reactions to stressful experiences. Psychosocial stress and vulnerability should also be studied in terms of their impact on various transitions in the clinical course of alcohol and drug use among adolescents, including initial use, regular use, transition to new substances, and abuse of alcohol and drugs. Finally, the role that psychosocial stress plays in changing use and abuse patterns requires further study, particularly how stress might interfere with efforts to reduce or discontinue alcohol and drug use, and whether stressful experiences can provoke efforts to stop drinking and using drugs.

REFERENCES

Allan, C. A., & Cooke, D. J. (1985), Stressful life events and alcohol misuse in women: A critical review. *J. Studies on Alcohol,* 46:147–152.

Billings, A. G., & Moos, R. H. (1983), Psychosocial processes of recovery among alcoholics and their families: Implications for clinicians and program evaluators. *Addict. Behav.,* 8:205–218.

Brody, G. H., & Forehand, R. (1992), Prospective associations among family form, family processes, and adolescents' alcohol and drug use. Paper presented at the annual meeting of the Research Society on Alcoholism, June.

Brown, S. A. (1985), Context of drinking and reinforcement from alcohol: Alcoholic patterns. *Addict. Behav.,* 10:191–196.

——— (1987), Alcohol use and type of life events experienced during adolescence. *Psychol. & Addict. Behav.,* 1:104–107.

——— (1989), Life events of adolescents in relation to personal and parental substance abuse. *Amer. J. Psychiatry,* 146:484–489.

——— (1993), Recovery patterns in adolescent substance abuse. In: *Addictive Behaviors across the Lifespan: Prevention, Treatment, and Policy Issues,* ed. J. S. Baer, G. A. Marlatt, & R. J. McMahon. Beverly Hills, CA: Sage Publications.

―――― Vik, P. W., & Creamer, V. A. (1989), Characteristics of relapse following adolescent substance abuse treatment. *Addict. Behav.*, 14:291–300.

―――― ―――― McQuaid, J. R., Patterson, T., Irwin, M. R., & Grant, I. (1990), Severity of psychosocial stress and outcome of alcoholism treatment. *J. Abnorm. Psychol.*, 99:344–348.

―――― ―――― Patterson, T. L., Grant, I., & Schuckit, M. A. (1995), Stress, vulnerability, and adult alcohol relapse. *J. Studies on Alcohol*, 56:538–545.

Bruns, C., & Geist, C. S. (1984), Stressful life events and drug use among adolescents. *J. Hum. Stress*, 10:135–139.

Burke, R. J., & Weir, T. (1978), Sex differences in adolescent life stress, social support and well-being. *J. Psychol.*, 98:277–288.

Burnside, M. A., Baer, P. E., McLaughlin, R. J., & Pokarny, A. D. (1986), Alcohol use by adolescents in disrupted families. *Alcoholism: Clin. & Exper. Res.*, 10:274–278.

Chwalisz, K., Altmaier, E. M., & Russell, D. W. (1992), Causal attributions, self-efficacy cognitions, and coping with stress. *J. Soc. & Clin. Psychol.*, 11:365–376.

Compas, B. E., & Wagner, B. M. (1991), Psychosocial stress during adolescence: Intrapersonal and interpersonal processes. In: *Adolescent Stress: Causes and Consequences*, ed. M. E. Colten & S. Gore. New York: Aldine de Gruyter, pp. 67–85.

Crutchfield, R. D., & Grove, W. R. (1984), Determinants of drug use: A test of the coping hypothesis. *Soc. Sci. Med.*, 18:503–509.

Doherty, W. J., & Needle, R. H. (1991), Psychological adjustment among adolescents before and after a parental divorce. *Child Develop.*, 62:328–337.

Dohrenwend, B. S., & Dohrenwend, B. P. (1974), *Stressful Life Events: Their Nature and Effects*. New York: Wiley.

Emery, R. E. (1982), Interparental conflict and the children of discord and divorce. *Psycholog. Bull.*, 92:310–330.

Finney, J. W., Moos, R. H. & Mewborn, C. R. (1980), Posttreatment experiences and treatment outcome of alcoholic patients six months and two years after hospitalization. *J. Consult. & Clin. Psychol.*, 48:17–29.

Forehand, R., Thomas, A. M., Wierson, M., Brody, G., & Fauber, R. (1990), Role of maternal functioning and parenting skills in adolescent functioning following parental divorce. *J. Abnorm. Psychol.*, 99:278–283.

Goldman, M. S., Brown, S. A., Christiansen, B. A., & Smith, G. T. (1991), Alcoholism and memory: Broadening the scope of alcohol expectancy research. *Psycholog. Bull.*, 110:137–146.

Gore, S., & Colten, M. E. (1991), Introduction: Adolescent stress, social relationships and mental health. In: *Adolescent Stress: Causes and Consequences*, ed. M. E. Colten & S. Gore. New York: Aldine de Gruyter, pp. 1–14.

Grant, I., Brown, G. W., Harris, T., McDonald, W. I., Patterson, T., & Trimble, M. R. (1989), Severely threatening events and marked life difficulties preceding onset or exacerbation of multiple sclerosis. *J. Neurol., Neurosurg., & Psychiatry*, 51:8–13.

Grizzle, K. (1988), *The Social Support Network of Substance Abusing Adolescents*. Unpublished Master's Thesis, San Diego State University, San Diego, CA.

Gross, R. T., & Duke, P. M. (1980), The effect of early versus late physical maturation on adolescent behavior. *Pediatr. Clin. N. Amer.*, 27:71–77.

Grych, J. H., & Fincham, F. D. (1990), Marital conflict and children's adjustment: A cognitive-contextual framework. *Amer. Psycholog. Bull.*, 108:267–290.

Hendren, R. L. (1990), Stress in adolescence. In: *Childhood Stress*, ed. L. E. Arnold. New York: Wiley.

Herman, G., Schuckit, M. A., Hineman, S., & Pugh, W. (1976), The association of stress with drug use and academic performance among university students. *J. Amer. Coll. Health Assn.*, 25:97–101.

Hetherington, E. M. (1979), Divorce: A child's perspective. *Amer. Psychologist*, 34:851–858.

Hodges, W. F. (1991), *Interventions for Children of Divorce: Custody, Access, and Psychotherapy*, 2nd ed. New York: John Wiley.

Holmes, T. H., & Rahe, R. H. (1967), The social readjustment rating scale. *J. Psychosom. Res.*, 11:213–218.

Hore, B. D. (1971a), Life events and alcohol relapse. *Brit. J. Addict.*, 66:83–88.

——— (1971b), Factors in alcoholic relapse. *Brit. J. Addict.*, 66:89–96.

Johnson, J. H., & McCutcheon, S. (1980), Assessing life stress in older children and adolescents. In: *Stress and Anxiety*, Vol. 7, ed. I. G. Sarason & C. D. Spielberger. Washington, DC: Hemisphere.

Johnson, J. L., & Rolf, J. E. (1990), When children change: Research perspectives on children of alcoholics. In: *Alcohol and the Family: Research and Clinical Perspectives*, ed. R. L. Collins, K. E. Leonard, & J. S. Searles. New York: Guilford Press.

Johnson, V., & Pandina, R. J. (1991), Familial and personal drinking histories and measures of competence in youth. *Addict. Behav.*, 16:453–465.

Kegan, R. (1982), *The Evolving Self: Problem and Process in Human Development*. Cambridge, MA: Harvard University Press.

Labouvie, E. W. (1986), Alcohol and marijuana use in relation to adolescent stress. *Internat. J. Addict.*, 23:333–345.

Lazarus, R. S., & Folkman, S. (1984), *Stress, Appraisal and Coping*. New York: Springer.

Litman, G. K., Eiser, J. R., Rawson, N. S. B., & Oppenheim, A. N. (1979), Differences in relapse precipitants and coping behavior between alcohol relapsers and survivors. *Behav. Res. & Ther.*, 17:89–94.

Maccoby, E. E., & Martin, J. A. (1983), Socialization in the context of the family: Parent–child interaction. In: *Handbook of Child Psychology*, Vol. 4, series ed. P. H. Mussen, ed. E. M. Hetherington. New York: Wiley.

Masten, A. S. (1989), Resilience in development: Implications of the study of successful adaptation for developmental psychopathology. In: *The Emergence of a Discipline: Rochester Symposium on Developmental Psychopathology*, ed. D. Cicchetti. Hillsdale, NJ: Lawrence Erlbaum.

Miller, W. R., Hedrick, K. E., & Taylor, C. A. (1983), Addictive behaviors and life problems before and after behavioral treatment of problem drinkers. *Addict. Behav.*, 8:403–412.

Morrissey, G. R., & Schuckit, M. A. (1978), Stressful life events and alcohol problems among women seen at a detoxification center. *J. Studies on Alcohol*, 39:1559–1576.

Myers, M. G., & Brown, S. A. (1990a), Coping and appraisal in potential relapse situations among adolescent substance abusers following treatment. *J. Adol. Chem. Depend.*, 1:95–115.
——— ——— (1990b), Coping responses and relapse among adolescent substance abusers. *J. Substance Abuse*, 2:177–189.
Newcomb, M. D., & Bentler, P. M. (1988a), *Consequences of Adolescent Drug Use.* Newberry Park, CA: Sage.
——— ——— (1988b), Substance use and abuse among children and teenagers. *Amer. Psychologist*, 44:242–248.
——— Harlow, L. L. (1986), Life events and substance abuse among adolescents: Medicating effects of perceived loss of control and meaninglessness in life. *J. Personal. & Soc. Psychol.*, 51:564–577.
——— Huba, G. J., & Bentler, P. M. (1981), Multidimensional assessment of stressful life events among adolescents. *J. Health & Soc. Behav.*, 22:400–415.
——— ——— (1986), Desirability of various life change events among adolescents: Effects of exposure, sex, age, and ethnicity. *J. Res. Personal.*, 20:207–227.
Nottelman, E. D., Susman, E. J., Inoff-Germain, G., Cutler, G. B., Lorianx, D. L., & Chrousos, G. P. (1987), Developmental process in early adolescence: Relationships between adolescent adjustment problems and chronological age, pubertal stage and puberty-related serum hormone levels. *J. Pediatrics*, 110:473–480.
Pandina, R. J., & Johnson, V. (1989), Familial drinking history as a predictor of alcohol and drug consumption among adolescent children. *J. Studies on Alcohol*, 50:245–253.
Richter, S. S., Brown, S. A., & Mott, M. A. (1991), The impact of social support and self-esteem on adolescent substance abuse treatment outcome. *J. Substance Abuse*, 3:371–385.
Rook, K. S., & Dooley, D. (1985), Applying social support research: Theoretical problems and future directions. *J. Soc. Iss.*, 41:5–28.
Rosenberg, H. (1983), Relapsed versus non-relapsed alcohol abusers: Coping skills, life events and social support. *Addict. Behav.*, 8:183–186.
Sroufe, L. A. (1989), Pathways to adaptation and maladaptation: Psychopathology as developmental deviation. In: *The Emergence of a Discipline: Rochester Symposium on Developmental Psychopathology*, ed. D. Cicchetti. Hillsdale, NJ: Lawrence Erlbaum.
Thoits, P. A. (1986), Social support as coping assistance. *J. Consult. & Clin. Psychol.*, 54:416–426.
Tschann, J. M., Johnston, J. R., Kline, M., & Wallerstein, J. S. (1989), Family process and children's functioning during divorce. *J. Marr. & Fam.*, 51:431–444.
Vik, P. W. (1991), *Interparental Conflict and Social Functioning in Young Adulthood.* Unpublished doctoral dissertation, University of Colorado, Boulder, CO.
——— Grizzle, K., & Brown, S. A. (1992), Social resource characteristics and adolescent substance abuse relapse. *J. Adol. Chem. Dependency*, 2:59–74.
Wagner, B. M., & Compas, B. E. (1990), Gender, instrumentality and expressivity: Moderators of the relation between stress and psychological symptoms during adolescence. *Amer. J. Commun. Psychol.*, 18:383–406.

———— ———— Howell, D. C. (1988), Daily and major life events: A test of an integrative model of psychosocial stress. *Amer. J. Commun. Psychol.,* 16:189–205.

Werner, E. E. (1986), Resilient offspring of alcoholics: A longitudinal study from birth to age 18. *J. Studies on Alcohol,* 47:34–40.

Wills, T. A. (1986), Stress and coping in early adolescence: Relationships to substance use in early urban school samples. *J. Health Psychol.,* 5:503–529.

Windle, M. (1992), A longitudinal study of stress buffering for adolescent problem behaviors. *Development. Psychol.,* 28:522–530.

Chapter 10
The Trauma
of Peer Victimization

ALLAN BEANE, PH.D.

IINTRODUCTION

According to Ryder (1993), approximately 3 million bullying incidents per year, or 1700 per day, are reported in the United States
by kindergarten to 12th grade students. This means that every 20
seconds a child is being harassed, taunted, assaulted, or abused.
Some researchers report that three out of five children have been
bullied by another child and two out of that five are bullied daily.
According to the National Association of School Psychologists,
one in seven children, male and female, is either a bully or victim
of bullying (Foltz-Gray, 1996). Since much of bullying occurs in
secret and children often do not report bullying, these statistics
may be underestimated. In fact, all children are affected by bullying. They are either bullies, victims, or concerned observers.
Bullying is an international problem that occurs at all grade levels
and in all sizes of schools and school districts. Psychologists and
school systems are beginning to realize the urgency in solving
this problem.

   According to the National Association of School Boards of Education (1994) bullying (including name-calling) is a form of

school violence and should be treated as such—all forms of bullying involve children hurting children. Carter (1989) calls such treatment *invalidation,* a general term that describes one person *injuring or trying to injure another.* Such actions can be physical, verbal, or nonverbal. As one teenage girl said, "Bullying is slow and painful torture." In fact, Floyd (1987) and Ryder (1993) consider bullying a form of terrorism that is making the lives of too many children miserable.

Children need to be loved and to love. They long for acceptance, meaningful interactions and relationships with their family, teachers, and peers. Therefore, not having these quality relationships can be hurtful and even disabling. It is not surprising that many children react to rejection by engaging in aggressive and rebellious behavior, running away from home, becoming depressed, developing health problems, turning to alcohol and other drugs, joining gangs and hate groups, withdrawing, or choosing to have a baby to create someone to love them and to have someone to love. Bullying not only has negative effects on the physical and mental health of children, it can also cost them their lives. The following stories illustrate the scope and intensity of the problem.

A child who was teased and rejected by her new classmates wrote, "With an empty body, and an empty soul, I stand and pack my books away. I feel a cold stone in the emptiness of my chest. That stone is my heart."

Heather is persistently teased for having small hands. She is ashamed and hides them by sitting on them.

Brandon is an angry ninth grader. He is tired of being harassed, belittled, teased and rejected. He decides to take a gun to school for protection.

Jacob is an eighth grader who feels rejected by his peers and family. He expects this rejection to continue because he feels he has been stamped DEFECTIVE. He wishes he could avoid his peers and his parents. Therefore, he feels that the only solution is to commit suicide.

Stories like these make the news and then are lost in the pool of breaking events considered more important. Unfortunately, events such as those described above happen every day.

DEFINITION OF BULLYING

Bullying can be defined as when one or more individuals engages in overt, aggressive, hostile, violent, hurtful, and persistent behavior that is intentional and designed to injure and create fear and distress in one or more persons who seem to be unable to defend themselves and this gives the bully some degree of satisfaction (Olweus, 1993). Bullying behavior ranges from being overtly teased and intentionally socially isolated to being harassed and assaulted (verbally and/or physically) by one or more individuals. According to Olweus (1993), for it to be said that bullying has occurred, there has to also be an imbalance of strength (power and dominance). Therefore, the victim has trouble defending him- or herself and feels helpless.

CHARACTERISTICS OF BULLIED CHILDREN

Children are not usually randomly selected to be victims, nor does any one particular characteristic or behavior *cause* them to become victims. The problem is the bully. If there were no bullies, there would be no victims. Bullies desire to have power and control over their victims.

However, there are a few characteristics that make bullies think an individual may be an easy target. For example, victims of bullying may be smaller and physically weaker than their bullies and they may appear to lack self-confidence. Also, children who are overly aggressive or always disrupting their peers, may also be rejected. Regardless of a child's characteristics, no one deserves to be bullied. Some characteristics (behaviors) that may indicate a child is being rejected or bullied, or that he or she may be a risk are: (1) often has erratic attendance (may refuse to go to school); (2) frequently ill (headache, stomachache, etc.); (3) isolated from others and lonely—unpopular and becomes withdrawn; (4) prefers the company of adults during recess, lunch, and other such times; (5) goes to recess late and comes back early; (6) talks about or attempts to run away from home; (7) talks about or attempts suicide; (8) develops an eating disorder or a sudden loss of appetite; (9) has problems sleeping, nightmares, and calls out "leave me alone"—may cry themselves to sleep; (10) sudden poor academic performance over time or performs at a lower-than-average level; (11) shows a lack of concentration; (12) has no or fewer friends than other children; (13) appears to be on the edge of his or her peer group; (14) shows unexplained signs of physical abuse (scratches, bruises, torn clothing, etc.) that can't be explained other than from mistreatment; (15) makes facial expressions revealing their anxiety, fear, distress during discussions about school or walking to school; (16) made fun of and laughed at; (17) picked on, shoved, hit, kicked, and involved in fights (but unable to defend themselves—may cry); (18) teased, called names, and belittled; (19) last one to be picked to be on a team; (20) has possessions (books, money, etc.) taken or damaged; (21) avoids going certain places at school and in the community; (22) frequently asks for more money; (23) takes weapons (guns, knives, forks, bottle openers, etc.) to school for protection; (24) starts stammering; (25) comes home starving (lunch money stolen); (26) begs to be driven to school and asks that he or she be taken and picked up—refuses to walk or ride bus; (27) unwilling to go to school; (28) changes walking route to school; (29) sudden loss of interest in homework; (30) extreme mood swings; (31) unable to trust others; (32) feels the bully knows a lot about them; (33) feels resentment because the bullies have taken all their friends away; (34) feels powerless against the bullies; (35) feels that the whole world is watching their situation and can do nothing about it; (36) sudden bed-wetting; (37) appears preoccupied and tense on Sunday afternoon-evening and

Monday morning or to and from school (Byrne, 1994); (38) abnormal obsession and anxiety regarding his or her height, weight, size of nose and ears, or appearance of hair; (39) wants to stay indoors a lot; (40) drops out of school-sponsored activities he or she enjoys; (41) over time may feel that he or she is to be blamed for being bullied; (42) considered "different" from classmates (unpopular)—differs from the "norm"—triggers negative expectations because of prejudice or biases; (43) low self-esteem and lacking self-confidence and assertiveness; (44) does not stand up for him- or herself, will not retaliate; (45) poor social skills, poor interpersonal skills, and poor manners; (46) may have a disability (moderate and mild learning difficulties); (47) moves without confidence and lacks assertiveness; (48) is quiet-shy and not very noticeable; (49) does not say much when pushed around; (50) may have overly protective parents—closer than normal relationship with the mother; (51) may be extremely cautious, insecure, and sensitive, does not assert him- or herself in a peer group; (52) physically weaker than boys in general and less agile than average—not involved in sports; (53) may be aggressive and disruptive—may have a hot temper; (54) appears nervous and sticks to him- or herself; and (55) academically successful and appears to be the teacher's pet or does poorly academically (the extremes).

Rationale for Prevention and Intervention Strategies

Bullying causes a variety of educational, personal, and social problems that impact families, schools, communities, and society. The following are only a few reasons prevention and intervention strategies need to be developed to rid communities and schools of peer rejection and other forms of bullying: (1) children have a right to protection; (2) lack of peer and teacher acceptance causes discipline problems (Dreikurs, Grunwald and Pepper,

1982); (3) ignoring the problem provides a bad example; (4) occurs in every classroom; (5) school personnel and parents are not always supportive (Olweus, 1993); (6) impacts physical and emotional health of children (Asher and Coie, 1990); (7) impacts sense of personal worth, self-confidence, and who children become; (8) causes loneliness (Weiss, 1982); (9) causes depression (Vosk, Forehand, Parker, and Rickard, 1982); (10) encourages children to commit suicide; (11) destroys a child's natural response (sensitivity, joy, desire to explore and learn); (12) robs children of important social skills (Ladd, Price, and Hart [1990], reported in Asher and Coie [1990, p. 107]); (13) encourages children to run away from home (Crespi and Sabatelli, 1993); (14) encourages children to use drugs; (15) encourages children to join gangs and to develop gangs (Kupersmidt [1983], reported in Asher and Coie [1990, p. 136]); (16) encourages children to join hate groups; (17) encourages teen pregnancies (Youngs, 1992); (18) encourages children to drop out of school (Youngs, 1992); (19) encourages poor school attendance (Garrity, Jens, Poter, Sager, and Short-Camillie, 1996); (20) encourages use of weapons; (21) encourages cynicism toward authority (Floyd, 1987); (22) impacts student morale and achievement (Floyd, 1987; Wolcott, 1991); (23) encourages inappropriate behavior; (24) prevents full-inclusion of children with disabilities; and (25) it has long-lasting effects and creates societal problems (Hartup, 1992).

PREVENTION AND INTERVENTION STRATEGIES

Bullying is a multifaceted and complex problem. Its complexity should not frighten or discourage professionals and parents, but should energize their search for solutions. To prevent bullying and to assist children already involved in bullying situations, a multifaceted program is required that develops, implements, and evaluates strategies focusing on establishing peaceable and caring environments in which children and adults feel psychologically and physically safe. The aim is to create environments where all adults and children model the importance of discipline-responsibility, encouragement, acceptance of differences, support, sensitivity, respect, and zero tolerance of bullying. Beane (1996) has developed such a model program that includes a bank of more than 250 strategies. The strategies are system-centered (communities and schools), personnel-centered, peer-centered, family-centered, and child-centered. His model emphasizes the importance of focusing on the "little things" that can make a difference (day-to-day attitudes and behaviors of those around the child) as well as the "big things" (i.e., peer mediation, conflict resolution, enhancing self-esteem, effective policies and procedures). Even though formal programs such as conflict resolution and social skills training are valuable components of any program, it is also the cumulative effect of the "little things" that are done that make a difference.

The strategies identified and developed by Beane (1996) go beyond common courtesy and etiquette and focus on changing policies and procedures as well as changing the attitudes, thinking, and behavior of school personnel, peers, parents, the victims of bullying, and the bully. All of the strategies and their rationale cannot be discussed in this chapter; however, the following is a sampling of the strategies.

System-centered Strategies

Bullying is a community problem that affects everyone. Therefore, a systems approach must be used. Everyone must support one another to effectively combat bullying and to develop safe and caring environments for children. This requires the examination of policies, procedures, and programs. Some of the system-centered strategies are:

1. Protect children through adequate supervision.
2. Establish and publicize an antibullying policy and regulations.

3. Examine current policies and procedures that are placing children in embarrassing situations during activities sponsored by the community and/or school system.

4. Establish and enforce rules that protect children. Classroom rules and schoolwide rules all should contain content relative to bullying. Rules for providing safe environments (e.g., recreational areas) in the community should also address bullying.

5. Use a *bully reporting box, bullying hotline/helpline,* or some other reporting procedure. Develop and utilize forms for reporting and for tracking efforts to address the problem.

6. Establish a bully court.

7. Implement strategies that add structure to less structured activities, such as recess and lunchtime. For example, separate bullies from the victim by staggering recess/play times and space. Some children may prefer a place on the playground designated as the "quiet place." Or, ask groups of children to plan an activity they will engage in prior to recess.

8. Establish a community-wide parent education program through interagency cooperation that addresses behavior that often contributes to the problem of peer abuse and rejection. One element of this strategy is to identify the professional programs and services that are already available to families.

9. Establish a peer mediation program.

10. Use video cameras to record all activity during a 24-hour period. Place video cameras in the community, on buses, and on school property.

PERSONNEL-CENTERED STRATEGIES

All school personnel play an important role in preventing peer rejection and other forms of bullying and in the implementation of intervention strategies. Therefore, to be effective, they must also serve as models of acceptance. This requires them to examine their attitudes, thinking, and behaviors. Some of the personnel-centered strategies are:

1. Personnel should examine their attitudes toward aggressive and disruptive children and be sensitive to their self-talk regarding these children.
2. Personnel should avoid favoritism.
3. Personnel should frequently ask themselves, "Am I giving everyone eye contact and attention?"
4. Personnel should identify and eliminate their own prejudices.
5. Personnel should examine their expectations and ignore warnings from others regarding specific children.
6. Personnel should examine the appropriateness and effectiveness of classroom rules, classroom management plans, and routines.
7. No surprises. Children should be warned of changes in structure (e.g., furniture arrangement, schedules, routines).
8. Develop "With-it-ness." Strive to be sensitive to the numerous social interactions of students and be alert to nonverbal signals that may indicate problems.
9. School personnel should examine their own self-esteems and strive to improve them.
10. School personnel should avoid mentioning how children are different (in a negative sense) from their parents and siblings.

PEER-CENTERED STRATEGIES

According to Hymel, Wagner, and Butler (1990; reported in Asher and Coie, 1990, p. 180), efforts to assist rejected children that focus solely on changing the child, address only part of the problem. Intervention efforts must also take into account not only the characteristics of the rejected–abused child, but also the receptivity of the peers. Therefore, strategies are needed to change their attitudes, thinking, and behaviors. Some of the peer-centered strategies are:

1. Use strategic seating assignments to increase the child's social contact with his or her peers. For example, do not permit rejected children to be seated at the periphery of the class.
2. Routinely take and display pictures of children working and playing together.
3. Design activities which require group effort and reward cooperative behavior rather than the result.
4. Communicate to students that bullying will not be tolerated.
5. Do not tolerate public comments from children, parents, or colleagues which degrade, condemn, or ridicule children.
6. Teachers should make sure students understand their commitment to provide a safe (physical and psychological) environment for them. Do not tolerate the teasing, threatening, or harassing behavior of children.
7. Engage several small groups of students in a variety of service projects.
8. Use sociometric procedures to identify children who are "stars" in the classroom. Then, invent ways to get the stars of the classroom to assume some cooperative role with rejected children. Be careful not to let these children become "bosses" or "taskmasters."
9. Never award special statuses or privileges to rejected children, except when to do so is absolutely necessary.
10. Provide effective illustrations and models of peer acceptance and discuss them with children in the classroom. For exampple, there may be a newspaper article or video focusing on how groups of children are assisting children with disabilities, homeless children, and others.

FAMILY-CENTERED STRATEGIES

The National Education Association (1996) believes that appropriate school behavior begins and is reinforced in the home. Programs that provide assistance and training in child development, effective parenting skills, and strategies for dealing with disruptive students should be available for parents-guardians. Schools can be instrumental in identifying and recommending strategies that can assist parents-guardians. Some of the family-centered strategies are discussed below.

Strategies for Parents of the Bullied

1. When parents first determine that their child is being bullied, they should be encouraged to avoid trying to be Mr. and Mrs. Fix-It.
2. When parents discover that their child is being bullied, they should take action. Their first step is to keep a diary. They should record the facts without interrogating their child.
3. No one deserves to be bullied, but parents should explore the possibility that their child is provoking the bullying. If appropriate, assure the child that the bullying is not his or her fault.
4. Tell parents they should not promise their children they will keep the bullying a secret. The parents should reassure their child that they will help them solve this problem in an appropriate manner.
5. Encourage the social interaction of the parents of bullied children with the parents of other children.

Strategies for Parents of the Bullies

1. Encourage the parents of the bully to stay calm and assure them that something can be done to help their child.
2. Encourage the parents of the bully to engage in meaningful conversations with their child to determine the reason he or she might be bullying and what might need to be done to stop it from reccurring. They should identify the facts without interrogating their child.
3. Parents should communicate their zero tolerance for bullying and parents must practice what they preach.
4. Tell parents that they should ensure that their child apologizes (verbally or in writing) to the child who is bullied or

work out some way for the child to make amends for his or
her behavior.

5. Encourage parents to be very observant of their child and
   to reward nonviolent behavior through praise and other re-
   inforcers.

Strategies for All Parents

1. Ask all parents to be sensitive to signs that their children
   may be victims of bullying.
2. Inform parents of the research regarding the impact infant–parent attachment can have on the child's development.
3. Do as much as possible to help parents create a positive and
   safe home environment.
4. Encourage effective *parenting styles* and educate parents
   about the effect such styles could have on their children.
5. Encourage effective *disciplinary techniques* and educate parents about the effect they could have on children.

CHILD-CENTERED STRATEGIES

There are several strategies for assisting the victims of bullying
and for assisting children who are bullies. Many of the strategies
may be appropriate for both the bullied and the bullies. In fact,
several strategies can be used with all children and serve as preventive measures. Some of the child-centered strategies that focus
on the victim are discussed below.

1. Help the rejected child develop a skill that has social value.
2. Encourage children to "sample" a variety of potential play
   partners in order to identify peers who can become suitable
   companions.
3. When a child is a newcomer to the school or school system,
   arrange for him or her to meet some of the classmates prior
   to the first day of school.

4. Give children a high dose of self-confidence and teach them to communicate this confidence. Teach them to say "Leave me alone!" or "Buzz off!" with confidence and anger and then to walk away with confidence. Self-defense courses have given a lot of children self-confidence and they learn it is not always appropriate to fight back.
5. Teach children to have positive social acceptance expectations regarding their own acceptance.
6. Give children social knowledge and skills (e.g., how to make friends, how to help others). Of course, this could be incorporated into the coaching strategy described above.
7. Create opportunities for children to bond with their grandparents as often as possible.
8. Teach children to control their anger through reframing and other techniques.
9. Teach children to emphasize similarities between themselves and their peers.
10. Work with children with disabilities to develop their willingness to talk openly about their abilities and characteristics.

CONCLUSION

Parents and professionals have felt helpless and frustrated when facing the problems associated with peer rejection and bullying. The resources are now available to give them the required knowledge. All they need is the will, the courage, and the wisdom to implement the strategies.

It is critical that professionals remember that crash courses are usually not effective. In order to effectively promote peer acceptance, a plan is needed that uses: (1) system-centered strategies; (2) personnel-centered strategies; (3) peer-centered strategies; (4) family-center strategies; and (5) child-centered strategies. Only then can they say they have done their best. As Helen Keller said, "When we do the best we can, we never know what miracle is wrought in our life, or in the life of another."

REFERENCES

Asher, S. R., & Coie, J. D., Eds. (1990), *Peer Rejection in Childhood.* Cambridge, MA: Cambridge University Press.

Beane, A. (1996), *A Handbook to Promote Acceptance of Diversity and Prevent School Violence.* Unpublished Manuscript.

Byrne, B. (1994), *Bullying: A Community Approach.* Mount Merrion, Blackrock, Co Dublin: Columbia.

Carter, J. (1989), *Nasty People.* Chicago: Contemporary.

Crespi, T. D., & Sabatelli, R. M. (1993), Adolescent runaways and family strife: A conflict-induced differentiation framework. *Adolescence,* 28(112):868–878.

Dreikurs, B., Grunwald, B., & Pepper, F. (1982), *Maintaining Sanity in the Classroom.* New York: Harper & Row.

Floyd, N. M. (1987), Terrorism in the schools. *School Safety,* Winter:22–25.

Foltz-Gray, D. (1996), The bully trap. *Teaching Tolerance,* 5(1):19–23.

Garrity, C., Jens, K., Poter, W., Sager, N., & Short-Camillie, C. (1995), *Bully-Proofing Your School: A Comprehensive Approach for Elementary Schools.* Sopris West: Longmont.

Hartup, W. W. (1992), *Having Friends, Making Friends, and Keeping Friends: Relationships as Educational Contexts.* Urbana, IL: ERIC, Clearinghouse on Elementary and Early Childhood Education ED 345 854.

Hymel, S., Wagner, E., & Butler, L. (1990), Reputational bias view from the peer group. In: *Peer Reflection in Childhood,* ed. S. R. Asher, & J. D. Coie. Cambridge, MA: Cambridge University Press, pp. 156–186.

Kupersmidt, J. B. (1983), Predicting delinquency and academic problems from childhood peer status. In: *Strategies for identifying children at social risk: Longitudinal correlates and consequences.* Symposium chaired by J. D. Coie at the biennial meeting of the Society for Research in Child Development, Detroit.

Ladd, G., Price, J., & Hart, C. (1990), Preschooler's behavioral orientations and patterns of peer contact: Predictive of peer status? In: *Peer Rejection in Childhood,* ed. S. R. Asher, & J. D. Coie. Cambridge, MA: Cambridge University Press, pp. 90–115.

National Association of State Boards of Education (1994), *Schools Without Fear.* Alexandria, VA: National Association of State Boards of Education.

Olweus, D. (1993), *Bullying at School: What We Know and What We Can Do.* Cambridge, MA: Blackwell.

Ryder, V. (1993), *The Bully Problem: Signs of a Victim.* Houston, TX: Ryder Press.

Vosk, B., Forehand, R., Parker, J. B., & Rickard, P. (1982), A multimethod comparison of popular and unpopular children. *Develop. Psychology,* 18:571–575.

Weiss, R. S. (1982), Loneliness: What we know about it and what we might do about it. In: *Preventing the Harmful Consequences of Severe and Persistent Loneliness,* ed. L. A. Peplow & S. E. Goldston. Rockville, MD: National Institute of Mental Health.

Wolcott, L. (1991), Relations: The fourth "R." *Teacher Mag.,* April:26–27.

Youngs, B. B. (1992), *The 6 Vital Ingredients of Self-Esteem: How to Develop Them in Your Students.* Rolling Hills Estates, CA: Jalmar Press.

Chapter 11
Posttraumatic Stress Disorder in Children and Its Treatment

WILLIAM YULE, PH.D.

It has long been recognized that children, like adults, react to stressful events, but until the last decade it had largely been assumed that such reactions in children were temporary adjustment reactions. Following a stressful experience, children were seen as reacting with more "nervous" symptoms such as bed-wetting, tics, and disturbed sleep. They required more reassurance and comfort from their parents. Such reactions were seen as temporary and time-limited, and carrying no implications for more severe psychopathology. Indeed, such a picture was reflected in the two major systems of psychiatric classification—the World Health Organization's International Classification of Diseases (ICD) (World Health Organization, 1991) and the American Psychiatric Association's *Diagnostic and Statistical Manual* (APA, 1980, 1987, 1994).

The concept of posttraumatic stress disorder (PTSD) was first developed in relation to studies of adult reactions to major stress. Major stress reactions had been recognized in soldiers in battle in the nineteenth century and in civilians following railway accidents, but it was not until the persisting problems of Vietnam veterans were better documented that it was realized that three major groups of symptoms, distressing recurring recollections of the traumatic event; avoidance of stimuli associated with the trauma; and a range of signs of increased physiological arousal, formed a coherent syndrome that came to be labeled PTSD (Horowitz, 1976; APA, 1980).

The introduction of the category and its first operationalization in DSM-III (APA, 1980) sparked a great deal of research as well as controversy. Posttraumatic stress disorder was classified as an anxiety disorder. It was increasingly described as "a normal reaction to an abnormal situation," and so, logically, it was queried whether it should be regarded as a psychiatric disorder at all (O'Donohue and Eliot, 1992).

While being predominantly an anxiety disorder, PTSD in adults differs from other anxiety disorders in important ways. Thus, Foa, Steketee, and Olasov-Rothbaum (1989) showed that the trauma suffered violated more of the patients' safety assumptions than did events giving rise to other forms of anxiety. There was a much greater generalization of fear responses in the PTSD groups, and, unlike other anxious patients, they reported far more frequent reexperiencing of the traumatic event. Indeed, it is this internal, subjective experience that seems most to mark out PTSD from other disorders (Jones and Barlow, 1992).

One question is whether there is a spectrum of posttraumatic stress disorders (Kolb, 1988). While many patients meet criteria as proposed in DSM-III, some show many but insufficient symptoms to meet full criteria. Some researchers and clinicians argue for an additional grouping to be recognized—Disorders of Extreme Stress Not Otherwise Specified (DESNOS) (Herman, 1992). To some extent, this category is being sought to encompass the complex symptomatology shown by people who have been incarcerated or otherwise suffered repeated traumatization, as in cases of child sexual abuse. To that extent, the distinction between PTSD and DESNOS is similar to the distinction drawn by Terr (1991) between her type I and type II PTSD in children (see below).

Thus, even in adult patients where the condition has been recognized for longer and many fundamental studies have been undertaken, there is still incomplete agreement on the phenomenology of PTSD and its overlap with other psychopatho-logical conditions. Indeed the two major classificatory systems disagree on the symptoms they include in the constellation, the criteria required to make the diagnosis, and the weight given to the different symptoms.

DSM AND ICD CRITERIA FOR PTSD

DSM-III-R (APA, 1987) describes Posttraumatic Stress Disorder as follows:

The essential feature of this disorder is the development of characteristic symptoms following a psychologically distressing event that is outside the range of usual human experience (i.e., outside the range of such common experiences as simple bereavement, chronic illness, business losses, and marital conflict). The stressor producing this syndrome would be markedly distressing to almost anyone, and is usually experienced with intense fear, terror, and helplessness. The characteristic symptoms involve re-experiencing the traumatic event, avoidance of stimuli associated with the event or numbing of general responsiveness, and increased arousal. The diagnosis is not made if the disturbance lasts less than one month [p. 247].

DSM-III-R goes on to note that PTSD can occur during childhood. Children may refuse to talk about the trauma, but they may well remember it vividly. They especially may show a marked change in orientation to the future, and they may show a variety of physical symptoms such as stomach- or headaches.

ICD-10 (WHO, 1991) describes PTSD as follows: "Arises as a delayed or protracted response to a stressful event or situation . . . of an exceptionally threatening or catastrophic nature, which is likely to cause pervasive distress in almost everyone" (p. 137). Predisposing personality traits or prior history are neither sufficient nor necessary to explain the onset of PTSD. ICD-10 lists similar symptoms as DSM-III-R, but emphasizes the repetitive

intrusive memories, stating that, "A conspicuous emotional de-
tachment, numbing of feeling, and avoidance of stimuli that
might arouse recollections of the trauma are often present but
are not essential for the diagnosis. The autonomic disturbances,
mood disorder, and behavioral abnormalities are all contributory
to the diagnosis but not of prime importance" (p. 138).

Thus, ICD places most emphasis on the troublesome reexperiencing phenomena and much less emphasis on the emotional
numbing which has proven difficult to elicit in many adults and
also proved difficult to define in children and adolescents. It
should also be noted that ICD says that PTSD should normally
only be diagnosed when it arises within 6 months of a major
trauma.

PTSD IN CHILDREN

The main problem with applying the working criteria of either
DSM or ICD to classifying problems presented by children and
adolescents after experiencing a major trauma is that the criteria
were not developed on the basis of studies of young people. Only
careful descriptive studies of representative groups of traumatized children studied over periods of time can establish the natural history of the disorder in children. It is important that
investigators keep an open mind about the range of symptoms
shown by children and do not merely enquire about symptoms
that are already incorporated in the official classifications.

Following my experience of assessing and working with child
and adolescent survivors of the capsizing of the *Herald of Free
Enterprise* car ferry (Yule and Williams, 1990) and those from the
sinking of the cruise ship *Jupiter* (Yule, Udwin, and Murdoch,
1990; Yule, 1992a), I noted the following common reactions:

Most children are troubled by repetitive, intrusive thoughts
about the accident. Such thoughts can occur at any time, but
particularly when the children are otherwise quiet, as when they

are trying to drop off to sleep. At other times, the thoughts and vivid recollections are triggered off by reminders in their environment. Vivid flashbacks are not uncommon. Sleep disturbances are very common, particularly in the first few weeks. Fears of the dark and bad dreams, nightmares, and waking through the night are widespread.

Separation difficulties are frequent, even among teenagers. For the first few days, children may not want to let their parents out of their sight, even reverting to sleeping in the parental bed. Many children become much more irritable and angry than previously, both with parents and peers.

Although child survivors experience a pressure to talk about their experiences, paradoxically they also find it very difficult to talk with their parents and peers. Often they do not want to upset the adults, and so parents may not be aware of the full extent of their children's suffering. Peers may hold back from asking what happened in case they upset the child further; the survivor often feels this as a rejection.

Children report a number of cognitive changes. Many experience difficulties in concentration, especially in school work. Others report memory problems, both in mastering new material and in remembering old skills such as reading music. They become very alert to danger in their environment, being adversely affected by reports of other disasters.

Survivors have learned that life is very fragile. This can lead to a loss of faith in the future or a sense of foreshortened future. Their priorities change. Some feel they should live each day to the full and not plan far ahead. Others realize they have been overconcerned with materialistic or petty matters and resolve to rethink their values.

Not surprisingly, many develop fears associated with specific aspects of their experiences. They avoid situations they associate with the disaster. Many experience "survivor guilt"—about surviving when others died; about thinking they should have done more to help others; about what they themselves did to survive.

Adolescent survivors report significantly high rates of depression, some becoming clinically depressed, having suicidal thoughts, and taking overdoses in the year after a disaster. A significant number become very anxious after accidents, although the appearance of panic attacks is sometimes considerably delayed. When children have been bereaved, they may need bereavement counseling.

In summary, children and adolescents surviving a life-threatening disaster show most of the same range of symptoms as adults do. There may be considerable comorbidity with depression, generalized anxiety, or pathological grief reactions.

EFFECTS ON YOUNGER CHILDREN

Many writers agree that it is very difficult to elicit evidence of emotional numbing in children (Frederick, 1985). Many do show loss of interest in activities and hobbies that previously gave them pleasure. Preschool children show much more regressive behavior as well as more antisocial, aggressive, and destructive behavior. There are many anecdotal accounts of preschool children showing repetitive drawing and play involving themes about the trauma they experienced.

Although parents and teachers initially report that young children do not easily talk about the trauma, recent experience has been that many young children easily give very graphic accounts of their experiences and are also able to report how distressing the reexperiencing in thoughts and images is (Sullivan, Saylor, and Foster, 1991; Berelowitz, Misch, and Yale, 1993). All clinicians and researchers need to have a good understanding of children's development to be able to assist them express their inner distress.

EFFECTS OF DIFFERENT DISASTERS

Reactions to disasters depend on preexisting adjustment as well as on factors in the child and in the disaster situation (Rachman, 1980). Some consensus is beginning to emerge on the nature of risk and protective factors (Yule, 1992b) and there is general agreement that girls show greater stress reactions than boys; that less able children are more affected than brighter children; that good support in families and schools protects against the effects of exposure; that children who feel their lives were threatened fare worse; and that there is an exposure–effect relationship such that those who are most exposed show the greatest reactions.

There are very few longitudinal studies so that one cannot describe the natural course of PTSD in childhood with any confidence. Indeed, the early studies were mainly clinical and anecdotal, used few standard measures, and suffered many methodological problems (Garmezy, 1986). This situation has improved rapidly in very recent years, to the point that it is becoming difficult to keep up with the expanding literature. The table below gives a summary of most of the published studies.

TREATMENT AND PREVENTION

Clinicians who first encounter a large number of children traumatized by some event may well feel overwhelmed and not know where to begin. They may feel that they do not know how to treat PTSD. However, a moment's consideration of the list of presenting symptoms outlined above should convince most clinicians that they already have a wide range of appropriate techniques in their therapeutic armamentarium.

While there are, as yet, few detailed accounts of treating PTSD in children, and no randomized control studies, nevertheless there are sufficient case studies with adults and some with children to warrant giving advice. Interventions fall into four main types: crisis intervention; intervention in groups; individual treatments; planning for prevention.

Crisis Intervention: Critical Incident Stress Debriefing

Debriefing was originally developed to assist emergency personnel adjust to their emotional reactions to events encountered in the course of their rescue work. It makes use of group support techniques within a predominantly male, macho culture where expressing and sharing feelings is not the norm. The technique has now been adapted for use with children following a wide variety of traumas (Dyregrov, 1991).

Within a few days of an incident, the survivors are brought together in a group with an outside leader. During the introductory phase, the leader sets the rules for the meeting emphasizing that they are there to share feelings and help each other, and that what goes on in the meeting is private. The information should not be used to tease other children. No one *has* to talk, although all are encouraged to do so. They then go on to clarify the facts of what actually happened in the incident. This permits the nailing of any rumors. They are asked about what they thought when they realized something was wrong, and this leads naturally into discussions of how they felt, and of their current emotional reactions. In this way, children share the various reactions they have experienced and usually learn that others have similar feelings. The leader labels their responses as normal (understandable) reactions to an abnormal situation. Many children are relieved to learn they are not the only ones experiencing feelings and so are relieved that there is an explanation and that they are not going mad. The leader summarizes the information arising in the group, and educates the children about what simple steps they can take to control some of their reactions. They are also told of other help available should their distress persist.

There is evidence that this structured crisis intervention is helpful in preventing later distress in adults (Duckworth, 1986; Dyregrow, 1988; Robinson and Mitchell, 1993). Yule and Udwin (1991) describe their use of critical incident stress debriefing with girls who survived the sinking of the *Jupiter*. Self-report data 5 months after the incident suggest that this reduced levels of stress, particularly those manifested in intrusive thoughts (Yule, 1992a). Stallard and Law (1993) show more convincing evidence that debriefing greatly reduced the distress of girls who survived a school bus crash. However, we still do not know when best to offer such debriefing to survivors of a disaster, nor indeed whether all survivors benefit.

Group Treatment

Where natural groupings exist in communities and schools, it makes sense to direct some therapeutic support through such groups (Farberow and Gordon, 1981; Galante and Foa, 1986; Ayalon, 1988; Yule and Williams, 1990; Yule and Udwin, 1991; Azarian, Miller, and Schriptchenko-Gregorian, 1994). The aims of such therapeutic groups should include the sharing of feelings, boosting children's sense of coping and mastery, and sharing ways of solving common problems.

Gillis (1993) suggests that it is optimal to work with groups of six to eight children. His experience following a school sniper attack was that it was better to run separate groups for boys and girls because of the different reactions they had to the attack. Boys showed more externalizing problems and girls showed more internalizing ones.

Different authors have imposed varying degrees of structure on their groups, with Galante and Foa (1986) adopting a fairly structured approach where different topics were tackled at each meeting, while Yule and Williams (1990) describe not only a very unstructured, problem-solving approach but also ran a parallel group for the parents. Different incidents will require different approaches.

Group approaches seem to be very therapeutic for many children but not all problems can be solved in the group. Gillis (1993) suggests that high-risk children—those whose lives were directly threatened, who directly witnessed death, who were physically injured, who had preexisting problems, or who lack family support—should be offered individual help. More generally, children whose problems persist despite group help should be treated individually.

Individual Treatment

To date, there is little evidence that drug treatments have a central role, so the focus has been mainly on cognitive behavioral treatments that aim both to help the survivor make sense of what happened and to master their feelings of anxiety and help-lessness.

Asking children to draw their experience often assists recall of both the event and the emotions (Newman, 1976; Blom, 1986; Galante and Foa, 1986; Pynoos and Eth, 1986). Drawings were not used as "projective" techniques, but as ways of assisting talking about the experience.

Most survivors recognize that sooner or later they must face up to the traumatic event. The problem for the therapist is how to help the survivor reexperience the event and the emotions that it engenders in such a way that the distress can be mastered rather than magnified. Therapeutic exposure sessions that are too brief may sensitize rather than desensitize (Rachman, 1980) so the therapist may need to use much longer exposure sessions than normal (Saigh, 1986). Fuller suggestions of useful techniques to promote emotional processing are given elsewhere (Rachman, 1980; Richards and Lovell, 1990; Yule 1991, 1992c; Richards and Rose, 1991; Saigh, 1992).

Exposure under supportive circumstances seems to deal well with both intrusive thoughts and behavioral avoidance. The other major symptom of child PTSD that requires attention is sleep disorder. A careful analysis will reveal whether the problem is mainly one of getting off to sleep or in waking because of intrusive nightmares related to the disaster. In the former case, implementing relaxing routines before bed and masking thoughts with music may help. In the latter, there are now some promising cognitive behavioral techniques for alleviating nightmares (Marks, 1978, 1987; Halliday, 1987; Seligman and Yellen, 1987; Palace and Johnston, 1989).

Ayalon (1983) suggests the use of stress-inoculation techniques (Meichenbaum, 1975, 1977; Meichenbaum and Cameron, 1983), among many others, to prepare Israeli children to cope with the effects of "terrorist" attacks. These ideas seem eminently sensible, but their implementation awaits systematic evaluation.

Case Example 1

Fifteen-year-old Tom had been looking forward to going on a cruise with his school to the eastern Mediterranean. He and his mates were excited about going abroad for the first time and as the cruise ship *Jupiter* set sail from Athens harbor, they gathered in the lounge to hear a lecture on safety on board. As the cruise leader began his talk, they all felt a bump and the ship lurched. Forty-five minutes later, it sank, killing one girl, one teacher, and two rescuers.

Tom later remembered the ship slowly keeling over. More and more people crowded into the lounge. Many were distressed and crying. Glasses were crashing off the bar. Furniture was sliding down. People were getting entangled in the furniture. Tom got separated from his mates and when they were asked to leave the lounge to make their way to the top deck, he remembers feeling afraid and alone.

Out on deck, there was a white railing running all the way round. The deck was listing so badly that they had to climb on the *outside* of the railing to keep balance, seeing the sea far below. Tugs had come out from the harbor and were wedged against the ship to keep it afloat for as long as possible. Children and teachers had to slide down the slippery, sloping deck to be able to jump over onto a tug and to safety.

Tom remembers standing at the top of the slope feeling terrified that he would miss the outstretched hand of an adult below and end up in the water. Fortunately, he made it onto the tug safely.

Back at school, he was unable to concentrate on anything. He became very irritable with everyone, especially if they talked about the disaster. His irritability escalated into anger and he had to be suspended after hurting a fellow pupil who had taunted him. At home, he was moody, anxious, unable to sleep, and constantly distressed by images of what had happened to him on the ship.

As can be seen in the graph, when he was first assessed a few months after the disaster, he was found to be extremely anxious, quite depressed, and to have a high level of distress caused by intrusive images of the disaster and by having to avoid things that reminded him of it. Arrangements were made for him to receive help locally.

Unfortunately, he did not engage with the local therapist and it was nearly 2 years before he came back for treatment. In the intervening time, his problems had not improved. But also in that time, we had experience of using cognitive-behavioral exposure therapy with adults from many other disasters and so he was offered this.

Exposure therapy assumes that the avoidance and distress are all signs of anxiety and that such anxiety needs to habituate when recalling the trauma in supportive, nonthreatening circumstances. Tom was asked to describe what had happened to him in great detail, paying attention to what he experienced in terms of what he saw, heard, felt, smelled, the movements he recalled, and so on, as well as what he was thinking and feeling at the time. His account was tape recorded and he was asked to listen to the tape every day between sessions. Each session was very distressing initially, but was long enough for the distress to fall a bit by the end.

In each session, Tom recalled more and more detail than he had been able to discuss initially. In one session, he told of having what appeared to be a panic attack at a railway station. The therapist asked him to close his eyes and to describe the station in detail to see if they could spot anything that had triggered off the attack. Tom had feared he was going mad but the therapist assumed there was some stimulus that had reminded him of the *Jupiter*. Sure enough, as he described the session, he started to describe a ramp leading to the car park and froze! It reminded him of the sloping deck on the ship. Once identified, he knew he was not going mad and he could control his reaction.

As can be seen, after only four sessions of exposure, his scores on intrusion and avoidance dropped dramatically. During the next four sessions he was able to go on a small pleasure boat on the Thames with the therapist, and while uncomfortable initially, he was able to control his discomfort and felt a great sense of achievement. Much later, he went on a cross-channel ferry with a friend. As luck would have it, the coach broke down on the sloping ramp! Tom began to feel uncomfortable, but quickly did his relaxation exercises and told himself this was not the cruise. He managed to control his reactions and was not only rightly proud of himself, he went on to enjoy a good day trip.

Case Example 2

David was the younger of two children living with their mother. All three in the family were fanatical football supporters and David accompanied his mother to see their team, Liverpool, play an important match at Hillsborough. His mother had to stand at the front of the spectators' enclosure as she was a short lady. Unfortunately, too many supporters were let into the enclosure and as an early goal was scored, they surged forward, crushing those at the front. Along with many others, David's mother died of suffocation.

He was helped by local services with his understandable grief reaction, but he developed other worrying symptoms and was referred 10 months after the accident. At that time, he still found it difficult to accept that his mother had died, and still "talked" to her. He had bad dreams about being crushed and these interfered with his sleep. He suffered intrusive thoughts about the disaster, increased irritability and aggression, and poor concentration at school. He achieved a score of 47 on the Impact of Events Scale, and was diagnosed as suffering from PTSD.

David was able to describe how he managed to climb over the fence to get away from the crush, only to be confronted with many dying and

TABLE 10.1
Summary of the Published Studies on PTSD in Children

Authors	Type	No.	Ages	Comment
War				
Macksoud, Dyregrov, & Raundalen (1992)				Review of effects of war on children
Swenson & Klingman (1993)				Review of effects of war on children
Saigh (1989)	Lebanon	840	9–13	273 of 840 children in Lebanese civil war had PTSD
Kinzie, Sack, Angell, Manson, & Rath (1986)	Cambodia			50% of adolescent refugees met PTSD criteria 6 years after the war
Nader, Pynoos, Fairbanks, Frederick, Al-Ajeel, & Al-Asfour (1993)	Gulf War, Kuwait	51	8–21	High levels of exposure to violence; highest Reaction Index scores in children who had hurt others
Ribicic & Gorsic (1992); Ribicic (1992)	Slovenia	167 191	7–14 13–14	Exposure-effect relationship found on Impact of Events in three areas in Slovenia
Natural Disasters				
Dam and mud slides				
Lacey (1972)	Aberfan	56		Clinical description of children presenting to local clinic after coal tip engulfed local school
Newman (1976); Green, Korol, Grace, Vary, Leonard, Gleser, & Smithson-Cohen (1991)	Buffalo Creek	179	2–15	37% received probable PTSD diagnosis after a dam burst
Earthquakes				
Galante & Foa (1986)	N. Italy	300	6–10	Group therapy provided but changes did not register on the Rutter Scale
Bradburn (1991)	San Francisco	22	10–12	6 had moderate PTSD and 8 had mild PTSD according to Frederick & Pynoos Reaction Index
Azarian, Skriptchenko, Miller, & Kraus (1994)	Armenia, Spitak	839	3–18	77% with anxiety disorders and depressive disorders, 31% survivor guilt, trauma accommodation syndrome

continued

TABLE 10.1 (continued)

Pynoos, Goenjian, Karakashian, Tashijian, Manjikian, Manoukian, Steinberg, & Fairbanks (1993)	Armenia	231	8–16	Strong exposure-effect relationship on Reaction Index

Hurricanes, Tornadoes, & Cyclones

Bloch, Silber, & Perry (1956)	Tornado, Vicksburg, Mississippi	183		56 showed mild to severe reactions and many played tornado games
Crawshaw (1963)	Cyclone, Oregon		2–16	Under 8's reflected parental reactions; 10–13 were excited; teenagers showed anxiety
Milne (1977a,b)	Cyclone Tracy, Darwin, Australia	647	2–18	More problems reported by parents in younger children; more in those evacuated
Piotrowski & Dunham (1983)	Hurricane Eloise, Florida	269	5th grade	Locus of control and semantic differential suggest that having coped with the reality they develop a more positive attitude toward hurricanes
Frederick (1985)	Tornado, Xenia, Ohio			Anecdotal description: attests difficulty in eliciting evidence of psychic numbing in children
Martin & Little (1986)	Tornado, Wichita Falls	30	9–10	Attempt to evaluate effects on school attainment
Lonigan, Shannon, Finch, Daugherty, & Saylor (1991)	Hurricane Hugo	5687	9–19	Standard battery used Strong exposure–effect relationship
Belter, Dunn, & Jeney (1991)	Hurricane Hugo			Parents report significantly fewer PTSD symptoms than children
Sullivan, Saylor, & Foster (1991)	Hurricane Hugo	632	preschool	Few clinically significant problems

Lightning strike

Dollinger, O'Donnell, & Staley (1984)	Lightning	29	10–13	Struck during football match, killed one. Subsequently children developed storm-related fears

Flood/blizzard

Earls, Smith, Reich, & Jung (1988)	Missouri & Mississippi rivers	32	6–17	Used DICA to estimate pathology. Children report more than parents. No relationship with exposure, but more with prior history of mental health problems

continued

TABLE 10.1 (continued)

Burke, Borus, Burns, Millstein, & Beasley (1982); Burke, Moccia, Borus, & Burns (1986)	Blizzards and floods		1st/5th grade	In younger group, boys more affected than girls; in older group, girls more affected than boys
Bush Fire				
McFarlane (1987); McFarlane, Policansky, & Irwin (1987)	Australian bush fire		5–12	Parents and teachers report less pathology, but more as time progressed; family factors seen as important in maintaining distress
Technological Disasters				
Yule (1993)				Review paper
Nuclear Plant Accidents				
Handford, Mayes, Mattison, Humphrey, Bagnato, Bixler, & Kales (1986)	Three Mile Island	35	5–19	3.5 years after, parents report less symptoms than children; but this was a silent disaster that fortunately did not happen
Shipping Disasters				
Yule & Williams (1990)	*Herald of Free Enterprise*	13	8–16	Clinical interviews and Impact of Events Scale used to establish high rate of PTSD; distress scarcely dropped over 15 months
Yule, Udwin, & Murdoch (1990); Yule & Udwin (1991); Yule (1992a)	*Jupiter* cruise ship	334	12–18	Standard screening battery established high rates of distress, exposure–effect relationship, and some evidence for value of early debriefing
Rail, Road, and Air Crashes				
Milgram, Toubiana, Klingman, Raviv, & Goldstein (1988)	Israeli school bus crash			High levels of initial distress; predicted levels at 9 months; stronger effect of knowing victims than of direct exposure

continued

TABLE 10.1 (continued)

Parry Jones (1992)	Lockerbie/ Pan Am Flight 102	121	5–18	No examples of delayed stress reactions; high levels of PTSD symptoms, 66% meeting PTSD criteria
Sugar (1989)	Kenner, Louisiana air crash	7	3–12	High levels of stress symptoms including posttraumatic play
Martini, Ryan, Nakayama, & Ramenofsky (1990)	Pittsburgh regatta	5	3–9	4 of 5 suffered PTSD according to Reaction Index, but only 3 met DSM criteria
Stallard & Law (1993)	School bus crash			Strong evidence of value of early debriefing
Canterbury, Yule, & Glucksman (1993)	Road traffic accidents			Evidence of increased stress reactions compared with hospital controls, but low returns make estimation of prevalence of PTSD difficult
Blom (1986)	Building collapse	156	5–12	5–10% children very distressed in first 2 weeks; by 7 months most recovered

Industrial/Chemical Accidents

Smith, North, & Price (1988)	St. Louis floods			Dioxin found in contaminated flood water. PTSD not related to severity of exposure. High frequency of stress symptoms but only 5% met DSM criteria for PTSD

Deliberate Attacks and Witness to Violence

Pynoos & Eth (1986); Pynoos, Frederick, Nader, Arroyo, Steinberg, Eth, Nunez, & Fairbanks (1987)	California school sniper	159	Av = 9 yrs	Sampled children exposed to fatal sniper attack on school. 40% had moderate to severe PTSD. Strong exposure-effect relationship
Nader, Pynoos, Fairbanks & Frederick (1991)				14 month follow-up, 74% of most affected group still had moderate to severe PTSD. Early reactions a good predictor of later outcome
Black & Kaplan (1988); Black, Kaplan, Harris, & Hendricks (1991) Pynoos & Nader (1988)	Child saw father kill mother	28, later 80		Children's needs often ignored in aftermath of murder; most children developed PTSD Used Reaction Index with children who had witnessed a wide range of injury and death

continued

natural history of PTSD in children. Better cross-sectional studies can also investigate the nature of risk and protective factors within the children themselves and their families. The international child mental health research community should agree on a common core methodology that can be applied in studying the effects of disasters on children, along the lines of that agreed with respect to adult studies (Raphael, Lundin, and Weisaeth, 1989).

REFERENCES

American Psychiatric Association (1980), *Diagnostic and Statistical Manual of Mental Disorders* (DSM-II), 3rd ed. Washington, DC: American Psychiatric Press.
—— (1987), *Diagnostic and Statistical Manual of Mental Disorders* (DSM-III-R), 3rd ed. rev. Washington, DC: American Psychiatric Press.
—— (1994), *Diagnostic and Statistical Manual of Mental Disorders* (DSM-IV), 4th ed. Washington, DC: American Psychiatric Press.
Ayalon, O. (1983), Coping with terrorism: The Israeli case. In: *Stress Reduction and Prevention,* ed. D. Meichenbaum & M. E. Jaremko. New York: Plenum, pp. 293–339.
—— (1988), *Rescue! Community Oriented Preventive Education for Coping with Stress.* Haifa: Nord Publications.
Azarian, A. G., Miller, T. W., & Skriptchenko-Gregorian, V. G. (1994), Childhood trauma in victims of the Armenian earthquake. *J. Contemp. Psychother.,* 24(2):77–85.
—— Skriptchenko, V. G., Miller, T. W., & Kraus, R. F. (1994), Childhood trauma in victims of the Armenian earthquake. *J. Contemp. Psychotherapy,* 24(4):38–42.
Belter, R. W., Dunn, S. E., & Jeney, P. (1991), The psychological impact of Hurricane Hugo on children: A needs assessment. *Adv. Behav. Res. Ther.,* 13:155–161.
Berelowitz, M., Misch, P., & Yale, W. (1993), Childhood trauma: Treatment and follow-up. In: *Trauma and Crisis Management,* ed. J. Ouston. ACPP Occasional Paper. London: Institute of Psychiatry.
Black, D., & Kaplan, T. (1988), Father kills mother: Issues and problems encountered by a child psychiatric team. *Brit. J. Psychiatry,* 153:624–630.
—— —— Harris B., & Hendricks, J. (1991), Children who witness parental killing. Paper presented at European Society for Child and Adolescent Psychiatry, London, September.
Bloch, D. A., Silber, E., & Perry, S. E. (1956), Some factors in the emotional reactions of children to disaster. *Amer. J. Psychiatry,* 133:416–422.

TABLE 10.1 (continued)

Terr (1979, 1983)	Chowchilla school bus kidnap		Clinical description of badly traumatized children who remained affected over 4 years later despite receiving help
Physical and Sexual Abuse			
Frederick (1985)	Sexual abuse	50	All suffered PTSD
Goodwin (1988)	Sexual abuse		Notes developmental differences but concludes many suffer PTSD
Wolfe, Gentile, & Wolfe (1989)	Sexual abuse		A PTSD formulation points way to more effective intervention with troubling symptoms
Kiser, Heston, Millsap, & Pruitt (1991)	Physical and sexual abuse	89	55% met DSM criteria for PTSD; difference between single event and chronic abuse
Sanders & Giolas (1991)	Trauma and dissociation		Significant relationship found
Famularo, Kinscherff, & Fenton (1991)	Borderline personality	19	Most reported significant traumatization and one-third met PTSD criteria

injured spectators laid out on the football pitch. He recalled one dying man who held out a hand to him, and David tried to comfort him. Later, he had to identify his mother's body from photographs in a makeshift mortuary. He recalled the funny pattern of marks on her face (from where she was pressed against the fence).

David was seen for seven sessions. While initially an exposure approach was taken, he reported that he was particularly upset whenever he heard phrases containing the words *hill* or *borough*. He was given a tape with many such words recorded on it and asked to listen to it over and over, twice every day. Within 2 weeks, his distress at hearing these words had habituated.

Eight months after treatment, David had resumed many of his sporting activities and was found to be much more relaxed. He was able to concentrate on schoolwork and obtained satisfaction from achievement. He had been able to attend a football match and could recall good times with his mother without getting upset. His score on the Impact of Events Scale had dropped to 7.[1]

---

[1] I would like to acknowledge the assistance of E. Citron, trainee clinical psychologist, in treating "David."

These two case examples illustrate the need to have a very detailed account of the child's experiences during an incident and also illustrate the use of techniques of anxiety management, relaxation, habituation, as well as exposure.

Planning for Prevention

Disasters, by their nature, are unexpected. However, those responsible for delivering community mental health services can reasonably anticipate that a variety of disasters, large and small, will hit their community each year. They need to plan ahead not only to decide on how to mobilize resources to deal with a disaster after it hits, but also to consider what preventive techniques should be implemented. As far as children are concerned, schools are the most obvious focus for such preventive work.

This is recognized by a number of authors (Johnson, 1987; Yule and Gold, 1993a; Klingman, 1993). Not only can schools plan ahead as to how they will deal with a variety of predictable events—such as the death of a teacher or pupil in school; deaths on a school outing; arson, sniper attack, etc.—they can consider how to deal with related events in the school curriculum. Thus, an actual crisis should not be the first time that teachers and pupils have discussed death and its surrounding rituals. Schools need to be aware of the variety of faiths practiced by students and their families so that they know which faiths welcome children at funerals and which do not.

Some consideration might be given to providing children with an introduction to simple stress management techniques which can be augmented when a disaster does strike.

Conclusions

Children's reactions to major stressors can last for many years and be quite disabling. In older children and adolescents, the

symptoms shown by children are very similar to those shown by adults and are usefully summarized under the construct of PTSD with its tripartite grouping of symptoms—reexperiencing the trauma, avoidance reactions, increased arousal. However, there are some symptoms such as loss of loving feelings that are not shown by children and there are others such as survivor guilt that are frequently shown. Thus, the construct of PTSD as operationalized in ICD and DSM is of value in guiding clinicians, but does not fully reflect the complex reactions of children. In particular, it does not adequately encompass the reactions of younger children. Thus, clinicians and researchers who merely treat child survivors by addressing only DSM symptoms are doing the children a disservice as such studies will never advance our understanding of the natural reactions of children to major stressors.

Despite these caveats, there have been major advances in recent years with more systematic studies of child survivors and victims using more standardized techniques (Finch and Daugherty, 1993). Such studies have established that, by and large, the more threatened a child feels during a traumatic event, the greater the risk of developing PTSD. The subjective appraisal of the risk is as important as the objective threat. On the whole, girls react with greater degrees of stress than boys, and less able children are more affected than bright children. Schoolwork can be badly affected and children can be thrown off the normal educational trajectory if they fail to achieve well in crucial examinations (Tsui, Dagwell, and Yule, 1993).

Schools form the natural focus of much crisis intervention and also have a role in prevention. Individual therapy will be needed by some children. At present, the most promising therapy is based on cognitive–behavioral principles and involves prolonged exposure to the feared, traumatic event (in imagination) together with positive steps to boost the child's own coping strategies.

It is difficult to undertake useful research in a traumatic situation, unless one has thought through beforehand what questions can reasonably be asked within a particular disaster. There is still a need for better cross-sectional descriptive studies, particularly if these lead on to longitudinal studies that can help establish the

TABLE 10.1 (continued)

Terr (1979, 1983)	Chowchilla school bus kidnap		Clinical description of badly traumatized children who remained affected over 4 years later despite receiving help

Physical and Sexual Abuse

Frederick (1985)	Sexual abuse	50	All suffered PTSD
Goodwin (1988)	Sexual abuse		Notes developmental differences but concludes many suffer PTSD
Wolfe, Gentile, & Wolfe (1989)	Sexual abuse		A PTSD formulation points way to more effective intervention with troubling symptoms
Kiser, Heston, Millsap, & Pruitt (1991)	Physical and sexual abuse	89	55% met DSM criteria for PTSD; difference between single event and chronic abuse
Sanders & Giolas (1991)	Trauma and dissociation		Significant relationship found
Famularo, Kinscherff, & Fenton (1991)	Borderline personality	19	Most reported significant traumatization and one-third met PTSD criteria

injured spectators laid out on the football pitch. He recalled one dying man who held out a hand to him, and David tried to comfort him. Later, he had to identify his mother's body from photographs in a makeshift mortuary. He recalled the funny pattern of marks on her face (from where she was pressed against the fence).

David was seen for seven sessions. While initially an exposure approach was taken, he reported that he was particularly upset whenever he heard phrases containing the words *hill* or *borough*. He was given a tape with many such words recorded on it and asked to listen to it over and over, twice every day. Within 2 weeks, his distress at hearing these words had habituated.

Eight months after treatment, David had resumed many of his sporting activities and was found to be much more relaxed. He was able to concentrate on schoolwork and obtained satisfaction from achievement. He had been able to attend a football match and could recall good times with his mother without getting upset. His score on the Impact of Events Scale had dropped to 7.[1]

[1] I would like to acknowledge the assistance of E. Citron, trainee clinical psychologist, in treating "David."

These two case examples illustrate the need to have a very detailed account of the child's experiences during an incident and also illustrate the use of techniques of anxiety management, relaxation, habituation, as well as exposure.

Planning for Prevention

Disasters, by their nature, are unexpected. However, those responsible for delivering community mental health services can reasonably anticipate that a variety of disasters, large and small, will hit their community each year. They need to plan ahead not only to decide on how to mobilize resources to deal with a disaster after it hits, but also to consider what preventive techniques should be implemented. As far as children are concerned, schools are the most obvious focus for such preventive work.

This is recognized by a number of authors (Johnson, 1987; Yule and Gold, 1993a; Klingman, 1993). Not only can schools plan ahead as to how they will deal with a variety of predictable events—such as the death of a teacher or pupil in school; deaths on a school outing; arson, sniper attack, etc.—they can consider how to deal with related events in the school curriculum. Thus, an actual crisis should not be the first time that teachers and pupils have discussed death and its surrounding rituals. Schools need to be aware of the variety of faiths practiced by students and their families so that they know which faiths welcome children at funerals and which do not.

Some consideration might be given to providing children with an introduction to simple stress management techniques which can be augmented when a disaster does strike.

Conclusions

Children's reactions to major stressors can last for many years and be quite disabling. In older children and adolescents, the symptoms shown by children are very similar to those shown by adults and are usefully summarized under the construct of PTSD with its tripartite grouping of symptoms—reexperiencing the trauma, avoidance reactions, increased arousal. However, there are some symptoms such as loss of loving feelings that are not shown by children and there are others such as survivor guilt that are frequently shown. Thus, the construct of PTSD as operationalized in ICD and DSM is of value in guiding clinicians, but does not fully reflect the complex reactions of children. In particular, it does not adequately encompass the reactions of younger children. Thus, clinicians and researchers who merely treat child survivors by addressing only DSM symptoms are doing the children a disservice as such studies will never advance our understanding of the natural reactions of children to major stressors.

Despite these caveats, there have been major advances in recent years with more systematic studies of child survivors and victims using more standardized techniques (Finch and Daugherty, 1993). Such studies have established that, by and large, the more threatened a child feels during a traumatic event, the greater the risk of developing PTSD. The subjective appraisal of the risk is as important as the objective threat. On the whole, girls react with greater degrees of stress than boys, and less able children are more affected than bright children. Schoolwork can be badly affected and children can be thrown off the normal educational trajectory if they fail to achieve well in crucial examinations (Tsui, Dagwell, and Yule, 1993).

Schools form the natural focus of much crisis intervention and also have a role in prevention. Individual therapy will be needed by some children. At present, the most promising therapy is based on cognitive–behavioral principles and involves prolonged exposure to the feared, traumatic event (in imagination) together with positive steps to boost the child's own coping strategies.

It is difficult to undertake useful research in a traumatic situation, unless one has thought through beforehand what questions can reasonably be asked within a particular disaster. There is still a need for better cross-sectional descriptive studies, particularly if these lead on to longitudinal studies that can help establish the natural history of PTSD in children. Better cross-sectional studies can also investigate the nature of risk and protective factors within the children themselves and their families. The international child mental health research community should agree on a common core methodology that can be applied in studying the effects of disasters on children, along the lines of that agreed with respect to adult studies (Raphael, Lundin, and Weisaeth, 1989).

REFERENCES

American Psychiatric Association (1980), *Diagnostic and Statistical Manual of Mental Disorders* (DSM-II), 3rd ed. Washington, DC: American Psychiatric Press.

—— (1987), *Diagnostic and Statistical Manual of Mental Disorders* (DSM-III-R), 3rd ed. rev. Washington, DC: American Psychiatric Press.

—— (1994), *Diagnostic and Statistical Manual of Mental Disorders* (DSM-IV), 4th ed. Washington, DC: American Psychiatric Press.

Ayalon, O. (1983), Coping with terrorism: The Israeli case. In: *Stress Reduction and Prevention,* ed. D. Meichenbaum & M. E. Jaremko. New York: Plenum, pp. 293–339.

—— (1988), *Rescue! Community Oriented Preventive Education for Coping with Stress.* Haifa: Nord Publications.

Azarian, A. G., Miller, T. W., & Skriptchenko-Gregorian, V. G. (1994), Childhood trauma in victims of the Armenian earthquake. *J. Contemp. Psychother.,* 24(2):77–85.

—— Skriptchenko, V. G., Miller, T. W., & Kraus, R. F. (1994), Childhood trauma in victims of the Armenian earthquake. *J. Contemp. Psychotherapy,* 24(4):38–42.

Belter, R. W., Dunn, S. E., & Jeney, P. (1991), The psychological impact of Hurricane Hugo on children: A needs assessment. *Adv. Behav. Res. Ther.,* 13:155–161.

Berelowitz, M., Misch, P., & Yale, W. (1993), Childhood trauma: Treatment and follow-up. In: *Trauma and Crisis Management,* ed. J. Ouston. ACPP Occasional Paper. London: Institute of Psychiatry.

Black, D., & Kaplan, T. (1988), Father kills mother: Issues and problems encountered by a child psychiatric team. *Brit. J. Psychiatry,* 153:624–630.

—— —— Harris B., & Hendricks, J. (1991), Children who witness parental killing. Paper presented at European Society for Child and Adolescent Psychiatry, London, September.

Bloch, D. A., Silber, E., & Perry, S. E. (1956), Some factors in the emotional reactions of children to disaster. *Amer. J. Psychiatry,* 133:416–422.

Blom, G. E. (1986), A school disaster—Intervention and research aspects. *J. Amer. Acad. Child Psychiatry,* 25:336–345.

Bradburn, I. S. (1991), After the earth shook: Children's stress symptoms 6–8 months after a disaster. *Adv. Behav. Res. Ther.,* 13:173–179.

Burke, J. D., Borus, J. F., Burns, B. J., Millstein, K. H., & Beasley, M. C. (1982), Changes in children's behavior after a natural disaster. *Amer. J. Psychiatry,* 139:1010–1014.

—— Moccia, P., Borus, J. F., & Burns, B. J. (1986), Emotional distress in fifth-grade children ten months after a natural disaster. *J. Amer. Acad. Child Psychiatry,* 25:536–541.

Canterbury, R., Yule, W., & Glucksman, E. (1993), PTSD in child survivors of road traffic accidents. Paper presented to Third European Conference on Traumatic Stress, Bergen, June 6–10.

Crawshaw, R. (1963), Reaction to disaster. *Arch. Gen. Psychiatry,* 9:157–162.

Dollinger, S. J., O'Donnell, J. F., & Staley, A. A. (1984), Lightning-strike disaster: Effects on children's fears and worries. *J. Consult. Clin. Psychol.,* 52:1028–1038.

Duckworth, D. (1986), Psychological problems arising from disaster work. *Stress Med.,* 2:315–323.

Dyregrov, A. (1988), Critical incident stress debriefings. Research Center for Occupational Health and Safety, University of Bergen, Norway. Typescript.

—— (1991), *Grief in Children: A Handbook for Adults.* London: Jessica Kingsley.

Earls, F., Smith, E., Reich, W., & Jung, K. G. (1988), Investigating psychopathological consequences of a disaster in children: A pilot study incorporating a structured diagnostic interview. *J. Amer. Acad. Child & Adol. Psychiatry,* 27(1):90–95.

Famularo, R., Kinscherff, R., & Fenton, T. (1991), Posttraumatic stress disorder among children clinically diagnosed as borderline personality disorder. *J. Nerv. Ment. Dis.,* 179:428–431.

Farberow, N. L., & Gordon, N. S. (1981), *Manual for Child Health Workers in Major Disasters.* DHHS Publication No. (ADM 81-10/0). Washington, DC: U.S. Government Printing Office.

Finch, A. J., & Daugherty, T. K. (1993), Issues in the assessment of posttraumatic stress disorder in children. In: *Children and Disasters,* ed. C. F. Saylor. New York: Plenum, pp. 45–66.

Foa, E. B., Steketee, G., & Olasov-Rothbaum, B. (1989), Behavioral/cognitive conceptualizations of post-traumatic stress disorder. *Behav. Ther.,* 20:155–176.

Frederick, C. J. (1985), Children traumatized by catastrophic situations. In: *Post-Traumatic Stress Disorder in Children,* ed. S. Eth & R. Pynoos. Washington, DC: American Psychiatric Press, pp. 73–99.

Galante, R., & Foa, D. (1986), An epidemiological study of psychic trauma and treatment effectiveness after a natural disaster. *J. Amer. Acad. Child Psychiatry,* 25:357–363.

Garmezy, N. (1986), Children under severe stress: Critique and comments. *J. Amer. Acad. Child Psychiatry,* 25:384–392.

Gillis, H. M. (1993), Individual and small-group psychotherapy for children involved in trauma and disaster. In: *Children and Disasters,* ed. C. F. Saylor. New York: Plenum, pp. 165–186.

Goodwin, J. (1988), Post-traumatic symptoms in abused children. *J. Traum. Stress,* 4:475–488.

Green, B. L., Korol, M., Grace, M. C., Vary, M. G., Leonard, A. C., Gleser, G. C., & Smithson-Cohen, S. (1991), Children and disaster: Age, gender, and parental effects on PTSD symptoms. *J. Amer. Acad. Child & Adol. Psychiatry,* 30:945–951.

Halliday, G. (1987), Direct psychological therapies for nightmares: A review. *Clin. Psychol. Rev.,* 7:501–523.

Handford, H. A., Mayes, S. O., Mattison, R. E., Humphrey, F. J., Bagnato, S., Bixler, E. O., & Kales, J. D. (1986), Child and parent reaction to the TMI nuclear accident. *J. Amer. Acad. Child Adol. Psychiat.,* 25:346–355.

Herman, J. L. (1992), Complex PTSD: A syndrome in survivors of prolonged and repeated trauma. *J. Traum. Stress,* 5:377–391.

Horowitz, M. J. (1976), *Stress Response Syndromes.* New York: Jason Aronson.

Johnson, K. (1987), *Classroom Crisis: A Readi-Reference Guide.* Claremont, CA: Turnpoint.

Jones, J. C., & Barlow, D. H. (1992), A new model of posttraumatic stress disorder. In: *Posttraumatic Stress Disorder: A Behavioral Approach to Assessment and Treatment,* ed. P. A. Saigh. New York: Macmillan, pp. 147–165.

Kinzie, J. D., Sack, W. H., Angell, R. H., Manson, S., & Rath, B. (1986), The psychiatric effects of massive trauma on Cambodian children: I. The children. *J. Amer. Acad. Child & Adol. Psychiatry,* 25:370–376.

Kiser, I. J., Heston, J., Millsap, P. A., & Pruitt, D. B. (1991), Physical and sexual abuse in childhood: Relationship with post-traumatic stress disorder. *J. Amer. Acad. Child Adol. Psychiatry,* 30:776–783.

Klingman, A. (1993), School-based intervention following a disaster. In: *Children and Disasters,* ed. C. F. Saylor. New York: Plenum, pp. 187–210.

Kolb, L. C. (1988), A critical survey of hypotheses regarding post-traumatic stress disorders in light of recent findings. *J. Traum. Stress,* 1:291–304.

Lacey, G. N. (1972), Observations on Aberfan. *J. Psychosom. Res.,* 16:257–260.

Lonigan, C. J., Shannon, M. P., Finch, A. J., Daugherty, T. K., & Saylor, C. M. (1991), Children's reactions to a natural disaster: Symptom severity and degree of exposure. *Adv. Behav. Res. Ther.,* 13:135–154.

Macksoud, M. S., Dyregrov, A., & Raundalen, M. (1992), Traumatic war experiences and their effects on children. In: *International Handbook of Traumatic Stress Syndromes,* ed. J. P. Wilson & B. Raphael. New York: Plenum.

Marks, I. (1978), Rehearsal relief of a nightmare. *Brit. J. Psychiatry,* 133:461–465.
———— (1987), Nightmares. *Integr. Psychiatry,* 5:71–73.

Martin, S., & Little, B. (1986), The effects of a natural disaster on academic abilities and social behavior of school children. *B.C.J. Spec. Ed.,* 10:167–182.

Martini, D. R., Ryan, C., Nakayama, D., & Ramenofsky, M. (1990), Psychiatric sequelae after traumatic injury: The Pittsburgh Regatta accident. *J. Amer. Acad. Child & Adol. Psychiatry,* 29:70–75.

McFarlane, A. C. (1987), Family functioning and overprotection following a natural disaster: The longitudinal effects of post-traumatic morbidity. *Austral. N.Z. J. Psychiatry*, 21:210–218.

—— Policansky, S., & Irwin, C. P. (1987), A longitudinal study of the psychological morbidity in children due to a natural disaster. *Psychol. Med.*, 17:727–738.

Meichenbaum, D. (1975), Self instructional methods. In: *Helping People Change*, ed. F. Kanfer & A. Goldstein. New York: Pergamon, pp. 357–391.

—— (1977), *Cognitive Behavior Modification: An Integrated Approach*. New York: Plenum.

—— Cameron, R. (1983), Stress inoculation training: Toward a general paradigm for training coping skills. In: *Stress Reduction and Prevention*, ed. D. Meichenbaum & M. E. Jaremko. New York: Plenum, pp. 115–154.

Milgram, N. A., Toubiana, Y. H., Klingman, A., Raviv, A., & Goldstein, I. (1988), Situational exposure and personal loss in children's acute and chronic stress reactions to a school bus disaster. *J. Traum. Stress*, 1:339–352.

Milne, G. (1977a), Cyclone Tracy: 1. Some consequences of the evacuation for adult victims. *Austral. Psychologist*, 12:39–54.

—— (1977b), Cyclone Tracy: 2. The effects on Darwin children. *Austral. Psychologist*, 12:55–62.

Nader, K., Pynoos, R. S., Fairbanks, L., & Frederick, C. (1991), Childhood PTSD reactions one year after a sniper attack. *Amer. J. Psychiatry*, 147:1526–1530.

—— Pynoos, R., Fairbanks, L., Frederick, C., Al-Ajeel, M., & Al-Asfour, A. (1993), A preliminary study of PTSD and grief among children of Kuwait following the Gulf crisis. *Brit. J. Clin. Psychol.*, 32:407–416.

Newman, C. J. (1976), Children of disaster: Clinical observation at Buffalo Creek. *Amer. J. Psychiatry*, 133:306–312.

O'Donohue, W., & Eliot, A. (1992), The current status of post traumatic stress syndrome as a diagnostic category: Problems and proposals. *J. Traum. Stress*, 5:421–439.

Palace, E. M., & Johnston, C. (1989), Treatment of recurrent nightmares by the dream reorganization approach. *J. Behav. Ther. Exper. Psychiatry*, 20:219–226.

Parry Jones, W. (1992), Children of Lockerbie. Paper presented at Guys Hospital meeting. London.

Piotrowski, C., & Dunham, F. Y. (1983), Locus of control orientation and perception of "hurricane" in fifth graders. *J. Gen. Psychology*, 109:119–127.

Pynoos, R. S., & Eth, S. (1986), Witness to violence: The child interview. *J. Amer. Acad. Child Psychiatry*, 25:306–319.

—— Frederick, C., Nader, K., Arroyo, W., Steinberg, A., Eth, S., Nunez, F., & Fairbanks, L. (1987), Life threat and posttraumatic stress disorder in school-age children. *Arch. Gen. Psychiatry*, 44:1057–1063.

—— Goenjian, A., Karakashian, M., Tashijian, M., Manjikian, R., Manoukian, G., Steinberg, A. M., & Fairbanks, L. A. (1993), Posttraumatic stress reactions in children after the 1988 American earthquake. *Brit. J. Psychiatry*, 32:407–416.

—— Nader, K. (1988), Psychological first aid and treatment approach for children exposed to community violence: Research implications. *J. Traum. Stress*, 1:243–267.

Rachman, S. (1980), Emotional processing. *Behav. Res. Ther.*, 18:51–60.
Raphael, B., Lundin, T., & Weisaeth, L. (1989), A research method for the study of psychological and psychiatric aspects of disaster. *Acta Psychiatr. Scand.*, 80 (Suppl.):1–75.
Ribicic, V. (1992), A scale of the influence of exceptional events. *Zdravstveno Varstvo*, 31:203–206.
────── Gorsic, N. K. (1992), The parents' perception of their child's reaction to war events. *Zdravstveno Varstvo*, 31:196–202.
Richards, D., & Lovell, K. (1990), Imaginal and in-vivo exposure in the treatment of PTSD. Paper read at Second European Conference on Traumatic Stress, Netherlands, September 1990.
────── Rose, J. (1991), Exposure therapy for post-traumatic stress disorder: Four case studies. *Brit. J. Psychiatry*, 158:836–840.
Robinson, R. C., & Mitchell, J. T. (1993), Evaluation of psychological debriefings. *J. Traum. Stress*, 6:367–382.
Saigh, P. A. (1986), In vitro flooding in the treatment of a 6-yr-old boy's posttraumatic stress disorder. *Behav. Res. Ther.*, 24:685–688.
────── (1989), The development and validation of the Children's Posttraumatic Stress Disorder Inventory. *Internat. J. Spec. Ed.*, 4:75–84.
────── (1992), *Posttraumatic Stress Disorder: A Behavioral Approach to Assessment and Treatment.* New York: Macmillan.
Sanders, B., & Giolas, M. H. (1991), Dissociation and childhood trauma in psychologically disturbed adolescents. *Amer. J. Psychiatry*, 148:50–54.
Seligman, M. E., & Yellen, A. (1987), What is a dream? *Behav. Res. Ther.*, 25:1–24.
Smith, E. M., North, C. S., & Price, P. C. (1988), Response to technological accidents. In: *Mental Health Responses to Mass Emergencies*, ed. M. Lystad. New York: Brunner/Mazel, pp. 52–95.
Stallard, P., & Law, F. (1993), Screening and psychological debriefing of adolescent survivors of life threatening events. *Brit. J. Psychiatry*.
Sugar, M. (1989), Children in disaster: An overview. *Child Psychiatry & Hum. Develop.*, 19:163–169.
Sullivan, M. A., Saylor, C. M., & Foster, K. Y. (1991), Post-hurricane adjustment of preschoolers and their families. *Adv. Behav. Res. Ther.*, 13:163–171.
Swenson, C. C., & Klingman, A. (1993), Children and war. In: *Children and Disasters*, ed. C. F. Saylor. New York: Plenum, pp. 137–163.
Terr, L. C. (1979), The children of Chowchilla. *The Psychoanalytic Study of the Child*, 34:547–623. New Haven, CT: Yale University Press.
────── (1983), Chowchilla revisited: The effects of psychic trauma four years after a schoolbus kidnapping. *Amer. J. Psychiatry*, 140:1543–1550.
────── (1991), Childhood traumas—An outline and overview. *Amer. J. Psychiatry*, 148:10–20.
Tsui, E., Dagwell, K., & Yule, W. (1993), Effect of a disaster on children's academic attainment. Invited presentation, Institute of Psychiatry, University of London, July 12.
Wolfe, V. V., Gentile, C., & Wolfe, D. A. (1989), The impact of sexual abuse on children: A PTSD formulation. *Behav. Ther.*, 20:215–228.
World Health Organization (1991), *International Classification of Diseases*, 10th ed. (ICD-10). WHO: Geneva.

Yule, W. (1991), Work with children following disasters. In: *Clinical Child Psychology: Social Learning, Development and Behaviour,* ed. L. Chichester. U.K.: Wiley, pp. 349–363.

―――― (1992a), Post traumatic stress disorder in child survivors of shipping disasters: The sinking of the "Jupiter." *Psychother. & Psychosom.,* 57:200–205.

―――― (1992b), Resilience and vulnerability in child survivors of disasters. In: *Vulnerability and Resilience: A Festchrift for Ann and Alan Clarke,* ed. B. Tizard & V. Varma. London: Jessica Kingsley, pp. 82–98.

―――― (1992c), Post traumatic stress disorder: Phenomenology and treatment. Paper presented at 22nd Congress of European Association for Behaviour Therapy, Coimbra, Portugal, September 9–12.

―――― (1993), Technology related disasters. In: *Children and Disasters,* ed. C. F. Saylor. New York: Plenum, pp. 105–121.

―――― Gold, A. (1993a), *Wise Before the Event: Coping with Crises in Schools.* London: Calouste Gulbenkian Foundation.

―――― ―――― (1993b), Wise before the event: Planning with schools to help child survivors of catastrophes. In: *Trauma and Crisis Management,* ed. J. Ouston. ACPP Occasional Paper. London: Institute of Psychiatry.

―――― Udwin, O. (1991), Screening child survivors for post-traumatic stress disorders: Experiences from the "Jupiter" sinking. *Brit. J. Clin. Psychol.,* 30:131–138.

―――― ―――― Murdock, K. (1990), The "Jupiter" sinking: Effects on children's fears, depression and anxiety. *J. Child Psychiat.,* 31:1051–1061.

―――― Williams, R. (1990), Post traumatic stress reactions in children. *J. Traum. Stress,* 3(2):279–295.

Concluding Comments

THOMAS W. MILLER, PH.D., A.B.P.P.

Important issues in stress adaptation are examined in this volume, as well as theoretical models that have broadened our awareness of the adaptation concept in stressful life events experienced by children. The detailed review of assessment and measurement of childhood trauma has given us clinical measures that should be helpful in our growing understanding of the impact of stressful life events.

Traumatization and stress in children, as well as adolescents, have been examined from a variety of perspectives, including family violence, sexual abuse, the impact of war-related posttraumatic stress disorder (PTSD), and natural disasters. Special attention has been paid to teenage pregnancy and the role of substance abuse and suicidal behavior in children and adolescents who are affected by trauma and stressful life experiences.

Finally, treatment models and prevention intervention measures have been examined in an effort to provide the clinician and researcher with a clear understanding of emerging models of treatment for children of trauma. In examining the content of this volume, one clearly realizes the importance of continued clinical research in studying the impact of stressful life events on the health of our children and adolescents. Recommendations that emerge include, but are not limited to, the following:

1. Clinical research continues to be needed to examine etiological factors, personality characteristics, and vulnerability

245

components in understanding the impact of stressful life events on children and adolescents.

2. Further research is needed to sort out the relative impact of stressful life events and the complexities of interaction effects in causation.

3. More focused epidemiological studies, including longitudinal studies, are needed to assess the magnitude and severity of the impact of various stressful life experiences on children.

4. Benchmark measures should be included in laboratory studies to permit generalization across studies. Biopsychosocial interactions must be examined if we are to better understand the impact of life stress and trauma in children.

5. To enhance scientific knowledge, funding agencies should make clinical field experiments a priority and should consider providing funding assistance to organizations that are willing to institute programs experimentally and subject them to independent evaluation.

Name Index

Subject Index

259